T0301987

ANARCHISM, ORGANIZATION AND MANAGEMENT

You might think that anarchism and management are opposed, but this book shows how engaging with the long history of anarchist ideas allows us to understand the problems of contemporary organizing much more clearly. Anarchism is a theory of organizing, and in times when global capitalism is in question, we need new ideas more than ever.

The reader of this book will learn how anarchist ideas are relevant to today's management problems. In a series of student-friendly short chapters on contemporary topics, the authors challenge the common sense that has allowed particular forms of organization and market to become globally dominant. Do we always need leaders? Is technological change always a good thing? Are markets the best way to arrange forms of exchange? This challenging book is essential for anyone who wants to understand what is wrong with business school theory and what we might do about it.

For students and teachers of management, the standard textbook reproduces the dominant ideas about the way that business should be done. This book turns those ideas on their head, asking awkward questions about authority, technology and markets and demanding that its readers think hard about whether they want to reproduce those ideas too. Students of management, like everyone else, know that the current global system is broken, but they don't know what they can do about it. This unique book uses 200 years of anarchist ideas to give readers a clear guide for building the organizations and businesses of the future and places choice and responsibility at the centre of making a new world for people and the planet.

Martin Parker is a professor in the School of Management, University of Bristol, and author of *Shut Down the Business School* (2018).

Konstantin Stoborod is an independent scholar based in Moscow.

Thomas Swann is a Leverhulme Early Career Fellow in Politics and International Studies at Loughborough University. His book *Anarchist Cybernetics* will be published in 2020.

'Have you been waiting for a management book that would help you in your work and planning? Or, have you, like me, spent many good hours imagining a working, living, breathing anarchist society? If so, then this book is for you. It is also for you, if you are curious about what lies in the parts of the maps of organizing, officially marked with "here be dragons." Or if you are tired of the assumption that there is no alternative, when everything in and around us is bursting with an abundance of alternatives, and the future of the planet happens to depend on using our imagination more often, and better? Yes, this book is it: a powerful and practical invitation to think about management and organization differently.'

Professor Monika Kostera, *The Jagiellonian University, Poland*

'Tackling conventional approaches to management with clarity and assurance, this collection invites students to re-think and re-imagine organisation by detaching "management" from bureaucratic, market principles. Parker, Stoborod and Swann outline a brilliant case for anarchist recuperation and the contributors to this collection provide a critical exploration of the mainstream that helps explain why so many of us find it hard to manage in our neat and tightly managed worlds.'

Professor Ruth Kinna, *Loughborough University, UK*

'This book aims to be an "antidote to management common sense." It fits the bill by being at once exciting and cultured, challenging and relevant. The chapters, crisply organized, juxtapose routine and contemporary management ideas and issues (e.g. culture, decision making, new technologies, innovation) with anarchist forms, inviting readers to meet different and stimulating realities of organizing that expand and struggle with notions of collective and individual freedom, autonomy and responsibility.'

Professor Alessia Contu, *University of Massachusetts, Boston, USA*

ANARCHISM, ORGANIZATION AND MANAGEMENT

Critical Perspectives for Students

Edited by Martin Parker, Konstantin Stoborod and Thomas Swann

Routledge
Taylor & Francis Group

LONDON AND NEW YORK

First published 2020
by Routledge
2 Park Square, Milton Park, Abingdon, Oxon OX14 4RN

and by Routledge
52 Vanderbilt Avenue, New York, NY 10017

Routledge is an imprint of the Taylor & Francis Group, an informa business.

British Library Cataloguing-in-Publication Data
A catalogue record for this book is available from the British Library.

Library of Congress Cataloging-in-Publication Data
Names: Parker, Martin, 1962– editor. | Stoborod, Konstantin,
    1987– editor. | Swann, Thomas, 1986– editor.
Title: Anarchism, organization and management : critical perspectives for
    students / Martin Parker, Konstantin Stoborod and Thomas Swann.
Description: First Edition. | New York : Routledge, 2020. | Includes
    bibliographical references and index.
Identifiers: LCCN 2019045455 (print) | LCCN 2019045456 (ebook) |
    ISBN 9781138044104 (hardback) | ISBN 9781138044111 (paperback) |
    ISBN 9781315172606 (ebook)
Subjects: LCSH: Anarchism—History. | Organization. | Business
    enterprises. | Management.
Classification: LCC HX833 .A5693 2020 (print) | LCC HX833 (ebook) |
    DDC 650.001—dc23
LC record available at https://lccn.loc.gov/2019045455
LC ebook record available at https://lccn.loc.gov/2019045456

ISBN: 978-1-138-04410-4 (hbk)
ISBN: 978-1-138-04411-1 (pbk)
ISBN: 978-1-315-17260-6 (ebk)

Typeset in Bembo
by Apex CoVantage, LLC

CONTENTS

List of contributors   *viii*

1 Introduction: management and anarchism, and organization   1
   Martin Parker, Thomas Swann and Konstantin Stoborod

PART I
Managers and management: history and present   **11**

2 An anarchist prehistory of management   13
   Nidhi Srinivas

3 Anarchy in management today   26
   Brian Wierman, Edward Granter and Leo McCann

PART II
People and organizations   **39**

4 Difference and diversity in organizations   41
   Claire Jin Deschner

5 Managing the self   57
   Peter Bloom

6 Business ethics 69
David Bevan

PART III
Structure and culture **83**

7 Decision making and power 85
Maarit Laihonen

8 Organizational culture 98
Elen Riot and Martin Parker

9 Leadership and authority 111
Lucas Casagrande and Guillermo Rivera

PART IV
Markets, finance and accounting **123**

10 Finance and value 125
Kenneth Weir and Christopher Land

11 Accounting in organizations and society 141
Anders Sandström

PART V
New technology and new economy **155**

12 The collaborative and sharing economy 157
Ozan Ağlargöz and Feyza Ağlargöz

13 Crowdsourcing and digital platforms 169
Andreas Kamstrup and Emil Husted

14 Trust, finance and cryptocurrencies 184
Enrico Beltramini

PART VI
Markets and exchange   **197**

15 Marketing, advertising and persuasion   199
    Amanda Earley

16 Innovation and entrepreneurship   212
    Alf Rehn

17 Exchange beyond the market   224
    Richard J. White and Colin C. Williams

18 Conclusion: what to do with this book   238
    Martin Parker, Thomas Swann and Konstantin Stoborod

Index   *244*

CONTRIBUTORS

Feyza Ağlargöz is an assistant professor of marketing in the Department of Business Administration at Anadolu University, Turkey. She received her PhD from Anadolu and has been a guest post-doctoral researcher at the School of Economics and Management, Lund University. She teaches marketing management, consumer behaviour and retail management at both the undergraduate and graduate levels. She is currently working on collaborative consumption, videography and voluntary simplicity. Her research interests are arts marketing, consumer culture, social marketing and sustainable consumption.

Ozan Ağlargöz is an assistant professor of management and organization in the Department of Business Administration at Anadolu University. He received an MSc from Lund University and PhD from Anadolu. He has been a guest post-doctoral researcher at Lund University and teaches management at the undergraduate level and leadership and qualitative research methods at the graduate level. He has published book chapters and journal articles and presented his research at international conferences worldwide. His primarily qualitative research problematizes working life in and around organizations through critical management studies, using concepts such as institutional work, leadership and identity.

Enrico Beltramini is currently senior lecturer in religious studies in the Department of Philosophy and Religious Studies at Notre Dame de Namur University, California. He holds doctoral degrees in business science (Manchester Business School), history (Royal Holloway, University of London), and theology (Vidyajyoti College of Theology). He primarily researches in the disciplines of theology and church history. His work on business and technology has been published in academic journals such as *AI and Society*, *Ephemera*, *Philosophy of Management*, and *Philosophy and Technology*.

David Bevan is the director of postgraduate and doctoral programmes in sustainability practice at Saint Martin's Institute of Higher Education in Malta. He first taught business ethics at King's College London School of Management during his doctoral training. He has since developed and delivered courses on corporate social (ir)responsibility in Paris, London, Chicago, Grenoble, Brussels, Shanghai and Hong Kong. He has written extensively in the field of business ethics and management. His research interests are pragmatically drawn from process ontology and action research practice.

Peter Bloom is the co-founder of the research group REEF (Research into Employment, Empowerment and Futures) at the Open University, UK. His books include *Authoritarian Capitalism in the Age of Globalization, Beyond Power and Resistance: Politics at the Radical Limits, The Ethics of Neoliberalism: The Business of Making Capitalism Moral, The Bad Faith in the Free Market: The Radical Promise of Existential Freedom, The CEO Society: How the Cult of Corporate Leadership Transform Our World* (co-written with Carl Rhodes), *Monitored: Business and Surveillance in a Time of Big Data* and *Disruptive Democracy: The Clash between Techno-Democracy and Techno-Populism* (with Alessandro Sancino).

Lucas Casagrande is a professor at the Federal University of Rio Grande do Sul (UFRGS) in Porto Alegre, Brazil. His main concerns are related to epistemology, ethics, organizational theory, organizing, degrowth and alternative forms of organization. His thesis was about immediatist anarchist organizations and the enchantment of the world. He was a professor at Federal University of Rio de Janeiro, a lecturer at the Federal and State universities of Rio Grande do Sul and a public project manager. He has also been involved with various social movements. Recent writings include a book about the theory of organization, an essay about Ivan Illich's work and an article about *Blade Runner.*

Claire Jin Deschner is a graduate research assistant at University of Leicester, School of Business. In her PhD, she explores performance discourses in anarchist organizing using participative theatre methods and activist ethnography. Claire is interested in interdisciplinary and co-operative research methods and reflections on radical self-organizing as sustainable and inclusive group processes. Her political interests lie in anti-racism, de-colonialism and queer-feminism. Her practical background lies in conflict facilitation and performance art.

Amanda Earley is a lecturer in marketing, politics and culture at the University of Leicester, School of Business. She did her doctoral work at the University of Missouri in marketing and cultural sociology and at York University, Canada, in marketing, cultural studies and communications. Her research examines the political and ethical dimensions of markets, often finding that powerful actors largely dictate the terms by which everyday people and smaller organizations operate. She also studies social movements which seek to resist the politics of the market. Her methods are tailored to the question at hand, ranging from ethnography and television studies to conceptual work and installation art.

Edward Granter is a senior lecturer in organizational behaviour at the University of Birmingham, UK. His research interests lie in the intersections of Frankfurt School critical theory and the sociology of work and organization. He has written on the future of work (*Critical Social Theory and the End of Work*, Routledge 2009) and the influence of critical theory on organization studies and critical social work. Edward's empirical research on health-care work and organization is reflected in co-authorship of *Deconstructing the Welfare State* (Routledge 2016). He is co-editor of *The Sage Handbook of the Sociology of Work and Employment* (2015).

Emil Husted is an assistant professor in the Department of Management, Politics and Philosophy at Copenhagen Business School. He has written on political parties and social movements from an organizational perspective and teaches courses on the intersection of politics, technology and organization. Emil has recently published a textbook called *Digital Organizing* with Ursula Plesner at Red Globe Press (you should probably buy it). Someone recently asked him about the biggest passions in his life, but he was unable to answer – a true academic, if nothing else.

Andreas Kamstrup is a research assistant at the Department of Organization at Copenhagen Business School. As part of his PhD, he examined how digital platforms work in organizations. He is interested in more or less anything that has something digital to it and has written about such diverse matters as crowdsourcing, digital architectural competitions and computer games. As he has realized that he will not write that single academic article that will change the world, he instead focuses his efforts on conceptualizing and unfolding digitally supported learning initiatives at Copenhagen Business School.

Maarit Laihonen is currently a postdoctoral researcher at the Department of Management, Aalto University School of Business. Her research interests and societal activity include, and recent and forthcoming publications concern, politics of large-scale industries, environmental governance, artistic knowledge creation, unorthodox and anarchist organizations, radical movements and higher education.

Christopher Land is a professor of work and organization at Anglia Ruskin University, where he mostly professes his dislike of work and mistrust of formal organization. He is interested in the values that motivate people organizing and 'doing stuff,' though personally he would rather think and read about 'stuff' than actually do any of it himself.

Leo McCann is a professor of management at the University of York. His research and teaching interests lie in the sociology of work and organization, focusing in particular on white-collar and uniformed professions. He has written widely about the impacts of neoliberal economic change on middle management and front-line skilled work across a variety of occupations. He is currently working on a major new book about the work of UK paramedics for Oxford University Press. He is the author of *A Very Short, Fairly Interesting, and Reasonably Cheap Book about Globalization* and is editor-in-chief of the journal *Competition and Change*.

Martin Parker is a professor of organization studies at the School of Management, University of Bristol. His previous book was titled *Shut Down the Business School* (Pluto, 2018), and he writes about alternative ways of imagining organization. He is the lead for the Inclusive Economy Initiative at the University of Bristol.

Alf Rehn has always wished to be a gentleman of leisure. Having failed miserably at this, he now suffers a professorship of innovation, design and management at the University of Southern Denmark.

Elen Riot is an associate professor of strategy at the Laboratoire REGARDS, Université de Reims Champagne-Ardennes. Trained as an anthropologist and a philosopher, she works on political economy in a multidisciplinary team of ethnographers, sociologists, economists and management scholars. She is a member of the ALCOR (alternative consumption research) network (http://alcor-institute. org). Her current fieldwork is with European art theatres and small farmers and fishermen cooperatives.

Guillermo Rivera is an associate professor at the School of Psychology in Pontificia Universidad Católica de Valparaíso in Chile. His main concerns are related to organizational studies in Latin-America, youth and employment and the subjectivity of work and self-management. He has developed social intervention and research in youth and employment policies in South America for more than ten years. In 2015, he was a visiting researcher in the School of Business and Management of the University of Leicester, UK. Recently he won a national fund for three years of research in vulnerable youth and employment programs in Chile (2018–2020).

Anders Sandström is a trained accountant with a degree from Uppsala University. He lives in Stockholm, where he works as the treasurer at SAAK, an unemployment office connected to the Swedish syndicalist trade union, SAC. Anders previously worked as an audit junior at KPMG and later as head of accounting and group finance controller in different companies. In 2010, Anders co-founded Parecon Sverige, an advocacy group for participatory economics, which is an economic system developed as a viable alternative to capitalism, and he is the author of *Anarchist Accounting: Accounting Principles for a Participatory Economy* (Routledge forthcoming).

Nidhi Srinivas is an associate professor of management at the New School and co-founder of the Parsons DESIS Design Lab. His research engages with critical theory through themes that include management historiography, international development and civic design. His research has been published in *Organization Studies*, *Non-profit and Voluntary Sector Quarterly*, *Management and Organizational History* and *Organization*. He has been an Erasmus Mundus research fellow at Roskilde University, Denmark; a BRICS research fellow at the BRICS Policy Institute in Rio de Janeiro, Brazil; and an India-China Institute research fellow and served as a visiting professor in universities in Brazil, India and Japan.

Konstantin Stoborod has been working at the School of Business, University of Leicester, as a teaching assistant and research fellow. He completed his PhD there in 2015 and has since been working on projects on well-being at work and hipster butchers. His broader research interests include alternative organizing, psychoanalysis, work and professions, popular culture and Russian political and social thought of the 19th century.

Thomas Swann is a Leverhulme Early Career Fellow in Politics and International Studies at Loughborough University. His work focuses on anarchist political theory and democratic organization. His PhD, completed in 2015, examined relationships between anarchism and cybernetics.

Kenneth Weir currently sells his labour power to Heriot-Watt University in exchange for a post as assistant professor in accounting. He is interested in the intersections of accounting and valuation and how such intersections shape social relations.

Richard J. White is a reader in human geography in the Department of Natural and Built Environment at Sheffield Hallam University, UK. Greatly influenced by anarchist praxis, Richard's main research explores a range of ethical, economic and activist landscapes animated by questions of social and spatial justice. His writings on anarchist economics have been published in a number of journals and books, which include *Sharing Economies in Times of Crisis* (Routledge, 2017), *The Handbook of Neoliberalism* (Routledge, 2016) and *The Accumulation of Freedom* (AK Press, 2014).

Brian Wierman is an independent scholar, consultant and US Marine. He consults with organizations in the US and Europe and teaches MBA and undergraduate business courses at several universities. Brian holds an MBA from Westminster College in Salt Lake City, Utah, and an MA in National Security Studies from the US Naval War College in Rhode Island. His forthcoming PhD on anarchism's influence on contemporary management is from the University of Manchester, UK. Brian and his family live in Park City, Utah, and Manchester, UK.

Colin C. Williams is a professor of Public Policy in the Management School at the University of Sheffield in the United Kingdom. Since 2016, he has been lead expert to the European Commission's European Platform Tackling Undeclared Work, providing support to the member states of the European Union and social partners in combating the undeclared economy. His research interests are in undeclared work, labour practices and entrepreneurship, subjects on which he has published some 30 books and over 450 journal articles over the past 30 years.

1

INTRODUCTION

Management and anarchism, and organization

Martin Parker, Thomas Swann and Konstantin Stoborod

Management *and* anarchism? Surely this should be management *versus* anarchism? Management, as one of the modern sciences of control, appears to be the opposite of a political movement which seeks the absence of government, which insists on personal and collective freedom and rejects the authority of the state and other centralized, dominating institutions (Marshall, 1993; Ward, 2004; Kinna, 2005; Guerin, 2005). How can they learn from each other when they are so opposed in their goals? Surely managers are always struggling against anarchy, and anarchists don't want to be managed?

This book is intended to persuade you not to jump to such assumptions too quickly. Indeed, we think that we can learn a great deal about management from a serious study of anarchist thought. However, the sorts of things that we learn cannot simply be added to management, as if they were new techniques that could be taught by university business schools and sold by management consultants. Management has a habit of doing this – taking various forms of thought and cultural references and then using them to rebrand clichés about leadership, marketing, careers or whatever. But this book is not suggesting that anarchist ideas can be used to help management. What we mean is different, in that we think that anarchism encourages us to rethink some of the fundamental assumptions of management, to turn management on its head and question many of the core assumptions and practices which comprise the common sense of business schools (Swann and Stoborod, 2014).

Most management textbooks, consultants and business magazines tell a story about the rise of management as pretty much the same as human progress. This is an account of the growth of large businesses and state bureaucracies that allow human beings to come together in ever more complex ways in order to achieve extraordinary goals. The Industrial Revolution, mass production, international trade, gigantic bridges spanning rivers, the Apollo moon landing and the latest iPhone – all these are achievements of complex coordination, the products of operations management, finance, logistics, strategy and so on. We are told that we now live in a managed world, a world which is made by management, and everything from the well-stocked supermarket to cheap air travel relies on the synchronization of people and technology under a central authority. That is why management is a growing subject at universities, and that is supposedly why managers deserve to be paid more than workers – because they hold great responsibilities and are experts in what they do.

It's a persuasive story, partly because it does contain some truths, but that doesn't mean that it is all true or that this a world which is inevitable or even desirable. Indeed, if we think about it, this story of 'managerialism' is usually told by people who have an interest in claiming that management is important. This is because they are managers or want to be managers or are selling some sort of knowledge which flatters managers (Parker, 2002). So they would say that, wouldn't they?

Part of the problem here is that *management* is a word which is used in some rather imprecise ways. Sometimes, we speak of management as a particular occupational group (the management), sometimes as a form of knowledge (such as the course that you might be studying right now) and sometimes as a kind of skill (managing). More often, it is used as a kind of condensation of all of these meanings, something which is everywhere, inevitable, and which we all do – managing our careers, our appearances, even our sex lives. Management seems to have become a word for any form of conscious patterning of human behaviour and something that is so common that denying its importance is like claiming that human beings don't need oxygen. How could we be against management? What sense does it make?

So let's try to be a bit more precise then. We want to use the word *management* to refer to an organizational form in which a specialist class of managers tell their subordinates how to organize themselves. Management – in this rather more specific sense – requires hierarchy. Power and reward are concentrated in a certain class of people, shaping the structure, space and strategies of managed organizations. This is reflected in an enduring distinction between the managers and those they manage, which can be marked out by special meetings in which people use a particular language, occupy separate parts of buildings and even wear different forms of clothing. This is an arrangement which relies on the assumption that the manager has expertise that the employee does not. Management in this sense is not democratic. It does not involve sharing information, status or rewards, and its authority cannot be challenged by ordinary workers. This sort of organizational arrangement also makes certain assumptions about people. It assumes that most of us are incapable of organizing ourselves and that we must be encouraged, cajoled and even punished to ensure that order is maintained. We are being persuaded that we need managing because we are being told that we can't manage ourselves.

These ideas about management configure the ways in which the very activity of business is imagined and taught. Many textbooks construct an 'ideal type' of organization, a picture of a company which is owned by shareholders, who are mainly interested in dividends, or owner managers who want to grow a business in order to make bigger profits by selling as much of a particular good or service as possible. This means that company strategy and human resource management attempt to maximize sales, minimize wages, maximize employment flexibility, minimize disobedience, maximize efficiency and avoid or externalize as many costs as possible. Entrepreneurs are important insofar as they are motivated to start companies which can grow into, or be bought by, corporations which are assumed to be the ultimate form of organization in commercial terms. The role of finance and accounting is therefore to serve the owners or shareholders by counting and distributing the financial value that is produced.

Most textbooks present 'management' in this organizational sense, as a social arrangement that has emerged over the last century or so and which has gradually replaced less efficient forms of organizing which generate lower profits, make decisions more slowly, don't grow quickly or whatever. The common sense of management assumes that managers are the ones who make decisions because most human beings need to be led, indeed that they rather like being subject to authority because they don't need to bear responsibility. Clever leaders don't even need to give direct instructions because they can also manipulate the culture of their organization in order to get people to share values that make them want to work harder for the firm. This ideal type organization will use sophisticated marketing in order to sell its products and services and innovative production, operations or digital technology in order to maximize its efficiency and open up new markets. If ethics is mentioned, it is usually in terms of not breaking the law or ensuring that potential customers or employees have a good impression of the firm by spending some money on social responsibility initiatives.

This is quite a specific picture and one that involves management disciplines which are each covered by the chapters in this book. This level of detail is important because 'management' is a particular way of arranging human beings, things and technologies, but that does not mean that it is the only way. Indeed, we think that the word does not describe all forms of organization. That would be like saying that because trees are plants, all plants are trees. It seems to us that people (and other animals) can actually organize themselves without many of the assumptions routinely built into management. Think about families, queues, flea markets or swarms of bees. Co-ordinated behaviour can happen on sports fields, in fairs and festivals and in mass migrations of animals. All of these examples are organized, in the sense of displaying recognizable patterns that endure across space and over time, but none of them are being directed by one form of central control, by a central brain that directs activity or by a particular cadre of people in suits who issue orders to everyone else.

Indeed, thinking about the concept 'organization' might be more helpful in understanding the world we live in, because many of the achievements of our modern human world, such as **open source software**, are certainly the results of complex forms of organization. Whether they are the results of management, in the specific sense we have defined it here, is quite another matter.

OPEN SOURCE SOFTWARE

Open source software comes with permission for anyone to use, copy, modify and redistribute. This freedom can only be exercised if users have access to the software source codes. 'Open' in this context does not necessarily mean free of charge but refers to users' freedom to alter the codes. A piece of software could be distributed freely but remain 'closed' or proprietary if the source codes are not disclosed. Open source software has its roots in the emergent hacker culture of the 1970s, but a landmark was Richard Stallman's announcement about the GNU software project in the early 1980s. The 'GNU Manifesto' (1985) was intended to 'bring back the cooperative spirit that prevailed in the computing community in earlier days.' To ensure that free software remained free and to prevent GNU software from being turned into proprietary software, free software licenses were developed; these open licenses are based on the idea of 'copyleft.' Copyleft uses copyright law but flips it over to serve the opposite of its usual purpose: instead of a means of privatizing software, it becomes a means of keeping software free. The central idea of copyleft is that it gives everyone permission to run, copy, modify and distribute the programme but not permission to add restrictions of their own.

The open software movement also uses more practical arguments that suggest the superior nature of the software development process when users are also involved as co-developers. The movement has inspired greater openness and participation in other media and communication fields, including creative **commons** licenses for published material (see box in Chapter 17). Open source breaks the barriers between information producers and consumers, between big companies and bedroom hackers, and enables all users to publish and edit news or information and act collectively in a decentralized way. Examples include the online encyclopaedia *Wikipedia*, the Linux computer operating system and versions of the distributed ledger system blockchain.

Anarchists are particularly interested in networks rather than hierarchies, in webs rather than bureaucracies, in patterns of people who collectively produce something which is intricate and robust, such as a piece of software, but do so without any central co-ordination. Anarchists generally don't like it when people tell them what to do, but this doesn't mean that they are against organization. Indeed, we think that this is a huge misunderstanding and that the long history of anarchist ideas provides a fantastic example of a sustained consideration of how human beings can come together to organize (Dunois, 1907; Ward, 1996; Parker et al., 2014; Swann and Stoborod, 2014). It is precisely because they wish to preserve individual and collective freedoms that anarchists are so interested in thinking and practicing different ways to organize themselves. They understand the costs and benefits of organization in a way that managerialists don't because the latter just assume that there is only one best way.

Given what we have said about anarchism's refusal of common sense, it shouldn't surprise you that anarchism is not one thing, not a single set of beliefs which is agreed upon. Perhaps it is better defined as a network or web of ideas. All anarchists would share an interest in thinking about independence from authority and agreeing on the rules they wish to live by, but there are lots of different versions of anarchism in these pages. All share a concern with the relationship between freedom and collective action, but their theories about people, markets and forms of organization are often quite different. Indeed, some anarchists aren't really interested in 'theory' at all, perhaps considering anarchism a practical activity that is tested by doing, not something that could be taught by textbooks. Unlike much management theory, which often suggests that there is 'best practice,' anarchists are usually happy enough with difference, acknowledging that there might be different anarchisms for different times or forms of organizing which will work at different scales or in different places.

Most management thinkers just assume that hierarchical authority by experts is the one best way, and so their writing consists of a small series of variations on this theme – charismatic leadership, strategic planning, centralized control of information, justification for huge inequalities in pay and status and so on. Anarchists, in contrast, suggest a much wider range of alternatives, many of which we will be exploring in this book. They encourage us to think about the importance of small and face-to-face forms of association, about collective forms of decision making and responsibility, but also about the possibilities of federations of the small to make something much bigger and the use of technology and social arrangements to enable voluntary co-operation. Anarchists think hard about the relationship, or balance, between personal freedoms and the collective good. They treat organizing as a form of politics.

When we call something 'political,' it means that a particular issue is – or should be – the subject of debate by the people it affects. This is a central principle of any institution that claims to be 'democratic.' In practice, this might involve voting in elections or referenda, donating money, having meetings, joining pressure groups, marching with banners and placards or liking particular causes on social media. Politics might include political parties, prime ministers, presidents and discussions in national institutions like parliaments or international ones like the European Union or the United Nations – the kind of thing we often see in the news. But politics can also be ordinary people getting involved in debating the issues that affect them and taking action to improve their situation, such as Extinction Rebellion or the open source software movement. Politics is a messy business in which people express different opinions about the way that the world should be arranged. It is not tidy, and it is often noisy and confusing. But to take any particular choice out of the realm of politics is to say that a decision should not be challenged and that the people who have made that decision know best and should be left to run the world in whatever way they want. On a large-scale level, this is what happens when we leave politics to big institutions, perhaps assuming that there is nothing that small people like us can do to shape the world that we live in.

This, we believe, is what conventional forms of management generally do. They assume that 'we' have no choice in the way that matters are organized, because the rules of efficiency, profitability or human nature inevitably drive us towards an arrangement in which managers tell other people what to do. We don't have the expertise, the power, the time and so leave the decisions to others, even if we are affected by them. This gives permission to others to tell us that we have no choice, that 'markets' or laws of nature determine what must be done and that only idealists or idiots would imagine that the world could be otherwise. We disagree, because we think that the future is open and only dictators or the unimaginative would think otherwise. Indeed, it is precisely those who benefit most from current arrangements who are keenest to tell us that they are natural and inevitable. They have the most to lose.

This book

The idea that animates this book is to show how anarchism could be used to think about management and organization differently. We are assuming that our audience are students who are currently studying for qualifications in management at one of the 13,000 business schools worldwide (Parker, 2018). We are also assuming that you will have textbooks which explain why best practice in management means that the world has to be arranged in certain ways. So in these texts, you will be taught about the importance of every organization having a leader or the necessity of arranging financial and accounting structures in ways that ensure shareholders and investors get a return on their money. Or you might be encouraged to think that strategy is something that only managers can do, whilst workers need to be motivated by human resource departments in order that they will work effectively.

Now these are credible ways of thinking about how people, things and money might be arranged, and they have had some remarkable successes – from the building of the 164-kilometre Danyang–Kunshan Grand Bridge in China to the intricate logistics that move shipping containers around the world. However, these aren't the only answers to how human beings can organize themselves, and this book will encourage our readers to be more imaginative and radical in thinking about how people and things can come together to achieve forms of co-ordination that improve their lives individually and collectively. It seems to us that this is the most important issue at the present time as we face the threats of climate change, global inequalities and a widespread sense of disengagement from conventional political institutions. Any form of thought that doesn't face these questions head-on is ignoring realities, betting instead on business as usual. But is more 'management' really the best way to address these questions? Can we manage our way out of the problems that management seems to be creating? Climate change, environmental degradation, gigantic global inequalities, populist politics, resource wars and forced migration are problems which are being produced by the current social and economic order. Whether you like it or not, addressing them means changing the way we do business with each other and, consequently, the ways that we think about organization.

The book is organized like a conventional textbook, to make it easier for you to use. We are also using text boxes to introduce important concepts and thinkers. Each chapter takes a standard management topic and begins by briefly rehearsing the sort of position that you are likely to find in the textbooks used in many management courses. After that, our authors then try to mess things up, by asking awkward questions, introducing unfamiliar and even revolutionary ideas and providing evidence that doesn't fit the standard management picture. Of course, not all textbooks are the same, and there are some that we would even recommend, but in general, this book is meant to be a kind of antidote to management common sense. Imagine the chapters here as engaged in a debate with your textbook – and perhaps with your lecturer too. We want you to question their assumptions, their evidence, and to ask whether the sort of world that they describe is the only one possible.

So, for example, if the textbook suggests that no great organization could exist without a leader, then we will be encouraging you to think about arrangements of human beings that do not rely on leaders to achieve co-ordination. Or if the text suggests that organizations need a unified culture in which everyone shares the same values, we will be encouraging you to think about whether we need to pretend that we believe certain things at work and whether open discussion and debate is possible within a work organization. Or if the text says that having pay inequalities is a good way to motivate people, we will draw your attention to organizations that seem to do well and still pay everyone around the same wages.

SUMA

Suma Foods is a worker **co-operative**, an organization owned and run by its members (Suma, 2017; see also Cannell, 2015; Roper, 2016, box in Chapter 8). It was founded in the Northern English city of Leeds in 1977 and is the largest independent wholefood wholesaler in the United Kingdom. In 2017, this co-operative was one of 7226 co-ops in the UK, employing 222 785 people and with a turnover of £36.1 billion (Co-ops UK, 2018). Suma specializes in vegetarian, organic, ethical and natural products. Suma stocks organic versions of everything they can and supports fair-trade as a licensee of the Fairtrade Foundation, and all their body care, cosmetic and household products are cruelty-free. They are also acutely aware of the impact that business has on the environment at local and global levels and hence try to keep carbon emissions to a minimum. Suma uses renewable electricity and motion sensors in rooms to switch the lights off when there is no activity. Sales representatives share a hybrid car, and their truck deliveries are optimized to reduce fuel consumption. They take back plastic and cardboard packaging from customers and what they are unable to re-use, they recycle.

Suma is owned by the people who work in it. There are no shareholders. Everyone is paid the same – in 2016, that was £40 000 a year for the 161 permanent members and over £11 an hour for temporary workers. Job rotation is simply assumed, with everyone collectively doing all the jobs that need doing, whatever they happen to be and regardless of status. This sort of multi-skilling also enables collaborative democratic decision making, as all members have at least some experience of every area and therefore practical knowledge on which to base discussion and decisions. In some ways, Suma is an unremarkable company. It buys, sells and moves a set of products that customers want. There is nothing particularly innovative about the core aspects of their business model, involving trucks and a warehouse. However, as is clear from the preceding, the way that they run the business denies hierarchical organization and refuses a permanent division of labour, asymmetries of knowledge and reward, the externalization of costs and even assumptions about growth. Members of Suma assume that the organizing principle is 'self-management,' not management by managers. This is a company which is clearly driven by idealism, with a vision of a different world, but which also deals with practical questions in ways that have been making its members a living for over forty years.

You will almost certainly disagree with many of the ideas being put forward in this book. Indeed, in a perverse way, that's what we want you to do, because it will encourage you think about your own assumptions. The beginning of creativity, of an innovative response to a situation, must involve a challenge to common sense, to what everyone else seems to think. That is what we think that anarchists encourage, a call to be radical and brave in our questioning of the world. Because if we don't do that, we might not have a world left that is worth saving.

Each of the 16 chapters that follows describes a common aspect of management and can be read alongside a similar chapter in your recommended textbook. As you move through the six sections of the book, you will also find text boxes that introduce you to famous anarchist and radical thinkers, as well as key concepts which anarchists use when describing what they do. There are cross-references to the text boxes in **bold** in each chapter. Even though the chapters are different in many ways, they are all inspired by well-known writers who have encouraged critical thinking about the importance of individual freedom and its relation to collective action. Anarchism is not one thing, and in these pages, you will meet lots of different forms of anarchism – green, feminist, primitivist, cyber, syndicalist, social and so on. Don't worry about these differences too much, but instead think of them as varied ways in which anarchists have responded to the challenges that they (and we) face but are still held together by a strong concern for individual and collective freedom and self-determination.

As you read about anarchist ideas, you will realise that woven through all the chapters is a big issue about 'human nature.' It can be simply expressed in terms of whether human beings are 'naturally' selfish or 'naturally' co-operative. How you answer this has a big influence on how you believe human beings should be organized. For example, do we always need hierarchies in business organizations and the state? Is decision making on the basis of democratic consensus always slow and inefficient? Are people only really motivated by money? The way that you answer these questions partly depends on what you believe to be our fundamental characteristics, our most basic drives and instincts. However, you might refuse the 'either/ or' implied by these questions, instead suggesting that there isn't something called 'human nature' because we are constructed by our societies, families, language, customs and religion. All the way through the book, we encourage you to think about these questions and then think about what anarchists claim is possible. Just as anarchists encourage us to question common sense, we should use that attitude to question anarchism too.

We started off by telling you that textbooks aren't always right, so perhaps an anarchist textbook is a contradiction in terms. Indeed, some anarchists, like Ivan **Illich** (see box in Chapter 10), are very suspicious of the education system itself, suggesting that we need to 'deschool society' in order to free people from the authority of teachers and the way that they prepare people to be workers and consumers within industrial capitalism (1971, see also **Michel**, box in Chapter 2). Paradoxically, we are claiming the authority of textbook authors in order to tell you to distrust authority. In our conclusion to the book, we will consider this problem some more and ask you what you can really do with books like this. After all, we want you to use it to help you pass an exam or write an essay, but that's not all that we want you to do with it. These ideas are too important to be left in books.

References

Cannell, B. (2015). "Doing It the Hard Way?" *Co-ops UK Blog.* Available at: www.uk.coop/ newsroom/bob-cannell-doing-it-hard-way (accessed 27 March 2017).

Co-operatives UK. (2018). *The UK Co-operative Economy 2018.* Manchester: Co-ops UK. Available at: http://reports.uk.coop/economy2018/ (accessed 26 June 2018).

Dunois, A. (1907). "Anarchism and Organization." *Anarchy and Organization: The Debate at the 1907 International Anarchist Congress.* Available at: http://theanarchistlibrary.org/library/ various-authors-anarchy-and-organization-the-debate-at-the-1907-international-anarchist-congres.

Guerin, D. (ed.). (2005). *No Gods, No Masters: An Anthology of Anarchism.* Oakland, CA: AK Press.

Illich, I. (1971). *Deschooling Society.* New York, NY: Harper and Row.

Kinna, R. (2005). *Anarchism: A Beginner's Guide.* Oxford: Oneworld Publications.

Marshall, P. (1993). *Demanding the Impossible: A History of Anarchism.* London: HarperCollins.

Parker, M. (2002). *Against Management.* Oxford: Polity Press.

Parker, M. (2018). *Shut Down the Business School.* London: Pluto Press.

Parker, M., Cheney, G., Fournier, V., and Land, C. (2014). *The Companion to Alternative Organization*. London: Routledge.

Roper, J. (2016). "Case Study: Total Pay Equality and Multi-Skilling at a Workers' Co-operative." *HR Magazine*, 1 September. Available at: www.hrmagazine.co.uk/article-details/case-study-total-equality-of-pay-and-multi-skilling-at-a-workers-co-operative (accessed 27 March 2017).

Stallman, R. (1985). "The GNU Manifesto." Available at: www.gnu.org/gnu/manifesto.en.html (accessed 26 June 2018).

Suma. (2017). "We Are Suma." Available at: www.suma.coop/about (accessed 26 June 2018).

Swann, T., and Stoborod, K. (eds.). (2014). "Management, Business, Anarchism." *Ephemera*, 14(4).

Ward, C. (1996). "The Organization of Anarchy." In L. Krimerman and L. Perry (eds.), *Patterns of Anarchy*. New York, NY: Anchor Books.

Ward, C. (2004). *Anarchism: A Very Short Introduction*. Oxford: Oxford University Press.

PART I

Managers and management

History and present

2

AN ANARCHIST PREHISTORY OF MANAGEMENT

Nidhi Srinivas

It might seem that anarchism and management are opposed. Very few textbooks on management contain even a reference to anarchism, when telling a story about how the modern science of management grew from 19th-century beginnings and became dominant and unquestioned. But is this silence justified? The fact is that ideas about 'management' and ideas about 'anarchism' emerged at the same time, in the context of the rise of industrial capitalism. So perhaps we need to understand the two as somehow related. This chapter will suggest that we can write a different history of management, one in which choices about who controls and benefits from industrial production are actively discussed. Opening management's prehistory (because this is something taking place before we can strictly identify a practice called 'management') provides us with a way of questioning some of its contemporary assumptions.

This chapter will focus on several examples that, on the surface, have little in common with each other, or indeed with management studies. Yet the social and work settings described, the interests of the actors involved and the sorts of organizations created were all animated by anarchist ideas. These anarchist ideas developed in the context of how work and production were organized in the late 19th century. Managers had to negotiate with workers inspired by anarchist politics, and this shaped the history of management ideas. However, the conventional history of management ignores these influences. Therefore, to discuss anarchism historically is also to offer an alternative account of how management ideas emerged and developed into the management common sense we find in textbooks today.

Common to these examples in this chapter is a shared sensitivity to organizing, accompanied by an acute sense of politics. Organizing is not simply about how to manage but about the institutions and relationships that shape the world we live in. The substance of these anarchist ideas about organizing was itself shaped by the fact that many anarchist intellectuals in the 19th century, when management came into being as a practice, were quite familiar with complex organizations and the challenges of coordinating them, and hence their anarchist ideas had direct organizational implications. This chapter explores these themes across three sections. I begin with a discussion of three examples – in Cuba, Egypt and Mexico – and what they tell us about anarchism and management theory. I then turn to the substance of anarchist ideas and the ideas' organizational implications. Finally, I discuss the significance of such a history and how it casts conventional textbook histories in a different light.

This chapter will

- discuss some examples of individuals who were inspired by anarchism and also held management positions,
- explore the similarities and differences between anarchism and management in how they responded to the changes in how work was performed and organized during and after the Industrial Revolution,
- provide an overview of anarchist forms of organization, and
- ask whether the history (or prehistory) of anarchism and management is important to how we currently understand management and its place in the business school education.

Three anarchist managers

In 1865, a cigar maker, Saturnino Martínez, started Cuba's first labour magazine, *La Aurora: Periodico Semanal Dedicado a los Artesanos* (Weekly Periodical Dedicated to Artisans). The periodical promoted worker associations and advocated *lecturas*, cigar factory readers who would read aloud relevant texts for the benefit of labouring (and illiterate) colleagues on the shop-floor. Its political approach would be sharply challenged by an alternative publication, started in 1887, *El Productor: Seminario consagrado a la defensa de los intereses económicos-sociales de la clase obrera* (Seminar Consecrated to the Defense of the Economic-Social Interests of the Working Class). Where *La Aurora* urged decentralizing control and empowering workers, *El Productor* condemned class inequality and urged worker control of factories for revolutionary ends (Daniel, 2015). One of *El Productor's* founders was Enrique Roíg San Martín, who had worked in the island's sugar mills, first as a labourer and ultimately as a manager.

A few decades later, in 1898, Pietro Vasai stepped off a ship in the Egyptian port city of Alexandria. A spate of Italian anarchists had arrived and allied themselves with local and migrant labour in the city. Listed in Italian police files as "anarchico pericoloso" ("dangerous anarchist"), Vasai had already managed the influential anarchist periodical *La Questione sociale* (The Social Question) (founded by the well-known anarchist Errico Malatesta). Vasai and colleagues, like Roíg in Cuba, wanted to create organizations to struggle with factory owners on behalf of workers. They organized strikes, exposed picket crossers (who would break strikes by going to work and thus undermining the power of the collective of all workers), established funds to help support workers on strike and the widows of deceased workers, set up sanitation and health services during cholera epidemics and held study circles (in wine shops that also served as libraries). Galvanized by these activities, cigarette, construction and print workers began to hold common meetings to coordinate worker resistance for their trades. A number of periodicals were started, including the bilingual *La Tribune Libre / La Tribuna Libera* (1901), which at its height published a thousand copies, more than half of which went to Italy (Khuri-Makdisi, 2010).

Shortly after the 1906 California earthquake, an Indian man, Pandurang Khankhoje, arrived in San Francisco via China. Fleeing the subcontinent for political reasons, he moved to Oregon and worked in a lumber mill. The mill manager had started an Indian Independence League, influenced by anarchist ideas, and Khankhoje would play an active role in it. During the First World War, he was sent in secret to the Iranian border to create a second front in the war. Failing in this effort, he retraced his route back, eventually arriving in Mexico City. Here he became an agricultural scientist. Appointed professor at the National School of Agriculture in Chapingo, Khankhoje researched hybrid corn and advised farmers on growing it. His close associates included Tina Modotti (who photographed the hybrid corn) and Diego Rivera (who painted the corn and Khankhoje into the mural *El pan nuestro*, at the Ministry of Education) (Sawhney, 2012).

The origins of anarchist ideas in the late 19th century

These historical examples share several themes. First, anarchist movements and the people involved in them were deeply connected to work, trades, factories, workplaces, industrial capital and the communities formed by industrial forces. Anarchists and those inspired by anarchist ideas frequently took up a number of roles in industry and trade, including as managers, which was the case here with Martínez, Roíg, Vasai and Khankhoje. Anarchism had direct organizational implications that greatly shaped the available goals and methods (which in anarchist and other circles are often referred to as ends and means) of anarchist struggle. They tended to be critical of authority structures reliant on hierarchical power, which was generally perceived as authoritarian. They also were critical of free markets and suspicious of the state. Instead, anarchists generally encouraged a focus on creating genuine agreement among workers on how to achieve their shared goals. These goals in turn involved a focus on collective groups and their needs and interests.

These anarchists had a particular way of looking at organizations, asking not just what these organizations should accomplish but also how they should go about it. This was an attention to the ends or goals of organization as well as the means or methods used within them. It meant that anarchist managers were critically aware of hierarchy and its dangers and sensitive to accusations of authoritarian decision making. At the same time, their organizations sought worker rights and directly challenged capitalist power (such as that of factory owners and allied government officials). The Italian anarchist Errico Malatesta explained that

> to become a convinced anarchist, and not in name only, he must begin to feel the solidarity that joins him to his comrades, and to learn to cooperate with others in the defence of common interests and that, by struggling against the bosses and against the government which supports them, should realise that bosses and governments are useless parasites and that the workers could manage the domestic economy by their own efforts.
>
> *(Malatesta, 1897/2015, p. 82)*

The close connection to work, and the attention to both means and ends, translated into a particular emphasis in thinking about organizing. It mattered how work was divided and brought together. The division of labour was a political act and had to be discussed in political terms. Efficiency was not a matter to be taken for granted, nor seen as outside the responsibility of the worker. Rather, the basic questions confronted by capitalist managers, when organizing the work in order to increase the market value generated by labour power, were questions to be taken up by all of those within the organization. If it mattered how work was divided and brought together, it also mattered what the work sought to achieve. Martínez, Roíg, Vasai and Khankhoje were deeply committed to the output of the work they did and supervised, whether cigars, sugar, construction or hybrid corn. But for them such output was not sufficiently understood solely in terms of market value. After all, who ultimately benefits from market value? Not the workers. The output was instead important as an opportunity for self-organizing, for prefigurative politics.

PREFIGURATION

"Prefiguration has been an important concept in the anarchist tradition since the late 19th century. However, the term itself was coined in the 1970s as a way of pointing to the importance of using organizational means or strategies that do not contradict the ends or purposes of an organization. Prefiguration has its roots in radical left and anarchist social movement practices. A distinctive quality of prefiguration is that it aims to achieve radical social and political change through an alternative approach to organization in the present. This distinguishes it from many other left-wing approaches that want to capture state power and promise a top-down social change at some point in the future". Management studies teaches us that organizations should separate actions and their consequences through formal hierarchies that hold some responsible for daily routines, practices and procedures and others responsible for matching such actions to expected and desired goals. The essence of prefiguration or prefigurative organizing is removal of a temporal distinction between what is being done right now and the desired outcome of this activity. There should be no distinction between what we want to achieve (ends) and how we plan to achieve it (means). The means we use should reflect the values we want to see solidified in the ends we are striving for. To put it simply, it is not OK to do something nasty right now in the name of some bright future to come. These principles underlying prefigurative organizing allow us, on the one hand, to understand how to facilitate progressive and liberatory forms of organizing and, on the other, to identify who we want to engage or ally with. In contemporary social movements and radical politics, prefiguration is often linked to ideas such as direct action or DIY – 'do it yourself' (or DIT, 'do it together').

Reflecting on how we should act in the first place has multiple consequences. First of all, it offers an opportunity for practical critique. Social life offers a variety of organizational encounters, from post offices and grocery stores, restaurants and online purchases, to the manner in which we earn a living and work with one another. Who shapes these encounters and towards what ends? Who decides these goals and how to go about meeting them? Second, it helps us recognize that politics and organization are intimately connected. The more we reflect on the way work is divided and responsibilities allotted, the more sensitive we become to the unequal distribution of rights and rewards in such work and its accomplishment. Finally, it helps us rehearse alternative possibilities. A willingness to reflect on goals and ways of meeting these goals also means an openness to test other ways of meeting such goals and generate conversations and forms of inclusion that enable shared learning, reducing the inequalities endemic to workplaces. Ultimately "such organizing is 'prefigurative', in the sense that it attempts to bring new forms of social relationships into being" (Parker et al., 2014, pp. 627–628), in a recognition that anarchism is "always immanent in existing social arrangements bubbling under the surface and waiting to re-emerge under the right conditions" (Reedy, 2014, p. 646).

These anarchist managers were prefigurative in the sense that they wanted to demonstrate the necessity and the benefits of workers taking up managerial roles on behalf of workers (as opposed to the capitalist). Such opportunities generated solidarity which in turn translated into credible benefits to the communities within which the workers lived, such as of health and schooling. Since the division of labour and the arrangement of the business (that is to say, hierarchy, work culture and leadership) were not neutral tasks because they conferred power and profits to capitalist owners, workers had to assert their own interests and ensure the terms of work were in their favour. Finally, it mattered how those doing the work were treated. Emphasized in these organizational efforts was a question of dignity, how those who did the work felt as they worked, reducing the gap between their aspirations and their treatment in their workplaces. Anarchist leaders were concerned with their workers' communities and their health, education and capacity to exercise political leadership and pressured capitalist owners for benefits to ensure some protection for these communities. Anarchists, as managers, were intensely practical. Organizations, and the work done in them, were assessed in terms of the goals sought and whom those goals served: whether they filled stomachs and kept communities together.

Second, because activists were intensely concerned with ideas and putting these ideas into practice, much of their activity involved translating and reading anarchist texts, discussing their key concepts and demonstrating their importance for actual organization. There was an acute practicality about all this, for achieving work results as well as political ones. Work goals spilled over into the social world surrounding the factory. Anarchist worker/managers were concerned about not only work conditions but the consequences of such work in terms of its effects on religious and national **identity** (see box in Chapter 4). Work was also about people, personalities, emotions, customs and conventions. Organizational activities were not locked into an instrumental relation between tasks, techniques, goals and their supervision; nor was work bounded by an organization that was distinct and separate from the social world. The cigar workers organized by Roíg in Florida would also welcome José Marti, noted poet, journalist and Cuban patriot, and encourage his triumphal (though fatal) return to Cuba to fight for the island's independence from the Spanish empire (Daniel, 2015). Work was also about customs and social conventions, including of religion and religious identity. Khankhoje and Vasai frequently negotiated with sectarian views in creating a shared set of work interests. Reading groups in Alexandria translated anarchist texts into Arabic, and they were discussed and debated in periodicals that saw no contradiction between these ideas and prevailing religious norms (Khuri-Makdisi, 2010). Ultimately, of course, work was about people and their emotions. The intense debates common to anarchist circles of the 19th century were personal, shaped by the charismatic individuals involved in them.

Finally, anarchist movements were connected to global networks as well as local associations. Activists were therefore concerned with a variety of overlapping social issues that cohered around work conditions but were also part of global radical currents concerned with anti-colonial resistance, gender equality and sexual critique, with ties that crossed boundaries of race and nation, creating radicalized communities of belief and friendship (see **Michel** this chapter and Gandhi, 2006). These shared themes meant that questions of management were raised in a particular way. Anarchist activism was intensely organizational, with an acute focus on the interplay between evaluating the means at their disposal and identifying the desirable ends to be achieved through acceptable means.

LOUISE MICHEL, 1830–1905

Louise Michel is perhaps the best known of the anarchists who took part in the Paris Commune from 1870 to 71. The Paris Commune refers to a period where following France's defeat by Prussia (a once dominant state in Europe that eventually unified with other states to form what we now know as Germany) in the Franco-Prussian War, the people of Paris took over control of the city and ran it themselves, defending it from attack by the French army. Michel was involved in arranging public services and in organizing the women who fought to defend Paris. The Paris Commune was ultimately defeated, and the French government took back control of the city, executing tens of thousands of Communards (the people who took part in the Commune). Michel was captured and exiled to New Caledonia. Central to Michel's anarchism was a belief in the ability of education to provide people with knowledge and to develop a virtuous character. While dominant ideas at the time saw Europeans as the most civilized and cultured people in the world, Michel argued that the ideals of European colonialism were more akin to barbarism and that a truly civilized education involved learning from folk history as much as from science. Through her experiences of being ridiculed when she tried to publish work on science, Michel saw a connection between how education could be misused to dominate people and how women were oppressed.

Anarchist ideas and their organizational implications

Errico Malatesta defined anarchist organization in the following terms:

> An anarchist organisation must, in my opinion [allow for] complete autonomy, and independence, and therefore full responsibility, to individuals and groups; free agreement between those who think it useful to come together for **cooperative** action [see box in Chapter 8], for common aims; a moral duty to fulfill one's pledges and to take no action which is contrary to the accepted programme.
>
> *(Malatesta, 1897)*

Peter Marshall (2008, p. 3) echoes this when he observes that

> while there are many different currents in anarchism, anarchists do share certain basic assumptions and central themes. If you dive into an anarchist philosophy, you generally find a particular view of human nature, a critique of the existing order, a vision of a free society, and a way to achieve it.

That last phrase, "a way to achieve it", is for anarchists the sphere of organization. It was also something that provoked discussion and disagreement.

What did these anarchists want? Martínez and Roíg would both have known the trade and production of cigarettes. They would have known the machinery in these factories, how it worked, its risks and how to repair it. They would have known how to ensure workers did the work they should. How to price cigarettes, where to source tobacco and how to keep machinery in good order were familiar matters to such practical managers. Both supported the rights of cigarette workers, including better work conditions and wages. Both felt it was essential that workers create associations to represent them. Where they differed sharply was in the manner and the goals in bringing these workers together, the means and ends of organization. These differences, in turn, were the consequence of a very different understanding of what anarchy constituted and how one went about it.

Martínez's great influence was the **mutualist** anarchist Pierre-Joseph Proudhon, who believed that workers should 'control their own means of production (see box in Chapter 17). They would form small as well as large associations, especially in the manufacturing and extractive industries.' Proudhon believed that as mutualist ideas spread, the 'State would eventually wither away' (Marshall, 2008, p. 243).

PIERRE-JOSEPH PROUDHON, 1809–1865

Proudhon, the son of an innkeeper, born in 1809, grew up in the Jura region of France, near the Swiss border. Largely self-taught, fiercely independent, he is one of the most influential thinkers of anarchism and often is considered its founding father. Proudhon's views also contributed to a lasting division on the left, between libertarian and authoritarian socialists. Both shared a recognition of capitalist exploitation but diverged sharply on their responses to its malaise. Those who followed Proudhon wished to create a mutually governed society without a state. Those who followed Karl **Marx** sought to create a communist state (see box in Chapter 11). Proudhon's vision was of a society governed by its members, and not through the authoritarian, violent, centralized power of the state. Rather than the individualistic urges of the market, a mutually agreed system would govern society, where workers would form associations to conduct economic activities. Through these associations, workers would set their own wages and product prices and share the profits made. There would be no need, eventually, for the state, and it would instead be largely these associations that governed society, with a minimal presence of the state. Although Proudhon's views on gender and race were reprehensible, it is important to remember that he made one of the most important contributions to the political economy of anarchism, sparked debates on the left and inspired many later anarchist thinkers.

At the same time, Martínez was also pragmatic when it came to relations with the owners of the factories. He believed worker associations offered a productive way of reforming cigarette factories, a channel for voicing suggestions for the owners to hear, enabling a mutually beneficial resolution of the interests of these parties. Strikes and related forms of industrial disruption were to be avoided where possible, and the emphasis instead was on reconciling the goals of owners and workers. This marks Martínez out as different from the other figures discussed here, and in this accommodation with the owners of industry, he seems to be moving away from anarchism, despite being explicitly influenced by its ideas (Fernández, 2001).

Roíg was rather more radical, a **syndicalist** (see box in Chapter 8) who saw the interests of capitalists and workers as incompatible and proposed that confederations of worker unions were the solution. The purpose of workers associating among themselves was in fact to overthrow the factory owners and take control of production. They would learn to run cigarette factories, share the profits and mobilize other workers to do the same. Their ultimate purpose would be to create a society that was worker-run, for the benefit of all. The great influence here was Mikhail **Bakunin,** who insisted that "true freedom can only be realized with the total destruction of the State" (Marshall, 2008, p. 277, see box in Chapter 7).

If the goals of organizing the workers were different, so were the espoused methods. That is to say not only ends but also the means differed. Mutualists and syndicalists both took the task of organization seriously and developed procedures to enable a greater range of worker voices to be heard. But where they differed was in their rationale for choosing certain tactics over others. Violence, strikes and other forms of disruption were not disavowed by syndicalists like Roig. Martínez, however, distanced himself from such 'extremism.' In a sense, the two groups, syndicalists like Roíg and mutualists like Martínez, shared an end, worker control of enterprise and society, but differed greatly about the acceptable means to attain it.

A prehistory of management

The term *prehistory* means both a time before written records and the events and conditions leading up to a phenomenon. Both these meanings are appropriate when considering the anarchist prehistory of management.

Two common assertions in management textbooks are that they offer universal, scientifically supported knowledge and that such knowledge proves that we need to create organizational hierarchies to coordinate shared purpose. But it is misleading to imagine a contradiction between anarchist ideas and the origins of management in the early factories of the Industrial Revolution. In reality, management and anarchism emerged in the same creative radical ferment, as the rapid spread of industrial capital raised questions of poverty, justice and equality in a fiercely contested light across the political spectrum.

Presentations of management ideas, such as in textbooks, suggest a period that existed prior to the formal recognition of management skills and knowledge. 'Management' is said to begin in the late 19th century, with the ideas and theories of luminaries such as Henri Fayol and Frederick Taylor. This is described as a moment when it was recognized that it was necessary to coordinate formal spaces of work (Shenhav, 2003). The history that emerges in such accounts tends to discuss the functional and market demands of technology and competition during the Industrial Revolution. What is usually missing in these depictions is a discussion of the intense conflict between those who owned the means of production (factory owners) and those who sold their labour to operate these means of production (workers). Or, when there is a discussion of industrial conflict, managers are generally depicted as intermediaries in such struggle, working on behalf of the interests of factory owners, extracting more work from the worker (Braverman, 1974).

But imagine for a moment you were a manager in one of these workplaces that extended across the globe in the late 19th century, including the cigar factories in Havana and Key West, the lumber-yards of Oregon and British Columbia, the print shops of Alexandria. Your job involved great familiarity and proximity with workers. You often lived in areas of workers, and your children grew up with them. More often than not, you were once a worker yourself who 'rose through the ranks.' You were capable of retaining varying levels of empathy with the conditions of such work and an awareness of the different interests of workers and capital. This varying empathy and awareness offered a context for sympathy that had multiple effects. Some of those who took on managerial roles in industrial workplaces developed anarchist views and even committed to anarchist struggle, making common cause with like-minded workers, such as Roíg. In this sense, organizational life radicalized them. Others left their industrial workplaces to start alternative organizations, applying their managerial experience in a different context, such as Khankhoje. Common to all of these boundary-crossers was a cross-pollination or mixing of ideas about how to divide work and whether to do so, how to ensure work was done, how to issue commands and how to establish rules and the conditions to challenge them. This all became a basis for debate and experimentation, prefiguring alternative ways of defining and running places of work. And these ideas moved between factory floors and offices, from the hands of workers to the commands of managers, voiced in negotiations and in direct struggle.

As the examples discussed in this chapter show, many of the ideas of management and ideas of anarchism emerged in shared historical experience. Such experience included the mass migration to enclaves like Beirut, Cairo and Alexandria of peasants, artisans, entertainers, craftsmen, wage and salaried workers. And as 'many of these migrants took their grievances, their struggles, and their methods of contestation to new destinations, they also brought back with them new methods of collective action and new ways of challenging the status quo' (Khuri-Makdisi, 2010, pp. 4–5). It also included the effort and intricacy required in coordinating materials and labour for progressive causes and of mobilizing shared identities towards political goals. Such shared experience led necessarily to mutual borrowing. Rather than two opposed sets of ideas, 'management' and 'anarchism' were initially promiscuous domains, borrowing ideas from one another, engaging in debate about how they defined and distinguished who they were and what they did.

For these reasons, it is a serious misunderstanding to treat anarchism as a subject apart from that of management. In fact, both forms of thought were indebted to the disruption caused by the Industrial Revolution and the manner in which industrial growth was interpreted and its impact on society assessed. The late 19th century was a period of colonization in most of the Global South, whilst within Europe and

North America, rapid industrial growth and trade generated severe dislocation and conflict and industrial unrest expressed itself through regular strikes and violence. High levels of worker migration profoundly shaped cities such as Alexandria and leading to conflict with occupational skills which were zealously guarded through regional and ethnic craft associations. This was the context in which anarchist ideas circulated among workers and managers separated by language, religion and income but brought to some affinity by an experience of work, a recognition that it was beneficial to assert their rights, to set conditions for such work, and especially, shape work life towards social ends that they felt were necessary for ethical and material well-being.

A common assertion of management textbooks is that management offers universally applicable knowledge – that is, knowledge that can be applied in any and all circumstances, regardless of differences in context. Even international or cross-cultural management basically treats context as a sort of interference to business as usual, that is to say, the creation of a hierarchical order that serves an organizational good. The management textbook, in this sense, offers a history that presents management knowledge and those certified as managers together, as united. However, as we have seen, some managers working with anarchist causes were greatly concerned about what organizations should do and how they should go about it. Their debates on the means and ends of organization exposed the limits of what was claimed as management. Rather than being neutral and transcendental, management had goals and was worldly, bounded by interests and locales. Those who spoke for an organization, and made claims of organizational good, who spoke a language of efficiency and necessity, were also political actors. They were not neutral but represented the goals of organizational owners. In these ways, the historical presence of these anarchist managers paints a different picture of the rise of management. They are the anarchist prehistory of management.

Conclusion

Management histories ignore forms of organizing that came before management. Textbooks give the impression that management emerged as the outcome of developments aimed purely at improvements in function, not a debate over differing political projects. According to this line of thinking, factories needed management ideas to enable better coordination and goal achievement, and managers come into being as a coordinating intermediate class between the capitalist owners of industry and the workers who labour for them. Gradually, this class acquired expertise, and a business school education is generated to serve their needs. In such a narrative, hierarchy is preserved and strengthened over time. To be a manager is to assert the need for hierarchy, seek better ways of separating means from ends and ensuring these means are followed to generate the end of profit for owners.

However, rather than a functional response, management ideas were also part of a political project, an effort to create a 'common sense.' They served as both a justification for capitalist rule and also as part of a defense mobilized in response to workers demanding better conditions. In this sense, an anarchist prehistory offers the possibility of a counter history of management, providing a view of possible alternatives that textbooks simply ignore. As cultural philosopher Walter Benjamin (1968, p. 254) famously reminded us, 'nothing that has ever happened should be regarded as lost for history.' The effort of remembering is important in the present, for Benjamin's demand is to hold on to history and consider it as showing possibilities for alternative presents. For this reason, an anarchist prehistory of management can ultimately challenge the professionalizing project of management (Srinivas, 2012), the ways in which management has become linked to an expectation of expertise and a specific education – in the form of business schools – that reinforces this expertise.

An anarchist prehistory also offers another challenge, this time to the historical project of the left political party which wishes to lead the state. Anarchist views have historically been quite consistent in favouring certain means over others. Because of an opposition to the central authority of a political party or other form of leadership, as you can see in this book, anarchists have preferred consultation, committee work and decentralization. The superiority of certain means for anarchism thus meant conflicts with other movements on the left that wished to act on behalf of people without committing to forms of direct democracy (Grubačić, 2011; Guillet de Monthoux, 1983). In this sense, an anarchist prehistory offers an important reminder of the alternative means available for all organizations, not just business organizations.

Questions for further study

1 Two of the figures discussed in this chapter, Roíg and Martínez, are both described as being inspired by anarchist ideas, but these ideas take them in different directions. What is the difference between them? How could this difference help you better understand what anarchism means, in theory and practice? What about how they follow their anarchist inspiration makes Roíg more of an anarchist and Martínez less of one?

2 What was it about the Industrial Revolution and the changes it brought that led to the common problems that anarchism and management tried to deal with? What did anarchism and management share here and what did they try and do differently?

3 Try to think of an example (from work or another part of life) that anarchism and management would find different ways of dealing with. What would anarchists and managers do differently? What might they do the same?

4 This chapter argues that understanding history is important to the present. What lessons do you think the interconnected history of management and anarchism has for us today? How could we think differently about management and organization in light of anarchist ideas?

References

Benjamin, W. (1968). *Illuminations: Essays and Reflections*. New York, NY: Schocken.

Braverman, H. (1974). *Labor and Monopoly Capital: The Degradation of Work in the Twentieth Century*. New York, NY: Monthly Review Press.

Daniel, E. M. (2015). "Cuban Cigar Makers in Havana, Key West, and Ybor City, 1850s – 1890s: A Single Universe?" In G. de Laforcade and K. Shaffer (Eds.), *In Defiance of Boundaries: Anarchism in Latin American History*, pp. 25–47. Gainsville, FL: University Press of Florida.

Fernández, F. (2001). *Cuban Anarchism: The History of a Movement*. Available at: https://the anarchistlibrary.org/library/frank-fernandez-cuban-anarchism-the-history-of-a-movement (accessed 13 February 2019).

Gandhi, L. (2006). *Affective Communities: Anticolonial Thought and the Politics of Friendship*. Ranikhet: Permanent Black.

Grubačić, A. (2011). "Libertarian Socialism for the Twenty-First Century." In S. Lilley (Ed.), *Capital and Its Discontents: Conversations With Radical Thinkers in a Time of Tumult*. Oakland, CA: PM Press.

Guillet de Monthoux, P. (1983). *Action and Existence: Anarchism for Business Administration*. New York, NY: John Wiley & Sons.

Khuri-Makdisi, I. (2010). *The Eastern Mediterranean and the Making of Global Radicalism, 1860–1914*. Berkeley, CA: University of California.

Malatesta, E. (1897/2015). "Il Risveglio." In V. Richards (Ed.), *Life and Ideas: The Anarchist Writings of Errico Malatesta*. Oakland, CA: PM Press.

Marshall, P. (2008). *Demanding the Impossible: A History of Anarchism*. New York, NY: Harper Perennial.

Parker, M., Cheney, G., Fournier, V., and Land, C. (2014). "The Question of Organization: A Manifesto for Alternatives." *Ephemera*, 14(4), 623–638.

Reedy, P. (2014). "Impossible Organisations: Anarchism and Organisational Praxis." *Ephemera*, 14(4), 639–658.

Sawhney, S. (2012). "Revolutionary Work: Pandurang Khankhoje and Tina Modotti." *South Magazine*, 8.

Shenhav, Y. (2003). "The Historical and Epistemological Foundations of Organization Theory: Fusing Sociological Theory With Engineering Discourse." In H. Tsoukas and C. Knudsen (Eds.), *The Oxford Handbook of Organization Theory*, pp. 183–209. Oxford: Oxford University Press.

Srinivas, N. (2012). "The Possibilities of the Past: Two Routes to a Past and What They Tell Us About Professional Power." *Management & Organizational History*, 7, 237–249.

3

ANARCHY IN MANAGEMENT TODAY

Brian Wierman, Edward Granter and Leo McCann

Hierarchy is a structure of management with a few people in command who can order those below them to carry out certain tasks. The idea that this is inevitable and that meaningful decision making is the privilege of this select few at the top of the organization may be taken as an obvious fact of life. Whether in a church, a business, or perhaps even our own families, we often think that all these arrangements should be organized in the same way. Wherever you go, normally someone is in charge, and others are following. A CEO, for example, complete with rank, title, authority and a great salary, is thought to be rightly in charge of a company's affairs. These people fought hard to get there, and many people might agree that they deserve our support and that we should obey them. This arrangement may be useful in certain types of organizations, and it is often associated with large-scale industrialization, but, as the previous chapter suggested, the existence of a class of managers is not necessary for complex organization. For much of human history, we can see forms of organizing that are less hierarchical, smaller and more democratic.

Anarchists propose an approach to human association that does not rely on a central authority to dictate a group's affairs, that does not assume the need for a hierarchy of power and authority. In this chapter (as in the rest of this book), we ask readers to suspend their prior judgements about anarchism, to put aside what they may have heard about it or what they think they know about it, and engage with what this philosophy could mean for a contemporary notion of management, one that is less reliant on a central mechanism of control, whether it be a CEO, a manager, a military general or some other body or group of powerful individuals.

Drawing on the work of scholars such as Kinna (2005), we begin by suggesting that anarchism has three distinct forms at different points in its history: 'classical,' 'practical' and 'postanarchist'. We view the broader field of anarchism as a sort of buffet from which to select the 'best' ideas from these three epochs. Next, we consider what is meant by 'management.' After this work of defining the terms *anarchism* and *management*, we will examine how they are used in two case studies which, on first impression, seem very different. The first is a US military headquarters. The second is Zappos, the US-based online shoe retailer now owned by Amazon and generally regarded as an early adopter of progressive, forward-thinking management ideas. Lastly, we will briefly explore why the manifestations of anarchism in these case studies are hidden or obscured but nonetheless very much present in practical terms.

This chapter will

- cover how anarchism can be defined as a rejection of hierarchical control of human affairs,
- discuss how this type of anarchism relates to definitions of management, and
- through two case studies, explore how a particular form of anarchism may be identifiable but often hidden.

Anarchism

Kinna (2005, p. 3) defines anarchism as 'a doctrine that aims at the liberation of peoples from political domination and economic exploitation by encouragement of direct or non-governmental action.' Faure (1858–1942), a French anarchist quoted in George Woodcock's *Anarchism* (1974, p. 11), was a bit broader when describing *who* an anarchist is: 'Whoever denies authority and fights against it is an anarchist.' We adopt a notion of anarchism as a collection of ideas that critique and work against centralized coercive power and activities and thought that encourage realization of a person's liberation. This definition draws together three main 'epochs' of anarchist thinking (see Table 3.1).

TABLE 3.1 Anarchism's three epochs, key thinkers, texts and ideas

	Key thinker(s)	Key text(s)	Main idea(s)
First epoch – classical anarchism	Peter Kropotkin	*Mutual Aid*, 1902	Humans are cooperative (versus just competitive).
Second epoch – practical anarchism	Paul Goodman and Colin Ward	*People or Personnel*, 1965; *Anarchy in Action*, 1973	Most human exchange is decentralized. Progress is expansion of already-existing decentralized spaces.
Third epoch – postanarchism	Todd May, Saul Newman, Jason McQuinn, Bob Black	*The Philosophy of Poststructuralist Anarchism*, 1994; *Postanarchism*, 2015; *Post-Left Anarchy*, 2003/2012; *Anarchism After Leftism*, 1997	Large collective revolutionary anarchism is no longer viable or valid. Realizing anarchist values/reality comes from personal/individual anarchist action. Identifying and seeing the above requires a nuanced view of power.

The first epoch, running roughly from the 1840s to the 1930s is 'classical anarchism' and is best captured by Peter Kropotkin's *Mutual Aid*, written in 1902. The second epoch, broadly centred around the 1960s and '70s, is 'practical anarchism,' and is best seen through Paul Goodman's *People or Personnel* (1965) and Colin Ward's *Anarchy in Action* (1973). We argue that the third and current epoch of anarchism is '**postanarchism**' (see box in Chapter 5). Its features are most clearly seen through the work of Todd May (1994) and Saul Newman (2015), but it also includes 'post-left anarchy' writers Bob Black (1997) and Jason McQuinn (2003/2012). This period began roughly in the 1990s and continues through to the present time.

Classical anarchism

Key currents of thought in anarchism's classical epoch suggest that the state – as an assemblage of institutions which govern us – is unnecessary and even evil. While most classical anarchists agree that centralized power is corrupt and coercive, our choice of Peter **Kropotkin** (see box) as an exemplar for this epoch (alongside other thinkers such as Mikhail **Bakunin** – see box in Chapter 7 – or the French geographer and anarchist Élisée Reclus) is based on his study of and emphasis on human nature. Whether humans can be trusted to rule themselves is a common anarchist starting point, partly because it is assumed not to be the case in political philosophy more generally and indeed studies of management and organization. In *Mutual Aid* (1902), Kropotkin establishes a case for a cooperative human nature. This case arose from his work observing animals and humans in the harsh climate of Siberia. At the time Kropotkin was writing, discussions of human nature were dominated by social Darwinists like Herbert Spencer, drawing on Darwin's ideas about competition and survival. A sense of human nature as essentially self-interested helps justify government, law, management and other features of control. In short, Kropotkin argued that a view of human nature too focused on competition was problematic because humans cooperate extensively, and a cooperative outlook is ideal under most circumstances. If Kropotkin's argument is to be believed, then we may find that there are circumstances where a governing force or form of management is not required, or at least not required to the degree we may assume and to which we have become accustomed.

PETER KROPOTKIN, 1842–1921

Kropotkin belonged to the highest Russian aristocracy. He was groomed for a sparkling career at the court of Russian Emperor Alexander II, but the young prince rejected this prospect. From an early age, he had despised power, exploitation and inequality and requested to be moved to Siberia to work in state service. While there, he got a taste of freedom from strong autocratic rule and had a chance to study animals, people and nature. This resulted in him (amongst many other achievements) developing a theory of cooperation, which became a foundation of his anarcho-communist political philosophy. With such political preferences, he was persecuted in his home country and wherever he went. While in the UK, he was offered a chair of geography at Cambridge University, on the condition he would cease his anarchist activities. He, of course, rejected the offer. Kropotkin earned his living by publishing scientific papers and returned to Russia towards the end of his life, only to discover another version of state tyranny offered by the new Russian revolutionary government. To this day, Peter Kropotkin remains an inspiration for all the people around the world fighting for a freer and more just society.

Practical anarchism

Practical anarchism asserts that expressions of freedom and autonomy in modern life indicate that everyday anarchism already exists. It reframes anarchism around the idea that people's natural tendency is free association. The state, the government and business bureaucracies curtail and suppress this freedom. Paul Goodman (1911–1972) and Colin Ward (1924–2010) are the key writers associated with practical anarchism. They equated anarchy with a less restricted and fairer existence. Both writers asserted that we are inherently free, but our lives are often shaped by the impositions of a hierarchical social order. White and Williams (2016 and in this book) discuss contemporary notions of the same idea. Even though we may feel surrounded and even oppressed by neoliberal capitalism, the reality of most economic exchange is voluntary and self-organizing, a practical form of everyday freedom. Both Goodman and Ward paid homage to classical anarchist writers, particularly Kropotkin. Indeed Ward suggested that Kropotkin 'was one of the most persuasive of anarchist writers [because of his] inventive and pragmatic outlook' (Ward, 2008, p. 10).

Ward discusses many examples of people **cooperating** to their collective benefit (see box in Chapter 8), from co-ops to gardening to voluntary work, and suggested that this type of behaviour was much more prominent and natural than competition. Indeed, for Ward, civil society is already largely anarchist, and we shouldn't allow the seeming dominance of capitalism to obscure the importance of everyday collaboration and **mutual** support (see box in Chapter 17).

> How would you feel if you discovered that the society in which you would really like to live is already here[? . . . A] society which organizes itself without authority, is always in existence, like a seed beneath the snow, buried under the weight of the state and its bureaucracy.
>
> *(2008, p. 23)*

For practical anarchists, humans cooperate all the time without the need of assistance or a watchful governing eye.

Postanarchism

Postanarchism focuses on the self, arguing that personal resistance to authority and power at a local level is a meaningful anarchist act. It traces its lineage to Max **Stirner** (see box in Chapter 16), a Bavarian philosopher who, in *The Ego and Its Own* (1844) worked to articulate an individual expression of socialism which contrasted with **Marx**'s (see box in Chapter 11) and others' more collective perspectives. For postanarchists, individuals can themselves enact productive anarchist behaviour without the precondition of change in the capitalist system. It is important to note that postanarchism does not necessarily mean 'after'-anarchism but rather seeks to include postmodern and poststructuralist thought and attitudes in anarchist philosophy. Todd May (1994) was arguably the first writer to discuss anarchism in this manner.

POSTSTRUCTURALISM

A body of philosophically informed thought which became prominent in the 1970s and stresses the importance of language and symbolism in constructing social life and that pays particular attention to the ways that power and history shape meaning. Unlike structuralists, who attempt to discover regular patterns of action that determine social life (such as **Marx**, see box in Chapter 11), poststructuralists (and postmodernists) emphasize the ways in which systems of meaning suppress certain sets of ideas and emphasize others. The making of meanings and the forms of action they encourage is therefore always political because it normalizes a particular way of understanding the world in which one side of a dichotomy is dominant over another – man/woman, white/ black, straight/gay and so on. Philosophers such as Jacques Derrida, Michel **Foucault** (see box in Chapter 4) and Judith Butler have explored the fluid politics of texts, institutions and meaning. In the context of **postanarchism** (see box in Chapter 5), poststructuralism has been influential in providing a theoretical foundation for a suspicion of institutions – particularly the political party – and stressing individual agency and responsibility.

Saul Newman (2015) expands May's ideas to include discussions about violence, which is always a problematic practical topic for anarchist and revolutionary ideas. He suggests that anarchist strategy very often focusses on forming groups that reject mainstream ideas and that actively revolt against established powers. Perhaps surprisingly, Newman argues that this type of anarchist expression is counter-productive. 'Not only does violence coerce and dominate others . . . but violent resistance against power always risks an even greater and more devastating counter-violence' (2015, p. 69). The violent acts of angry youths clad in black, so this argument goes, works against the freedom of others by giving 'the right' or 'the state' justification for violent counter-reaction. For Newman, the most productive realization of anarchism is to identify things about yourself that need further freedom and expression. Doing this is a rejection of the power others may have over you, and it can be done immediately, needing no permission from a group, collective or ideology.

Other authors also suggested that anarchism needed to be understood more in terms of personal liberation. 'Post-Left anarchists' like Bob Black (1997) and Jason McQuinn (2009) seek to reject ideology, collectivism, party, revolution, and most of the terms that feature in political discourse. They argue that we should not worry about labels or rallying people to their expression, instead suggesting that individuals should begin to operate in ways that liberate them. Provided you do not harm others, you would be acting in an anarchist manner. Liberation of the self, even from the supposedly liberating ideas of others, is their goal, and working to include oneself in broader politics is not only yesterday's politics but ultimately foolish and counterproductive.

What is management?

Whether classical, practical or post, anarchism promotes autonomy, liberty and a profound opposition to coercion and control. It is almost the antithesis of what is usually associated with management. Management is about control, the word derived from *manus* (hand) or *maneggiare* (to handle, especially a horse). Management is the ideology, practice, technology, and interest group involved in reining in, harnessing and controlling organizations and their members. The large organizations that developed in the industrial age were bureaucratic, hierarchical, process-driven and coercive, as documented in endless 20th-century writings about de-humanizing factories and office blocks inhabited by the obedient *Organization Man* (Whyte, 1956).

But what is the nature of this control? Who exerts it over whom? In the Marxist tradition, management is understood as capital's instrument for the control of work in the interests of expanding profit, partly by maximizing control over the design, execution and measurement of labour. One way of thinking about this is as a 'frontier' of control (Edwards, 1980). This frontier represents the line drawn between workers and managers over the nature and degree of workplace control that each tries to assert. Management attempts to control workers in the interests of profit, while workers attempt to restrict managerial influence over their work tasks, autonomy and rewards. This frontier has changed through history, as managers attempt to shape the times and spaces of labour, as well as effort, **identity** (see box in Chapter 4), emotions and even a worker's sense of self.

Management will often deny that their interests are opposed to those of their workers and will suggest that enlightened managers and leaders put in place advanced arrangements such as 'high-performance work systems' (see Appelbaum, Bailey, and Berg, 2000) that maximize efficiency and operator discretion while also minimizing worker exploitation and boredom. These might include such innovations as self-managed teams, task autonomy and empowerment. These are now often framed by the idea of a post-industrial era based on a knowledge or creative economy which supposedly moves away from a simple structure of management controlling a workforce. However, despite these accounts, working people know only too well the competitive pressures of the global information economy and are forced into 'self-exploitation' in order to be successful (Fleming and Cederstrom, 2012). Social entrepreneurs, tech professionals or business consultants discipline themselves through self-branding and the selling of themselves as innovative, cutting-edge and trustworthy, making up a 'portfolio career' that spans dozens of employers in a 'reputational economy' (Reich, 2001; Florida, 2002; Barley and Kunda, 2004; Gandini 2016).

This means that management control remains a dominant force experienced by those employed in or by organizations, either directly or via outsourcing and the gig economy. 'Management' might now be called 'leadership,' understood simply as the most current and dominant manifestation of 'neo-management' (Boltanski and Chiapello, 2005) in which organizations are coordinated not by means of direct command but through supposedly benign or benevolent forms of 'inspiration' and 'vision.' Neo-management and 'leadership' discourses suggest a releasing of control. Contemporary organizations are often characterized by the injunction to 'just be yourself,' promoting themselves as liberal spaces for smart, autonomous professionals, where bureaucratic rule-books have been cast aside (Fleming and Sturdy, 2009). At least rhetorically, cutting-edge employers claim to be responsive, agile and flexible, which on some level corresponds with anarchism's promotion of self-actualized, autonomous spaces where coercive centralized control has been rejected.

But, of course, a considerable proportion of management knowledge and practice is mostly rhetorical (McCann, 2015), or simply 'bullshit' (Spicer, 2018). Companies have certainly undergone near-constant transformation through downsizing, delayering, culture change and the introduction of self-managed teams, but managerial control persists and in many ways is tighter than ever. A very significant element of this control remains firmly in the coercive, centralized realm of key performance indicators, big data, management by objectives, rankings and measurements of progress. Even the 'funky' intangibles, such as 'brand value,' are increasingly measured and ranked, and 'authenticity' is but one metric placed in a basket of comparable indicators (Willmott, 2011).

Management is essentially – perhaps inescapably – a form of surveillance and control and often a coercive one. But anarchism holds out the promise of human liberation from costly, coercive and needless control, so can it work within formal structures of control? The next section of this chapter explores the ways in which two particular organizations have tried to adopt elements of anarchy into their daily practices.

Two case studies of organizational anarchism

US Marine Corps Forces Europe and Africa

Our first case will illustrate how anarchist themes are even found in strongly hierarchical organizations. While the anarchism here is always contained and questioned, it does exist in a very dynamic and agile way, almost as if it is constantly trying to break free. This may confirm what Kropotkin and Ward suggest, that anarchism is basically a 'natural' way for humans to interact and that hierarchy, rules and authority suppress these fundamental tendencies.

US Marine Corps Forces Europe and Africa (MFE/A) is a 250-person organization housed in three Nazi-era structures just outside Stuttgart, Germany. It is headed by a two-star major-general. One of the present authors is a reserve marine officer affiliated with MFE/A since 2010, and this provided the opportunity to conduct ethnographic research, including participant observation and interviews.

Like many organizations of this size, corporate and otherwise, there are the usual tensions around the sharing of information, clarity around tasks and jobs and anxieties around how the organization itself is supposed to work. 'Substitute the uniforms for suits, and it would look like any other corporate-America place,' said one person working there. Men and women of various ranks and experiences arrive each morning for an eight- to 12-hour day. They work from desks or office spaces similar to any company, use phones and emails to correspond, and move around the building solving all sorts of problems, some very important for the organization's success, many others mundane but necessary to keep the organization functioning. Most of the 'things' created are knowledge oriented: a report on another nation's amphibious doctrine, a letter drafted to an ally's military liaison and various work that churns inside the broader US Department of Defense. Most of the work is designed around helping the commander of the organization make decisions. In short, MFE/A is largely indistinguishable from any other organization of similar size. We can observe anarchism's role at MFE/A in two main ways. The first are anarchisms associated with its design; we may term this the organization's 'DNA.' The second are anarchisms arising from its members' activities.

According to its official handbook, *Warfighting*, the US Marine Corps prides itself on a notion of initiative and action, called 'Mission Tactics' (MT). 'Mission tactics [is] assigning a subordinate a mission without specifying how the mission must be accomplished' (Marine Corps, 1989, p. 87). This is the best example of 'DNA-oriented' anarchism in the Marine Corps, and it can be framed primarily around a notion of decentralization. '[We] should decentralize execution planning to the lowest possible levels so that those who must execute have the freedom to develop their own plans' (Marine Corps, 1996, p. 125). MT originates in the Prussian concept of *Auftragstaktik* (a literal English translation is 'Assignment Tactics'). Hill (2012) notes the paradox of using a military 'command' system as a management innovation but argues that the 'important lessons for business are very similar to those taught by management revolutionaries. Much of the time, leaders must trust juniors to take decisions without first reporting back up the chain to headquarters' (2012). Readers will recall that in our earlier discussion of anarchism, decentralization is a common goal. Indeed, some anarchist writers themselves appear aware of the possibilities for anarchist dynamics to further the goals of corporations: 'General Motors is a classic example – [it can] shrewdly decide to delegate a measure of autonomy to its corporate parts, because more flexible enterprising is more profitable in the long run' (Goodman, 1965, p. 23).

At MFE/A, the Marines operate daily with an MT-oriented mindset but (according to one employee) are often frustrated by a 'corporate' environment that 'tends to stifle this initiative by punishing work that is off-message.' When pressed to determine the organization's mission and message, personnel often responded, 'You tell me; it seems to change often.' Staff members entrusted to close contact with MFE/A's commander seemed to possess better morale and well-being, but others were disenfranchised, and it largely stemmed from frustrated MT-oriented breakdowns; 'This is not the real Marine Corps. [*The situation here*] is actually harder to manage than being in combat,' said one disgruntled officer. 'One day I am told to be more purposeful and energetic in my work, in another I'm told I was off-message or acting outside my lane. Which is it?' This officer was not alone in voicing this concern. That said, there was certainly a wealth of evidence that the staff members of MFE/A operate with little guidance or used institutional guidance such as the doctrine of MT in place of more direct supervision to conduct their work. 'I talk to my boss often, but more to just let him know what I am working on,' said another officer. 'He knows I am the [*Subject-Matter Expert*] for [*my job*]; I just come in and do my thing.' This type of work operates largely outside of other central priorities at MFE/A, and so it seemed that staff conducting it had more autonomy than others. The commander's priorities were very rigidly controlled, and staff close to that work often felt the most enfranchised and appreciated but also operated with the least amount of personal autonomy. Though uneven and contested, this case illustrates how even strongly hierarchical organizations have an abundance of agile and dynamic anarchism 'buried' underneath their bureaucracy and process.

Zappos

Zappos, a US-based online clothes retailer, tells a story about entrepreneurial growth and success (Spicer, 2018, pp. 54–58). Tony Hsieh, the celebrity CEO of Zappos, discussed in his book, *Delivering Happiness*, how he grew the company from almost failing to the dramatic US$1.2billion sale to Amazon in July 2009, a somewhat unique deal that still provides him with tremendous freedom for what he wants to do with the company (Hsieh, 2010). This case illustrates how anarchism is influencing 'progressive' or 'post-management' ideas in mainstream organizations. Similar to MFE/A, Zappos has both structural 'DNA' and member behaviour that are anarchist, but once again, there are also countercurrents.

Zappos' structural or 'DNA'-oriented anarchism is extensive. The well-documented and observed adoption of 'Holacracy' at Zappos in 2015, a management style intent on 'having no managers' and 'getting rid of job descriptions,' is the primary example (Robertson, 2016). In this, Zappos seems to share Kropotkin's view of people as 'naturally' cooperative and as having no innate need for hierarchy. We could also mention Douglas McGregor's ideas about Theory X and Theory Y here. In this well-known mainstream theory, McGregor asserts that two common notions of management persist: Theory X suggests that people need constant monitoring and supervision, whereas Theory Y says that people work best with less supervision and direction (McGregor, 1960). It could be argued that Kropotkin's and Ward's anarchisms, as well as McGregor's Theory Y all speak to an anarchist suspicion of bureaucracy as a form of control.

We spent some time with the Zappos 'Insights' group, which functions as a sort of marketing arm to '[share] the Zappos culture with the world' (see zapposinsights.com). For this group, as one might expect, the core beliefs around Holacracy, reminiscent as they are of many anarchist impulses, are accepted as overwhelmingly positive. Additionally, the Insights group itself operates largely detached and decentralized from 'big Zappos.' It rotates its leadership roles – the 'Lead Link' of the group – sets its own hours and place of work and determines how it will conduct its role of evangelizing and spreading the wisdom of its management style. However, those involved do accept that the transition to post-hierarchy has not been completely smooth. In 2015, during the transition to Holacracy, 18% of the company took a severance option and left the organization rather than be part of the transition (McGregor, 2016).

Despite the apparently heavy element of anarchism in Zappos' explicitly re-engineered DNA, the anarchism of Zappos member-activity is harder to discern. The Insights group represents the organization as consistently Holacratic, or at least moving towards egalitarian and democratic leadership and decision making. One of the staff members at Zappos Insights said, '[Holacracy] is not perfect, it's not utopia, it's not a panacea to all organizational woes. It is a way to improve – maybe only marginally – the usual tensions around inefficient hierarchies and the inherent disrespect [hierarchy] has towards employees.' While not without some hierarchy, Zappos' use of Holacracy, with its emphasis on roles and notions of employees 'owning' certain tasks regardless of seniority, appears to be a step towards aspects of anarchism, with elements of concern for minimizing coercion and building ethical and respectful relationships. Employees at Zappos spend significant time on the 'how' of their organization; that is, they appear to be actively engaged in shaping it and their individual roles within it. In short, the emphasis, however imperfect in execution, to at least try to be more egalitarian and democratic, is noteworthy.

Counter-narratives to Zappos' corporate depiction of Holacracy have emerged, however. We saw earlier that many employees opted to bow out rather than adapt to this 'radically new' (anti)management system, with *Fortune* magazine suggesting that the transition has left employees 'confused, demoralized, and whipsawed by the constant pace of change' (Reingold, 2016). Does this suggest that people, after all, do not seek freedom from hierarchy and authority? As the journey to Holacracy continues, some have argued that it remains 'trapped by the dictates of bureaucracy' (Spicer, 2018, p. 57). Holacracy may be leaderless, but it is a system, and systems have processes and rules. If workers find themselves unable to distribute their 'people points' (workload) across various 'circles' (formerly known as teams), they 'either enter "Hero's Journey," in which a team helps you find a new raison d'être. Or you enter "Transition Support" to help you join another circle. If that doesn't happen in two weeks, you transition out of Zappos entirely' (Reingold, 2016). Other commentators have focused on the potentially dehumanizing effects of adopting a system that appears to treat human beings as software – Holacracy at Zappos is aided by special software called *Glassfrog*, developed and marketed by Holacracy's original founder, Brian Robertson (Gouveia, 2016).

Although her experience was at another company adopting Holacracy rather than Zappos itself, Julia Culen has branded the system 'not safe enough to try':

> I felt like being part of a code, operating [within] an algorithm that is opti-
> mized for machines, but not for humans. Instead of feeling more whole,
> self-organized and more powerful, I felt trapped. The circles I was being part
> of did not feel empowering at all but taking away my natural authenticity as
> well as my feeling of aliveness. It was fully unnatural and we were disciplined
> by rigorous protocols and procedures.
>
> *(Culen, 2016)*

Conclusion

The notions of decentralization, co-operation and individual self-direction at MFE/A and Zappos do not loudly declare their political relationships to key anarchist ideas. We have shown, however, that some features of anarchism exist in the sphere of state and corporate organization. These features of anarchism exist not as violent or chaotic disorder but rather as elements of organizational practice which represent attempts to give people in an organization a say in how the organization is run, or possibly free them from the notion of hierarchical organization altogether. As many of our anarchist authors suggest – Ward, Goodman and Newman in particular – expanding our democratic and anarchist spaces is not only reasonable but useful in achieving complex goals. In this respect, finding hidden anarchisms within contemporary organizations is a heartening prospect (see also Chapter 17). But the research discussed in this chapter also raises the question of whether anarchism is compatible with the management of market capitalism and, in the case of the Marine Corps, the military machine. In the case of the MFE/A, devolved decision making appears to clash with the boundaries of prescribed 'messages' or 'lanes' in which people should operate. For the US military, like the corporations it both inspires and is inspired by, models of tactical decentralization that seem to reduce hierarchical control are often found when people break with procedure more than when they follow it to the letter (Sennett, 2007). Zappos has embarked upon a bold experiment in organizational design, but it remains a capitalist corporation. It has adopted Holacracy, with its echoes of anarchist notions of self-management, partly based on the desires for freedom and autonomy of the organization's members but largely driven by its celebrity senior manager's vision and strong personality – admirable though these may be.

Organizations, from cutting-edge innovators to military bureaucracies, appear increasingly paradoxical – at once embracing self-managed teams and visionary leadership, while also grasping for ever-wider control over every feature of an organization, particularly its employees. It is in this grey area of control and autonomy that we suggest the insights of anarchism might have the most potential. They can help us make sense of the new constraints and possibilities of post-industrial management. Anarchistic elements exist in some elements of the employment and work of autonomous, self-managed professionals, but organizations typically always fall back on the anxious, clawing, paranoid forms of management that will not and really cannot give up hierarchical control (Grint, 2010).

The case studies examined in this chapter show that anarchism does exist in contemporary organization but in obscured, attenuated forms rather than in a pure or politically consistent way. 'Really existing' organizational anarchy might show signs of some of the aspects of anarchism in how it moves towards rejecting hierarchies, but it lacks above all the voluntarism and authenticity advocated by anarchist thinkers. It is not impossible, however, to imagine and to explore the possibilities for a fuller, truer expansion of anarchism by rethinking contemporary forms of organizing.

Questions for further study

1   The US Marine Corps case may illustrate that anarchism exists 'naturally' in even very hierarchical organizations. Do you agree or disagree? Do you have a personal work or organizational life experience that illustrates the authors' claim?

2   The authors of this chapter view modern management critically – that is, they suggest its primary goal is control and manipulation. Do you see management this way? Why or why not?

3   What might an anarchist concept of modern management be? Would it be a modern corporation simply more aware of the negative aspects of hierarchy, control and manipulation? Would it be something else entirely? What kind of organization would it be?

4   Based on the evidence presented, has Zappos done something radically new and innovative or not?

References

Appelbaum, E., Bailey, T., and Berg, P. (2000). *Manufacturing Advantage: Why High-Performance Work Systems Pay Off.* Ithaca, NY: Cornell, ILR Press.

Barley, S. R., and Kunda, G. (2004). *Gurus, Hired Guns and Warm Bodies: Itinerant Experts in a Knowledge Economy.* Princeton, NJ: Princeton University Press.

Black, B. (1997). *Anarchy After Leftism.* Columbia, MO: C.A.L. Press.

Boltanski, L., and Chiapello, E. (2005). *The New Spirit of Capitalism.* London: Verso.

Culen, J. (2016). "Holacracy: Not Safe Enough to Try." April. Available at: https://pazifika.com/2016/04/03/holacracy-not-safe-enough-to-try/ (accessed 14 November 2017).

Edwards, R. (1980). *Contested Terrain: The Transformation of the Workplace in the Twentieth Century.* London: Heinemann.

Fleming, P., and Cederstrom, C. (2012). *Dead Man Working.* London: Zero Books.

Fleming, P., and Sturdy, A. (2009). "Just Be Yourself! Towards Neo-Normative Control in Organizations?" *Employee Relations,* 31(6), 569–583.

Florida, R. (2002). *The Rise of the Creative Class*. New York, NY: Basic Books.

Gandini, A. (2016). *The Reputation Economy*. London: Palgrave Macmillan UK.

Goodman, P. (1965). *People or Personnel*. New York, NY: Random House.

Gouveia, L. B. (2016). "Holacracy as an Alternative to Organisations Governance." Available at: www.researchgate.net/publication/310449491_Holacracy_as_an_alternative_to_organisations_governance (accessed July 2019).

Grint, K. (2010). "The Cuckoo Clock Syndrome: Addicted to Command, Allergic to Leadership." *European Management Journal*, 28(4), 306–313.

Hill, A. (2012). "Business Lessons From the Front Line." 8 October. Available at: www.ft.com/content/96963fdc-0e2e-11e2-8d92-00144feabdc0 (Accessed 14 November 2017).

Hsieh, T. (2010). *Delivering Happiness*. New York, NY: Business Plus.

Kinna, R. (2005). *Anarchism: A Beginner's Guide*. Oxford: Oneworld.

Marine Corps. (1989). *Warfighting*. Washington, DC: U.S. Marine Corps.

Marine Corps. (1996). *Command and Control*. Washington, DC: U.S. Marine Corps.

May, T. (1994). *The Political Philosophy of Poststructuralist Anarchism*. University Park, PA: Pennsylvania State University Press.

McCann, L. (2015). "From Management to Leadership." In S. Edgell, H. Gottfried, and G. Granter (Eds.), *The Sage Handbook of Sociology of Work*. London: Sage Publications.

McGregor, D. (1960). *The Human Side of Enterprise*. New York, NY: McGraw-Hill.

McGregor, J. (2016). "Zappos Says 18 Percent of the Company Has Left Following Its Radical 'No Bosses' Approach." 14 January. Available at: www.washingtonpost.com/news/on-leadership/wp/2016/01/14/zappos-says-18-percent-of-the-company-has-left-following-its-radical-no-bosses-approach/?utm_term=.9dfc604a4395 (accessed 14 November 2017).

McQuinn, J. (2009). "Post-Left Anarchy: Leaving the Left Behind." *Anarchist Library*. Available at: https://theanarchistlibrary.org/library/jason-mcquinn-post-left-anarchy-leaving-the-left-behind (accessed 9 December 2019).

Newman, S. (2015). *Postanarchism*. Cambridge, UK: Polity Press.

Reich, R. B. (2001). *The Future of Success*. New York, NY: Random House.

Reingold, J. (2016). "How a Radical Shift Left Zappos Reeling." 4 March. Available at: http://fortune.com/zappos-tony-hsieh-holacracy/ (accessed 14 November 2017).

Robertson, B. (2016). *Holacracy: The New Management System for a Rapidly Changing World*. New York, NY: Henry Holt.

Sennett, R. (2007). *The Culture of the New Capitalism*. New Haven, CT: Yale University Press.

Spicer, A. (2018). *Business Bullshit*. Abingdon: Routledge.

Stirner, M. (1844/1995). *Stirner: The Ego and Its Own*. Cambridge: Cambridge University Press.

Ward, C. (1973/2008). *Anarchy in Action*. London: Freedom Press.

White, R. J., and Williams, C. C. (2016). "Everyday Contestations to Neoliberalism: Valuing and Harnessing Alternative Work Practices in a Neoliberal Society." In S. Springer, B. Kean, and J. Macleavy (Eds.), *The Handbook of Neoliberalism, Routledge International Handbooks*. Abingdon: Routledge.

Whyte, W. H. (1956). *The Organization Man*. New York, NY: Simon & Shuster.

Willmott, H. (2011). "Considering the 'Bigger Picture': Branding in Processes of Financialization and Market Capitalization." In M. J. Brannan, E. Parsons, and V. Priola (Eds.), *Branded Lives: The Production and Consumption of Meaning at Work*. Cheltenham: Edward Elgar.

Woodcock, G. (1974). *Anarchism*. New York, NY: New American Library.

PART II
People and organizations

4

DIFFERENCE AND DIVERSITY IN ORGANIZATIONS

Claire Jin Deschner

We are often told that companies are now attentive to discrimination and that they are working to produce a more diverse workforce, whether in terms of gender, race, ethnicity, sexuality or other characteristics. But at the time of writing, of the 100 most profitable companies in the UK, more were led by a man named 'David' or 'Stephen' than by female CEOs in total (CIPD, 2017). Are the five female CEOs in this list just exceptional women? Are their companies exceptionally advanced in equal opportunity management? What happened in the other 95 leading companies so that their leadership is so male-dominated? If most top management positions are held by men across companies, is inequality then an issue for society as a whole, beyond the ability of a single organization to tackle? What does this mean for inequality and diversity at the workplace?

This chapter will first question how differences in social identities are produced by introducing the idea of 'othering.' Second, it will provide a short introduction to the material differences between social groups by outlining how occupational segregation works within companies and within the labour market generally. Following this, I will explore different diversity practises within corporations and then, from an anarchist perspective, I will question how difference is managed or even re-created through these diversity practices. Does diversity management actually allow more difference within an organization, or does it merely manage a threatening 'otherness' and squeeze it into a new normal? Can an anarchist practise overcome the social categories of 'we' and 'other'?

This chapter will

- introduce the concept of 'othering' and the distinction between a 'norm group' and an 'out group,'

- examine how this distinction operates in the workplace and in relation to occupational segregation, and
- discuss diversity practices in corporations and in anarchist organizations and ask whether anarchist practices can overcome the problem of 'othering' and exclusion.

Who's diverse?

Diversity management concerns the processes dealing with the relationship between a social norm group and social out-groups. What 'social groups' are is a key question. Let's take an example. First-year students are a group of people who discover university life for the first time. This group is created on different levels. The university administration will have created the group on an institutional level, creating the category of 'first years' and will have various institutional processes which apply to this group, for example, registration in different modules. Membership to the group is partly socially attributed as lecturers and other students will treat the 'first years' accordingly by, for example, welcoming them or making fun of their disorientation. Members of the group can also self-identify as a group based on the shared experience of discovering university life. This experience differentiates them from other people working and studying in the university.

A social group can only be defined in relation to other groups. We differentiate between people of different genders, ages, ethnicities and lots of other categories. Although these groups are socially constructed, members might share certain experiences based on this membership (Young, 1990), and through the effects of stereotyping, members of a social group can seem to share not only experiences but also characteristics. The concept of social groups is related to the idea of individual identities. A member of the group of first-year students is identified as such on an individual level. While this identity usually would only last one year, membership of other social groups can be perceived as stable and fixed, as in the groups of women and men or citizens and immigrants. Many social theorists have argued that these identities are not as stable as they might seem to us in daily life. We might not simply be born as female or male, black or white, able or disabled, but we are brought up and conditioned into these identities in society.

For example, the post-colonial scholar Edward Said (2003) argued that categories of western and non-western are created through processes of 'othering': whiteness needs the exotic 'other' to establish itself as white and normal. It needs the 'other' to establish itself as a social identity because social groups are relational: they are only definable in a relation to another group. Often negative characteristics are attached to these 'others,' and because 'they' are 'different,' they can be treated as 'less' (Prasad, 1997). In a similar vein, feminist theorist Simone de Beauvoir (2011) argued that the category of women is created as everything the male is not. It has likewise been argued that people in poverty are 'demonized' as an under-class, which then legitimizes their removal from the category of 'citizens' (Jones, 2012). What these identity differences have in common is that they are all created with the effect of placing 'the other' below 'the norm.' People within the powerful group can be perceived as the normal, a 'norm group,' while people not belonging to this group can be perceived as otherwise, an 'out-group.'

ANARCHA-FEMINISM

Anarcha-feminism (or anarcho-feminism) is a branch of radical feminism that has its primary origins in the work of Emma **Goldman** (see box in Chapter 12). Patriarchy is argued to be the original form of oppressive authority from which all others develop. Most anarchists (with some exceptions, such as **Proudhon**, see box in Chapter 2) connected the liberation of women to the freedom of humanity. Feminists should thus struggle against all forms of hierarchy, whether expressed in language or social structure, and work towards forms of decentralized free association. This involves an opposition to domination, exploitation, aggression and competition, ideas which are integral to hierarchical forms of organization and often assumed to be 'masculine' in their character. By contrast, cooperation, sharing, compassion and sensitivity are values which anarcha-feminists would want to encourage, even though they are regarded as 'feminine' and hence devalued in public lives in the Global North. This involves paying particular attention to the politics of production and reproduction, the divisions between domestic and civic spaces and enduring forms of violence against women.

In everyday life, it becomes difficult to separate oneself from these social identities. This might be because identity categories are maintained and disciplined by powerful institutions (Foucault, 1982), because we have no choice but to be recognizable as something which is already known (Butler, 1999) or because we have learnt to accept ourselves as deviant, as somehow different from the norm (Fanon, 2008). If the social group is oppressed in society, movement to another identity might face resistance. In other cases, changing group membership or even being in multiple groups might be easier. For example, if you do not perform well in your first year, you might need to retake some first-year classes, and the group labels of first- and second-year students might become meaningless to you. Changing your identity from that of a migrant to a citizen might be more difficult. People might define your accent as foreign, or even the colour of our hair, skin and eyes as identities can be attached to our bodies against our will.

It is important to recognize that some relationships between groups are defined by significant power imbalances, and this can be called structural inequality or oppression. In this case, assumptions made via stereotyping are called prejudice. Some social groups have been fighting for the recognition of power imbalances based on their group membership, for example, women; homo-, trans- and inter-sexual people; people of colour; or working-class people (see Lucy **Parsons**, box in Chapter 5). This means we need to ask, who is in the position to define some iden-tities as 'other'? Even though 'otherness' of identities might be socially constructed, the results of inequalities between groups are very much present in everyday life, for example through the segregation of labour.

Difference and inequality in labour markets

To address inequalities between social groups within an organization, larger soci-etal structures need to be understood. These include occupational segregation and the distinction between paid productive labour and mostly unpaid reproductive labour involving care within families (see Chapter 17). While inequalities manifest in multiple ways, this chapter focuses on the question of work. A person's wage is a decisive leveraging power for other inequalities outside employment, such as access to health care, education, housing and mobility.

Segregated labour

Labour markets are segregated in racialized, gendered and classed ways. For exam-ple, outside what is traditionally considered the labour market is the sphere of unpaid reproductive labour, or care. Caring labour has been given as a reason why women should not, could not or would not want to engage in paid labour, and when women do work, they are considered for roles more suitable to their caring nature. The career choices of men are not discussed in relation to their gender, as their status as workers is naturally assumed. However, women traditionally work by providing unpaid reproductive labour power rather than the paid labour typically considered as work.

Reproductive labour includes all the work which produces and reproduces the ability to conduct waged labour, such as giving birth to and raising workers, feeding, dressing and healing them. This contributes to the economy by making waged work possible. There would be no workers without this labour. Even if this care work is considered as 'outside the market,' it is part of the economic system (Fraser, 2016). Caring is often assumed as a natural characteristic of women, even a characteristic that marks out femininity itself. Feminists have argued that women are brought up to believe that doing work for others without reciprocation is love. Women, they argue, are therefore exploited for their free labour for their entire lives (Federici, 2012b). Even when in formal employment, societal norms can pressure women to choose between a family and a career or to be super-human and manage both (Sørensen, 2017). As the standard expectation of a professional is still based on a husband with a housewife and the standard expectation of a 'good parent' is based on a wife committing full time to care work while living on her husband's wages, it is unrealistic that anyone could fulfil both expectations at the same time.

Even if they are in paid employment, women in the UK earn on average 9.1% less than men in full-time employment (ONS, 2017). Connected to this pay gap is the phenomenon of occupational segregation, 'the systematic concentration of groups of workers (e.g. women, people of colour) in particular jobs' (Gauchat, Kelly, and Wallace, 2012, p. 720). These are low-paid jobs with little upward mobility (Kirton and Greene, 2010). The labour market is also segregated vertically as even within mixed or mainly female industries, higher positions tend to be taken by men. Even if women enter management positions, they are paid on average 23% less than their male colleagues in the UK (CIPD, 2017). As women still do most of the unpaid care work, they tend to work more part-time, which again limits career advancement.

Shifts in the labour market can benefit some social groups on the expense of others. While the average income and access to the labour market has increased for middle-class white women, the reproductive labour still needs to be done. This leads to families on higher wages buying the reproductive labour of poorer families as cleaners, child minders, cooks and so on. This work is mostly conducted by women, again, who experience the double pressure – producing and reproducing labour – as they have to do their own caring labour on top of working for someone else. This chain of care work has become a part of the global economy as families in the Global North buy the cheaper labour power of migrants (Ehrenreich and Hochschild, 2003).

This is where the **intersection** (see box in Chapter 5) of gender, class and race becomes visible. 'Professional jobs' are not only better paid, but it is prestigious to work in an office and have 'others' serve you at home. Young argues that this division has a strong racist connotation, as people of colour in the US carry out the majority of menial labour.

> Menial labour usually refers not only to service, however, but also to any servile, unskilled, low-paying work lacking in autonomy, in which a person is subject to taking orders from many people.
>
> *(Young, 1990, p. 52)*

Reproductive and productive labour therefore divides not only the male and the female but also the professional and the servant. Pay inequality between the category of white and people of colour is less well researched. The racial pay gap in the UK has been indicated as up to 35% less in average household income for Bangladeshi families than for white families (Corlett, 2017). Ethnic minorities are barely present in the list of top CEOs in the UK, but their absence does not receive an annual media outrage as it does in the case of gender representation.

Segregated jobs

Most organizations are hierarchically organised in their pay and decision making. This hierarchy is justified through an emphasis on individual performance in which the best workers should lead. There are a few problems with this. First, workers do not lead in most companies. While some organizations claim a new, flat organizational design for decision making, ownership and control is not distributed. Working hard on a salary is unlikely to bring in enough money to buy a significant part of a modern company. Second, job design within companies is already shaped by socio-economic class. It is rare that a person without a university degree is on the board of directors or even within top management. Individual performance is not just based on personal effort but also on formal education, and access to and success within the education system is largely dependent on the class position of a child's parents (Savage, 2015).

Third, it is not easy to say who does the best job. Professional jobs require a complex skill set and some intuition. Performance reviews are carried out by supervisors, and these qualitative reviews are likely to be influenced by personal relationships. Performing a professional identity – based on the norm of the white cis-male heterosexual, middle-class, able-bodied university graduate – can become more important than conducting the actual work (Hodgson, 2005). Finally, standards of professionalism expect employees, especially top managers, to be 'unencumbered' of any additional responsibilities outside work (Acker, 2012). For the highest grades of success, the level of commitment requires employees to work overtime and attend networking events in their free time. This pace is difficult to sustain if you care for children or other dependants after work. Informal communication and informal learning, and therefore, knowledge exchange outside meetings, is invaluable for an organization to function (Manuti et al., 2015). This informal communication is not neutral but follows cultural norms. If the norm is to go to a pub and drink beer after work, this might unintentionally, but systematically, exclude people who do not drink for religious or health reasons.

It is clear that jobs are distributed, and segregated, according to social group membership. While part of this might be due to external factors, organizations replicate this 'us' and 'them' through job assignment, job design and pay systems. For example, in some organizations, jobs assigned to women might contain a more limited range of tasks than those assigned to men (Acker, 2012). These simplified jobs would leave them with less opportunity to advance. They also pay less, because they arguably require a smaller set of skills. Similarly, Coleman (2003) found that a racial pay gap between white men and men of colour measured in a study on urban inequality across four US cities could not be explained by a difference in skill or education. Even explicitly performance-based pay systems can still replicate racial discrimination by under-rating performances or by hampering performance of out-groups (Koskinen Sandberg, 2017). So, given the problems of segregation, within both organizations and labour markets, what have diversity initiatives tried to do about it?

Inclusion management

Within management theory, there are two main strategies to overcome occupational segregation. The first strategy aims to create equal opportunities for all employees. The second strategy tries to profit from difference. Let's consider them in turn.

Equal opportunities

Equal opportunities management aims to equalize uneven circumstances and give employees the chance to show their 'true merit.' Differences between groups should be harmonized with the underlying assumption that difference needs managing. This equalization is attempted by eliminating biases in the recruitment and evaluation process. Names and photographs in CVs can bias recruiters, so a common technique to eliminate biases is blind recruitment aimed at ensuring that gender and ethnicity are invisible. Other equal opportunity programs support outsiders to become similar, for example by providing targeted training for underrepresented social groups, which recognizes that a material inequality exists and is not only a matter of biases. However, these approaches deal with the symptoms of inequality while maintaining its structure. As discussed earlier, as long as the 40-hour job is not fundamentally re-designed, these obstacles remain. As long as organizations are hierarchical, they keep on producing unequal circumstances in job security, wages and benefits.

A more radical approach is 'affirmative action,' which favours members of specific out-groups against equally qualified applicants in the norm group. In practise, job adverts might include sentences such as "People of colour, women, homosexual and disabled candidates are favoured in case of equal qualifications." The objective is here to get those who are different, or 'other,' into the organization. If the 'other' is allowed inside, then the organization can potentially be changed to allow more 'others' in, although within the bounds of normal employment and job design. There is a chance that the previous organizational norm group is replaced by a new, more diverse norm group. Of course, this does risk of tokenism, where outsiders are included for appearances, but their input is not taken seriously, partly because of a backlash by norm groups, who can feel threatened and disadvantaged (Pierce, 2012).

Good business?

A different starting point is the 'business case' for diversity, which departs from the idea of a norm group and instead claims to value the diversity of individuals as business assets, suggesting that diverse teams bring together a larger range of experience, supporting creative problem solving. The model 'dimensions of diversity' by Gardenswartz and Rowe (2008, p. 33) centres around personality as an individual characteristic which is enclosed by an 'internal' dimension – including gender, age and race; an 'external' dimension – with aspects ranging from 'recreational habits' to 'geographical location'; and finally the 'organizational' dimension, which includes factors such as management status and department. Diversity is here not a social justice question but one of competitive advantage, a battle to recruit talent (Litvin, 2006).

The often-cited book by Roosevelt Thomas (1991) *Beyond Race and Gender* was published in a period of backlash against affirmative action programs in the US.

The business case could be understood as a strategy by diversity managers to keep their initiative on the agenda (Litvin, 2006). Preferential treatment of employees categorized as 'diverse' might be better accepted by colleagues if their difference is justified in terms of business reasons instead of social justice reasons. However, broadening out the definition of diversity can obscure the fact that some differences between social groups have a different quality than others. Being the only brown-skinned person in a company or being the only person who has changed career can affect your work and might have to be treated with support and care. But what importance does each experience have on a social justice level? Indeed, the business case for diversity tends to reinforce stereotypes, such as hiring a woman on the assumption that women have stronger social skills than men.

The enthusiasm for diversity management might also be part of workplace branding. Modern employers try to apply the principles of product branding to attract talent. This branding is taken on by the media through 'Best Employer' rankings, providing them with free publicity. The criteria for these rankings include the factors of internal trust and employee commitment (Love and Singh, 2011). A discriminatory image would raise problems for companies in these rankings, and so there is an incentive for companies to present themselves as diverse, as a place where anyone can belong, and commit to giving their best. Independent of race, gender and sexuality, employees should feel like they fully belong to the organization, and that will result in high performance.

All this being said, in practice, diversity management is only applied to a part of the workforce in most organizations – the programmers, engineers, designers, top managers. To understand the globalized workforce, it can be useful to differentiate between 'foreign born citizens,' the global specialists earning high wages, and 'foreign born non-citizens,' immigrants without formal qualifications (Wallace, Gauchat, and Fullerton, 2011). A citizen, for example a software engineer who migrated from India to the UK, would probably benefit from diversity management. This might include legal support with the immigration process, reimbursement for relocation costs, regular flights to the country of origin, financial bonuses, private health insurance and flexible working hours. A non-citizen, for example a security guard from the same country working in the same building, would likely be treated rather differently. The recruiter is likely to only interview people with an already approved working visa and only offer fixed-term contracts. The team leader will distribute the shifts with very limited flexibility. Benefits and pay-rises would be non-negotiable. Diversity management is not part of the HR strategy here. If security guards do not like the job, they are easily replaceable.

I am not your 'other'

Diversity management techniques – whether based on equal opportunities or the business case – do not dissolve the distinction between the norm group and out-group. Instead, they are an attempt to manage the other (Litvin, 2006). But why does this other have to be managed? Because of 'the danger of otherness, or the possible loss of otherness' (Czarniawska and Höpfl, 2002, p. 6)? Does the norm group need the other? The social theorist Michel Foucault would argue that the effect of institutions is to establish 'standards and norms against which difference could be identified' (Fournier, 2002, p. 81). The current celebration of differences within management might be nothing more than a continuation of this urge to create categories of difference to manage and maintain control of employees.

MICHEL FOUCAULT, 1926–1984

Foucault was born into a comfortable middle-class setting in the small city of Poitiers, France. His entire career and life are marked by eccentricity, rebellion against established cultural and scholarly norms and ardent personal and intellectual radicalism. After holding a series of academic positions in France and around the world, Foucault was elected a chair in the History of Systems of Thought at the prestigious Collège de France. Despite being trained formally as a philosopher, Foucault's ideas evaded easy classification in his lifetime, and his intellectual legacy is still difficult to pin down. Through exploring such subjects as sexuality, medicine and repressive institutions (e.g., prisons), Foucault demonstrated that what was or is considered a 'norm' (things like heterosexuality, acceptable social behaviour or a healthy personality) is historically contingent. Perhaps, crucially, he identified that the concept of 'man' as having a certain essence, which was traditionally posited in sciences, not just never existed but could not exist even in principle. Given that you will find multiple examples of essentialist claims pervading mainstream organizational thinking on the pages of this book, Foucault is a good author to go to if you want to challenge such claims.

Maybe the question should not be how to include an outsider, but why have a differentiation in the first place? As anti-racist scholar James Baldwin said, 'I'm not a nigger, I'm a man. If you [the white person] think I am a nigger that means you need him. . . . and you have to find out why' (Baldwin, 2017, p. 109). Whether or not you are allowed to ask this question – why do you need an 'other' – is crucial to understanding power and privilege in any given society. We could begin by suggesting that all humans are inherently different from one another. Living our lives every day, we are bound to share some experiences with some people while not sharing them with others. In contrast to the historical gendered, racialized and classed society, the anarchist tradition suggests that differences should not be structured in a hierarchical manner. But this does not mean a society where everybody is considered the same, and difference is somehow managed or smoothed away.

If social identities are constructed through power imbalances, then in order to address power, we need to question identity. For many anarchists, the point is that we cannot remain *male* and *female* or *black* and *white*, because we then remain the worker and the housewife, the slave and the owner. But who are we then, truly? Once you take away the labels of gender, race, class, ability – who are you? Anarchists often argue from a humanistic perspective, suggesting that people can recognize each other as unique if the right circumstances are created. Of course, there is always power, which defines identities, but most anarchists would argue that power needs to be made visible in order that it can be challenged.

IDENTITY

This is one of these concepts that features profusely in writings and debates on current affairs. However, it is not so easy to define it straightforwardly. It enjoys wide usage in such disciplines as sociology, psychology and philosophy; however, the meaning attached to it is always slightly different. A more psychological understanding of identity would focus on an individual's self-perception, for example, 'I am a woman; a father; a worker.' The totality of one's perceptions about oneself would be a possible understanding of identity. Yet, there is also more sociological and cultural understanding of identity. For example, when you are considered to be Christian or African or working-class, you might internalize such identifications and feel accordingly, or you might negotiate them throughout your life or simply change them by changing gender, occupation, social status and so on. This highlights the fact that identity is almost never something fixed but instead is always in a state of flux. It is always up for contestation, affirmation or reassembling. The main take away point for you here is that identity is not something given or fixed but instead socially constructed.

A refusal to be recognized and established as 'the other' can be practised by moving between identities by choice, sometimes simply to be contradictory and uncomfortable (Ziv, 2010) and to leave whoever is doing the labelling in a state of confusion (Fournier, 2002). You do not know what I am, because I refuse to be known by you. Whether identity labels should be reclaimed or rejected is a difficult topic within radical politics. Are you proud to be a fag, a paki, a crip, or do you reject these categories? What about indigenous identities? Should they be rejected or embraced? Following the idea of **prefiguration** (see box in Chapter 2), **postanarchist** practice (see the box in Chapter 5) starts with you and a reflection on your position and the people around you (see Chapter 3). This includes a reflection on privileges, a question which is not 'solved' by anarchism but is clearly at the heart of the questions it asks. Who gets to define positions of privilege and disadvantage? Perhaps it is not the inclusion of diverse people into the dominant norm-group that is important but diversity as the recognition of difference. This can of course include people who belong to the social norm-group category if they also seek to transcend this category. No one is free until all are free. Your freedom is bound together with mine.

While oppressions of different social groups are not necessarily the same, they share some characteristics of oppression, such as exploitation, marginalization, powerlessness, cultural appropriation and violence (Young, 1990). If an oppressed group does not work in solidarity with other oppressed groups, they might replicate these oppressions themselves. Audre Lorde (2009) described how she experienced oppression within the US feminist movement in the 1970s as a black person, oppression within the black power movement as a woman and finally oppression within the black feminist movement as a lesbian. In her view, people needed to recognize that the mechanisms of oppression are similar and that for oppression to disappear, the very idea of differences between these groups needed to be overcome. Anarchist practise based on this is a balancing act between overcoming the hierarchical separations between people in the collective to give everyone equal standing while recognizing the differences in experience.

It is not easy to refuse identities given to you. An obvious problem is the practical reality of oppression. The social group with more power defines the conditions for the group with less power, and this other group can do very little about it within the conditions given. Or as Black Power activist Assata Shakur (2001, p. 139) said, "Nobody in the world, nobody in history, has ever gotten their freedom by appealing to the moral sense of the people who were oppressing them." If one cannot achieve acceptance through the conditions given, either because one is too marginalized to participate or because one's participation is restricted to diversity tokenism, then one needs to build alternative conditions where this experience can be expressed.

How not to include

If we refuse to engage in giving certain groups identity labels, how do we then deal with differences in experience, especially with experiences of oppression and exclusion? How do we approach the questions of diversity and inclusion discussed in this chapter?

One way anarchist practise has addressed this is **consensus** decision making (see Chapter 7 and the box in Chapter 9). This practise became popular in radical politics for its potential to build alternatives to institutional bureaucracy (Cornell, 2011). While this focus on process can become a problem when people hold the method of conversation as more important than the people and practicalities in the conversation (Nunes, 2005), a consensus process begins with the assumption of difference. In opposition to diversity management, which asks how the 'different' individual benefits the collective – or the company anarchist practice asks how the collective can support different individuals – the very idea of consensus decision making is based on the assumption that people have different needs and interests and that these can be negotiated (Gordon, 2008, and Chapter 5). This negotiation is solved through discussion instead of majority voting, because voting by definition creates a dominant majority and a marginalized group. Similar to diversity management, which supports a diversity of perspectives for creative problem solving, consensus discussions should in theory bring about the best-informed course of action. The difference lies in the effort to make people express their differing opinions and leads to the principle of non-hierarchical organizing. Unequally distributed power can prevent people from speaking and produces decisions based on incomplete information. It relies on an already marginalized individual arguing against a perceived majority. An already visible diversity of opinions within a group can ease such an expression of difference.

People do not automatically leave behind their gendered, racialized or classed identities once they sit in an anarchist assembly, and neither do they leave behind the associated behaviours and expectations which come with them. Many accounts of gendered, racialized and classed exclusions within anarchist groups exist (for example, Lagalisse, 2010; Ünsal, 2015, and Chapter 8). Through their informality, these exclusions can be difficult to challenge (Freeman, 1972), and consensus decision making therefore has to begin with an assumption of solidarity between social groups. It relies on those in positions of informal power accepting claims of inequality when they are made. As in most organizations, the relationship between the person in an informal power position and the person claiming inequality replicates a structural inequality. Whether or not the collective accepts this and is willing to change their practise relies on its political analysis. Conflicts about the justification of such claims test each member's understandings of the group and can disrupt collectives up to the point of splitting. Ideally, such conflicts result in a new organizational practice which attends to the previous exclusion. In this way, the destruction of existing categories can give room to new relationships within a group.

Anarchist practices are not free from the dangers of tokenism and a sort of 'Oppression Olympics,' comparing who is the 'most oppressed.' While there are clearly differences in power, it is important to assert that there is no hierarchy of oppression (Lorde, 2009). A feeling of exclusion might be justified, but it does not leverage against other claims. The aim is not to find out who is 'the most different' but how we can create structures that allow difference to be expressed in a way that avoids a hierarchy of oppressions. Anarchist practice therefore relies on the tension between naming and not naming differences between social groups. Practising a daily life without anyone in charge giving orders can mean refusing to call people around you 'different' and therefore avoiding the creation of an out-group. Ironically, we sometimes need to call ourselves different to challenge normalized practises. This is seldom a comfortable process. It can be very personal and include conflict, but it offers the possibility of creating less hierarchical organizations.

Rejecting work

To return to the discussion of work in the first sections of this chapter, arguing for inclusive employment can be a bit of a contradiction from an anarchist perspective.

Of course, the right of women to enter paid work without requiring their husband's consent has been an important stepping stone in feminism. If a woman achieves financial independence, she can make her own life decisions, and joining the workforce could also bring women into the public sphere, hence allowing them to play a role in designing the world. However, employment also means dependence on your employer. Leaving the role of the stay-at-home wife to become a stay-at-the-office worker might be a marginal improvement in the situation but not necessarily a free way of life (see box on Goldman in Chapter 12).

This argument is not new. Feminist **Marx**ists (Dalla Costa and James, 1975; Federici, 2012a, see box in Chapter 11) have demanded a freedom from reproductive or caring work as well as alienated wage labour (see Chapter 10). Unfortunately, instead of doing neither, women now need to do both. Discussions of 'female employment' often still rely on the notion of two genders. They rest on the assumption of a nuclear family with two heterosexual parents without problematizing this or exploring alternative forms of living and caring. This leads to the question, do you want to be included in work at all? The anarchist writer Bob Black (2009) argues that work in formal organizations within a capitalist context cannot be reformed but has to be abolished completely because it produces a situation where managers dictate the times, spaces and contents of labour (see **De Cleyre**, box in Chapter 10). Instead, he proposed to distribute actions based on what people felt that they wanted to do, calling for a playful life, a labour of joy.

Conclusion

Black is presenting a very challenging post-work future, but the question he asks us is a painful one. Leaving aside fears of unemployment, how do you want to spend your life? Leaving aside fears of failing a job interview, do you really want to be accepted into a corporate norm, to become an organization person? Diversity management aims at normalizing difference without challenging the structures which produce it. It ignores how "[e]ntire epochs of slavery, patriarchy and colonization have resulted in some social identities lacking the skills, confidence and institutional support to enter into and advance within organizations" (Prasad, Pringle, and Konrad, 2006, p. 8). Diversity management ignores the fact that the conditions of advancement and norms of achievement are in favour of those who are already in power, and these conditions are mirrored within both education systems and the design of jobs (see Louise **Michel**, box in Chapter 2).

Anarchism questions this dynamic of a normed majority and marginalized others, with all the hierarchies that implies. However, consensus decision-making practices are limited in their ability to overcome this dynamic by themselves. Anarchist practice must include ongoing reflection on exclusion and aim to keep positions of power easily challengeable and changeable, and this requires social transformation, not just new forms of human resource management. Diversity can be branded as progressiveness while decision making and financial structures remain unchanged. That being said, even if equality management can be seen as simple reformism rather than something that brings about a revolutionary change in society, gradual improvements for specific workplaces are nevertheless desirable and possible. The mere act of identifying and naming exclusions and inequalities can be a significant act, but, more significantly, challenging the positions of social norm groups and outsiders is always a radical act.

We can even illustrate this by looking at this chapter's references. You will find that most authors have female or non-western names. Statistically, this is odd, as there are fewer publications by female academics or academics of colour in management research generally (Nielsen, 2017). It seems that the 'other' is not encouraged to write about management unless they focus on 'diversity.' Diversity itself can become a token, failing to threaten the categories of norm group and out-group: members of the out-group are restricted to what the norm-group defines as out-group activities, for example, writing chapters on diversity for books like this.

Questions for further study

1   What is the difference between a 'norm group' and an 'out group'? How does the idea of 'othering' help us understand this difference? What examples of 'othering' and of norm and out groups can you think of?
2   How does this process of 'othering' work in terms of occupational segregation? How do corporations and other organizations reinforce differences between norm groups and out groups?
3   In what ways is diversity defended in mainstream business and management contexts?
4   How do anarchists approach the issue of diversity? How can anarchist organizational practices help in dealing with the distinction between norm group and out group?

References

Acker, J. (2012). "Gendered Organizations and Intersectionality: Problems and Possibilities." *Equality, Diversity and Inclusion: An International Journal*, 31(3), 214–224. https://doi.org/10.1108/02610151211209072

Baldwin, J. (2017). *I Am Not Your Negro: A Major Motion Picture Directed by Raoul Peck* (R. Peck, Ed.). St. Ives: Penguin Books.

Beauvoir, S. de. (2011). *The Second Sex*. London: Vintage.

Black, B. (2009). "The Abolition of Work." Available at: https://theanarchistlibrary.org/library/bob-black-the-abolition-of-work (accessed 30 April 2018).

Butler, J. (1999). *Gender Trouble: Feminism and the Subversion of Identity*. New York, NY: Routledge.

CIPD. (2017). *Executive Pay: Review of FTSE 100 Executive Pay Packages (Research Report)*, p. 13. London: Chartered Institute for Personnel Development (CIPD). Available at: www.cipd.co.uk/Images/7571-ceo-pay-in-the-ftse100-report-web_tcm18-26441.pdf.

Coleman, M. G. (2003). "Job Skill and Black Male Wage Discrimination★." *Social Science Quarterly*, 84(4), 892–906. https://doi.org/10.1046/j.0038-4941.2003.08404007.x

Corlett, A. (2017). *Diverse Outcomes: Living Standards by Ethnicity*. London: Resolution Foundation. Available at: www.resolutionfoundation.org/app/uploads/2017/08/Diverse-outcomes.pdf.

Cornell, A. (2011). *Oppose and Propose! Lessons from Movement for a New Society*. Oakland, CA; Washington, DC: AK Press; Institute for Anarchist Studies.

Czarniawska, B., and Höpfl, H. (2002). "Casting the Other: Introduction." In B. Czarniawska and H. Höpfl (Eds.), *Casting the Other: Maintaining Gender Inequalities in the Workplace*, pp. 1–6. Hoboken, NJ: Routledge.

Dalla Costa, M., and James, S. (eds.). (1975). *The Power of Women and the Subversion of the Community* (3rd Edition). Bristol: Falling Wall Press Ltd.

Ehrenreich, B., and Hochschild, A. R. (eds.). (2003). *Global Woman: Nannies, Maids, and Sex Workers in the New Economy*. London: Granta Books.

Fanon, F. (2008). *Black Skin, White Masks* (New Edition). London: Pluto Press.

Federici, S. (2012a). *Revolution at Point Zero: Housework, Reproduction, and Feminist Struggle*. London: PM Press.

Federici, S. (2012b). "Wages Against Housework." In *Revolution at Point Zero: Housework, Reproduction, and Feminist Struggle*, pp. 15–22. London: PM Press.

Foucault, M. (1982). "The Subject and Power." *Critical Inquiry*, 8(4), 777–795. https://doi.org/10.1086/448181

Fournier, V. (2002). "Keeping the Veil of Otherness: Practising Disconnection." In B. Czarniawska and H. Höpfl (Eds.), *Casting the Other: Maintaining Gender Inequalities in the Workplace*, pp. 68–87. Hoboken, NJ: Routledge.

Fraser, N. (2016). "Contradictions of Capital and Care." *New Left Review*, 100, 99–117.

Freeman, J. (1972). "The Tyranny of Structurelessness." *Berkeley Journal of Sociology*, 17, 151–165. https://doi.org/10.1353/wsq.2013.0072

Gardenswartz, L., and Rowe, A. (2008). *Diverse Teams at Work: Capitalizing on the Power of Diversity*. Alexandria, VA: Society for Human Resource Management.

Gauchat, G., Kelly, M., and Wallace, M. (2012). "Occupational Gender Segregation, Globalization, and Gender Earnings Inequality in U.S. Metropolitan Areas." *Gender & Society*, 26(5), 718–747. https://doi.org/10.1177/0891243212453647

Gordon, U. (2008). *Anarchy Alive! Anti-authoritarian Politics From Practice to Theory*. London: Pluto Press.

Hodgson, D. (2005). "'Putting on a Professional Performance': Performativity, Subversion and Project Management." *Organization*, 12(1), 51–68. https://doi.org/10.1177/1350508405048576

Jones, O. (2012). *Chavs: The Demonization of the Working Class*. London ; New York, NY: Verso.

Kirton, G., and Greene, A. M. (2010). *The Dynamics of Managing Diversity: A Critical Approach* (3rd Edition). Amsterdam: Butterworth-Heinemann.

Koskinen Sandberg, P. (2017). "Intertwining Gender Inequalities and Gender-Neutral Legitimacy in Job Evaluation and Performance-Related Pay: Intertwining Inequalities in Pay Systems." *Gender, Work & Organization*, 24(2), 156–170. https://doi.org/10.1111/gwao.12156

Lagalisse, E. (2010). "The Limits of 'Radical Democracy': A Gender Analysis of 'Anarchist' Activist Collectives in Montreal." *Altérités*, 7(1), 19–38.

Litvin, D. R. (2006). "Diversity: Making Space for a Better Case." In A. M. Konrad, P. Prasad, and J. K. Pringle (Eds.), *The Handbook of Workplace Diversity*, pp. 75–94. London; Thousand Oaks, CA: Sage Publications.

Lorde, A. (2009). "There Is No Hierarchy of Oppression." In R. P. Byrd, J. Betsch Cole, and B. Guy-Sheftall (Eds.), *I Am Your Sister: Collected and Unpublished Writings of Audre Lorde*, pp. 219–220. Oxford: Oxford University Press.

Love, L. F., and Singh, P. (2011). "Workplace Branding: Leveraging Human Resources Management Practices for Competitive Advantage Through 'Best Employer' Surveys." *Journal of Business and Psychology*, 26(2), 175–181. https://doi.org/10.1007/s10869-011-9226-5

Manuti, A., Pastore, S., Scardigno, A. F., Giancaspro, M. L., and Morciano, D. (2015). "Formal and Informal Learning in the Workplace: A Research Review." *International Journal of Training and Development*, 19(1), 1–17. https://doi.org/10.1111/ijtd.12044

Nielsen, M. W. (2017). "Gender and Citation Impact in Management Research." *Journal of Informetrics*, 11(4), 1213–1228. https://doi.org/10.1016/j.joi.2017.09.005

Nunes, R. (2005). "Nothing Is What Democracy Looks Like: Openness, Horizontality and the Movement of Movements." In D. Harvie, K. Milburn, B. Trott, and D. Watts (Eds.), *Shut Them Down!*, pp. 299–319. Leeds; Brooklyn, NY: Autonomedia. Available at: www.shutthemdown.org/Resources/Ch%2030.pdf.

ONS. (2017). *Annual Survey of Hours and Earnings: 2017 Provisional and 2016 Revised Results.* London: Office for National Statistics. Available at: www.ons.gov.uk/employmentandlabourmarket/peopleinwork/earningsandworkinghours/bulletins/annualsurveyofhoursandearnings/2017provisionaland2016revisedresults#gender-pay-differences.

Pierce, J. L. (2012). *Racing for Innocence Whiteness, Gender, and the Backlash Against Affirmative Action.* Stanford, CA: Stanford University Press.

Prasad, A. (1997). "The Colonizing Consciousness and Representations of the Other." In P. Prasad, A. Mills, M. Elmes, and A. Prasad (Eds.), *Managing the Organizational Melting Pot: Dilemmas of Workplace Diversity*, pp. 285–311. Thousand Oaks, CA: Sage Publications.

Prasad, P., Pringle, J. K., and Konrad, A. M. (2006). "Examining the Contours of Workplace Diversity: Concepts, Contexts and Challenges." In A. M. Konrad, P. Prasad, and J. K. Pringle (Eds.), *The Handbook of Workplace Diversity*, pp. 1–22. London; Thousand Oaks, CA: Sage Publications.

Said, E. W. (2003). *Orientalism* (Reprinted with a new preface). London: Penguin Books.

Savage, M. (2015). *Social Class in the 21st Century.* London: Pelican, an imprint of Penguin Books.

Shakur, A. (2001). *Assata: An Autobiography.* Chicago, IL: L. Hill Books.

Sørensen, S. Ø. (2017). "The Performativity of Choice: Postfeminist Perspectives on Work-Life Balance: The Performativity of Choice." *Gender, Work & Organization*, 24(3), 297–313. https://doi.org/10.1111/gwao.12163

Thomas, R. R. (1991). *Beyond Race and Gender: Unleashing the Power of Your Total Work Force by Managing Diversity.* New York, NY: AMACOM.

Ünsal, N. (2015). "Challenging 'Refugee' and 'Supporters': Intersectional Power Structures in the Refugee Movement in Berlin." *Movements: Journal Für Kritische Migrations- Und Grenzregimeforschung*, 1(2). Available at: http://movements-journal.org/issues/02.kaempfe/09.Ã¼nsal – refugees-supporters-oplatz-intersectionality.html.

Wallace, M., Gauchat, G., and Fullerton, A. S. (2011). "Globalization, Labor Market Transformation, and Metropolitan Earnings Inequality." *Social Science Research*, 40(1), 15–36. https://doi.org/10.1016/j.ssresearch.2010.07.001

Young, I. M. (1990). *Justice and the Politics of Difference.* Princeton, NJ: Princeton University Press.

Ziv, A. (2010). "Performative Politics in Israeli Queer Anti-Occupation Activism." *GLQ: A Journal of Lesbian and Gay Studies*, 16(4), 537–556. https://doi.org/10.1215/10642684-2010-003

5

MANAGING THE SELF

Peter Bloom

The idea of 'freedom' is at the heart of management, whether in terms of managers being able to manage, employees being able to select jobs or consumers being able to choose products and services. Yet there is a contradiction here. Management also speaks to the regulation of human existence – particularly for the purposes of maximizing profit. It is more often than not linked to capitalist values of efficiency and profitability. It evokes an image of employees working like machines on an assembly line or as drones in an office cubicle.

Such contradictions, between management as freedom and management as control, are also reflected in the emerging literature on the relation between organization and anarchism (Swann and Stoborod, 2014; Reedy, 2014; Rhodes, 2014). For anarchists, it is not mainstream capitalist management that promotes freedom but alternative forms of social organization. Anarchist methods of organizing are often built on the idea of 'self-management,' where individual and collective freedom are genuinely enhanced (see Dolgoff, 1974; George, 1993; Pickerill and Chatterton, 2006). Self-management stands for giving power and decision making to individuals and democratic communities rather than governments or managers. It is an attempt to administer social and political relations in a way that is inclusive, non-coercive and **horizontal** (see box in Chapter 9). Anarchist self-management is contrasted with mainstream forms of management, which show concern for freedom in name but reinforce hierarchical control and manipulation in practice.

Yet this ideal of anarchic self-management does not say much about identity – such as race, gender, class, ethnicity, culture and sexual orientation among others (see Chapter 4). Importantly, given that each of us is part of multiple social categories (we can be defined by society in terms of combinations of identities, e.g. someone might be a black, working-class woman or a white, upper-class gay man), we each have multiple different identities. 'Intersectional' perspectives highlight how a person is composed of a diverse set of 'selves' linked to diverse social categories (like those mentioned earlier, see box in Chapter 4). We can be a woman and black or a Muslim and gay. These different selves or identities are interconnected in how a person experiences freedom and the absence of it.

INTERSECTIONALITY

This is a term originally coined by the American legal scholar Kimberlé Crenshaw in the late 1980s. Originally, it referred to a very specific American legal context in which the law didn't account for the cases of domestic violence involving black women. Intuitively, you can guess that 'intersectionality' refers to a situation of overlapping, crossing, perhaps contradictory identities. This takes place on the level of an individual. One individual can and always will embody multiple identities (see box in this chapter) and therefore can be subject to various simultaneous forms of discrimination or oppression. Those can be classed, racial, religious or gendered, as well as predicated on ability, age and so on. As a methodological and theoretical framework, intersectionality basically allows you to appreciate that an individual can be affected by several institutional or organizational disadvantages, which highlights the complexity of given circumstances. For further theoretical discussion of intersectionality and its relevance for organization studies and management, see the special issue 'Intersectionality' of the open access journal *ephemera*.

So rather than self-management, when thinking about **identity** (see box in Chapter 4), it is perhaps better to discuss 'selves-management,' an idea that reflects our diverse identities and social roles. This explores the potential to experience and have the power to manage an expansive set of identities. Anarchism, here, is focused on the efforts to challenge the dominance in our thinking of single identities, opening the space to explore a diverse range of lifestyles and ways of being. It focuses on creating the material conditions and subjective opportunities for people to engage in multiple possibilities for experiencing and engaging with our society and world. Anarchism thus allows for a complete transformation of management, shifting it from a hierarchical exercise in coercion and exploitation into a continual process of testing and going beyond the limits of what is normally considered possible. It does this through engagement with many different potential selves (see Bloom, 2016).

This chapter will

- review how contemporary notions of capitalist 'self-management' are economically exploitive and socially oppressive,
- provide an overview of the ways the anarchist ideal of 'self-management' challenges this capitalist concept,

- examine how we can separate the concept of management from managerial-ism based on anarchist ideals of 'self-management,'
- introduce the concept of 'anarchic selves-management' that focuses on expanding the opportunities a person has to experience multiple identities and lifestyles, and
- explore how this idea of 'selves-management' can guide the creation of alternative forms of anarchist organizing and organization.

Capitalist 'Self-Management'

The idea of 'self-management' may sound new but has deep historical roots. One of its most prominent influences is the idea of 'responsible autonomy' first proposed by Andy Friedman in his 1977 article 'Responsible Autonomy Versus Direct Control Over the Labour Process.' In the article, he argues that employee resistance to the coercions of direct control has led to the granting of certain workers greater control over how they perform their job. In principle, such 'responsible autonomy' is based on the idea that individuals will have the freedom to do their tasks and make decisions based on their own judgements yet will be held accountable for their outcomes. Importantly, this still remains a form of capitalist management in that employees are judged based on how much they are maximizing profit and contribution to the overall value of the firm. Modern companies usually use a mixture of 'responsible autonomy' for higher-level employees and 'direct control' for lower-level ones. The ideal of 'responsible autonomy' has served as the foundation for the broader promotion of capitalist 'self-management.'

Indeed, capitalism is often portrayed as the ultimate expression of individual autonomy. It promises nothing less than the complete freedom of people to pursue their individual happiness and personal dreams. However, in practice, capitalism traditionally has required a quite regulated workforce. Alongside its romanticized ideals of upward mobility – the freedom to use one's talents and hard work to better oneself socially and economically – lies a regulative and coercive organizational reality marked by demanding rules, strict managerial oversight and pressurized production expectations (see for instance Boje and Winsor, 1993). If the dream of capitalism is individual agency, its waking moments are most often made up of submitting to hierarchical authority and a constant worry about money and status.

Recently, such managerialism and top-down bureaucracy have been dramatically challenged as ineffective and even unethical. Ideas of post-bureaucracy have become increasingly accepted – admittedly more often in principle than reality – promoting values of flexibility, less top-down authority and even personal creativity (see Courpasson and Reed, 2004). However, this shift should not be mistaken for greater employee power in the workplace. Instead, it is a changing form of managerial control to monitor that their workforce are using their relative freedom appropriately. As Courpasson and Clegg (2006, p. 319) observe, 'bureaucracy far from being superseded, is rejuvenating, through complex processes of hybridism in which supposedly opposite political structures and principles, the democratic and oligarchic, intermingle and propagate.'

Put differently, these less-hierarchical organizations continue to promote the power of elites (e.g. corporate board members, CEOs, managers) and demand that people shape their behaviour in order to maximize their efficiency and the firm's profitability. This has been referred to as 'capitalist self-management' (Breevaart, Bakker, and Demeroutti, 2014; Sacks, 2017). For many, this is now the age of the 'autonomous worker,' or even the gig worker who uses technology to move from job to job and can complete a project without the need for direct supervision (see Cooper and Baird, 2015; De Menezes and Kelliher, 2017, and Chapter 12).

These appeals to individual freedom mask a governed and insecure 21st-century economy. They often lead to greater work intensification and paradoxically a feeling of less rather than more autonomy (Alvesson, 2000; Caproni, 2004; Healy, 2004). They also enhance the pressure on individuals to fulfill close to impossible job tasks in light of their privileged status as free 'self-managing' workers. Freedom, according to theorist Nikolas Rose, is dominantly viewed as a choice, stressing autonomy, self-responsibility and the obligation to maximize one's life as a kind of enterprise (Rose, 1996).

Mainstream ideas of workplace control usually focus on the power that managers have over employees. The traditional image is of an overseer or supervisor closely monitoring the workforce so as to ensure they are doing their jobs properly and efficiently. However, control can also include the shaping of people's values to reflect those of the companies. Here, the idea is to invoke a sense of loyalty and shared vision in order to induce employees to work harder for the good of the firm. Yet there is another type of control that directly connects up to the notion of 'self-management.' In 2009, critical management scholars Peter Fleming and Andrew Sturdy introduced the concept of 'neo-normative control.' Here, employees were encouraged to simply 'be yourself' – asked to bring their different backgrounds and identities into the workplace. Based on their experiences observing a call centre in Atlanta, the authors reveal how not only was this supposedly free expression strictly prohibited from criticizing the company or its leaders in any serious way, it also threatened people with having all aspects of their lives (not just their professional 'selves') being exploited by management for profit.

Organization scholars, in this vein, have developed the concept of 'identity work' to explain the way that the self can become treated as a kind of project, or brand. On the one hand, it refers to the efforts by individuals to constantly live up to the demanding expectations of an existing identity in their organizational and working lives. On the other, it depicts the ways that all our various identities – from being a parent to being a friend to being from a certain place or from a specific cultural heritage – becomes a 'managed' identity too, often with quite destructive effects. Importantly, the influence of capitalism and its current extreme version, often called 'neoliberalism,' is not merely confined to the shaping of someone's economic 'employable' self. It becomes an experience of governing selfhood overall, of being an individual. So being someone, someone who matters and counts, becomes oriented towards 'market' priorities – maximization, optimization and productivity. In trying to become a self, we manage ourselves.

Anarchist self-management

In contrast to these neo-normative management strategies, which encourage the management of the self, there are longstanding anarchist ideas of 'self-management' which show us how the concept could be understood quite differently. Historically, for anarchism, 'self-management' refers to the ability of workers to individually and collectively make their own rules and control their own working lives free from external authorities. It directly challenges the organization and values of a capitalist system that puts managers and profits over workers and their freedoms.

In 1896, the19th-century Russian anarchist Peter **Kropotkin** (see the box in Chapter 3) proclaimed,

> That is why Anarchy, when it works to destroy authority in all its aspects, when it demands the abrogation of laws and the abolition of the mechanism that serves to impose them, when it refuses all hierarchical organisation and preaches free agreement – at the same time strives to maintain and enlarge the precious kernel of social customs without which no human or animal society can exist.

And these are by no means mere utopian sentiments. Amidst the general dominance of the free market globally, there are many longstanding examples of 'self-managing' working collectives, such as Suma in the introduction to this book (Kanter, 1972; Rocker, 2004), which stand as vibrant and real alternatives to the oppressive form of capitalist 'self-management.' As well as this more direct form of anarchist 'self-management' (i.e. workers owning and controlling their own activities), anarchist perspectives also hold the potential to dramatically transform our personal and collective relationship with 'ourselves' as individuals. In particular, they challenge the very foundations of our current 'disciplining' society in which we become our own police officers, our own prison wardens. Established forms of top-down coercive power (such as from managers) are augmented and to an extent replaced by an

> Ensemble formed by the institutions, procedures, analyses and reflections, the calculations and tactics that allow the exercise of this very specific albeit complex form of power, which has as its target population, as its principal form of knowledge political economy, and as its essential technical means apparatuses of security.
>
> *(Burchell, Gordon, and Miller, 1991, pp. 102–103)*

For thinkers like Michel **Foucault**, this change in how we are socially controlled is associated with the economic and organizational growth of capitalism (see box in Chapter 4). We are disciplined as a means for making us more 'productive' and 'valuable' citizens as well as more pliable employees.

Nowadays, this has expanded into a form of 'self-discipline' in which our multiple and intersecting identities must conform to prevailing market logics. It can even be the case that asserting one's cultural, sexual or ethnic identity involves intentionally promoting it to increase our employability in a globalizing labour market. Our personal desires become marketable ideas that can lead us to untold riches. Our ethical commitments evolve into new lucrative opportunities for entrepreneurship.

By contrast, anarchism is suspicious of capitalist demands for 'self-discipline' as a form of 'self-management' in favour of an individual and collective life focused on experimentation and exploration. As such, it frees our multiple selves from having to fit within or conform to market and managerial demands and expectations. Anarchist forms of 'self-management' directly challenge capitalist notions of 'self-management.' They present a different vision of how to organize labour and society, emphasizing collective ownership and control, not the individual as enterprise. Nevertheless, they remain rather wedded to the singular identity of people as workers. Their focus is understandably on the progressive evolution of an individual from a controlled employee to a free individual through embracing anarchy in action. But because anarchism has often been historically focused on changing how we work and how labour is organized, it often neglects the multiple versions of selfhood that people have, including the many ways that our identities are not necessarily always related to the workplace.

To counter this quite narrow concentration on 'class,' as it is often presented, recent anarchist theories have instead emphasized individual identity. Commonly referred to as 'post-anarchism,' this is an attempt to open up the possibilities of anarchism in more personal ways (see Chapter 3). It is a call for individuals to explore and seek to enact a wider sense of what it means to be human – liberated from the dominant pull of social ideologies and the constraining influence of common sense and tradition. It channels the spirit, if not always the radical politics, of historically renowned early 20th-century anarchist Emma **Goldman** (see box in Chapter 12):

> Anarchism, then, really stands for the liberation of the human mind from the dominion of religion; the liberation of the human body from the dominion of property; liberation from the shackles and restraint of government. Anarchism stands for a social order based on the free grouping of individuals for the purpose of producing real social wealth; an order that will guarantee to every human being free access to the earth and full enjoyment of the necessities of life, according to individual desires, tastes, and inclinations.
>
> *(1917, p. 7)*

POST-ANARCHISM

Post-anarchism is a term that, despite its name, does not seek to do away with or move beyond anarchism but rather evolve it. The philosopher Hakim

Bey first introduced the idea in 1987 to criticize contemporary anarchism for becoming too academic and ignoring concrete social realities. These ideas have been further developed by a wide range of present-day anarchist theorists, such as Saul Newman and Bob Black. Notably, Todd May sought to combine anarchist ethics of freedom with **poststructuralist** ideas of power (see box in Chapter 3) as a pervasive cultural force for shaping **identity** (see box in Chapter 4). Lewis Call has similarly drawn on continental philosophers such as Nietzsche to propose a theory of anarchist 'becoming' in which the goal of anarchy is not to achieve a final end state but rather to continually create new and different social arrangements. Though a loose term, it covers a variety of approaches that emphasize an everyday attempt to think about personal liberation, as well as an awareness of the ways that building new institutions can all too often mean building new power structures.

'Post-anarchism' could be criticized for being seemingly apolitical. This runs directly counter to previous interpretations of anarchy that explicitly espouse an anti-authoritarian or anti-capitalist agenda. For older versions of anarchism, there was a clear and necessary relationship between the overthrow of capitalism and the creation of a free anarchist society. By contrast, many – though certainly not all – recent anarchists eschew such revolutionary desires as outdated and counterproductive. They argue that violence begets violence, and ideological commitments, even those that are radically oriented, lead to dogmatism and repression. Quoting the contemporary radical theorist John Holloway (2002, p. 19),

> The notion of capturing positions of power, whether it be governmental power or more dispersed positions of power in society, misses the point that the aim of the revolution is to dissolve relations of power, to create a society based on the mutual recognition of people's dignity. What has failed is the notion that revolution means capturing power in order to abolish power. What is now on the agenda is the much more demanding notion of a direct attack on power relations. The only way in which revolution can now be imagined is not as the conquest of power but as the dissolution of power.

They are seeking, in this respect, a revolution of the self not society. However, it would be wrong to dismiss post-anarchism as merely a 'personal' turn in anarchist thinking. The prioritization of the self helps to expand the scope of anarchism and update it to reflect an era where people's identities are not so exclusively associated with that of their employment status, that is to say, people do not see themselves as workers first and foremost. It points to the possibilities of redirecting anarchist perspectives on the development of 'oneselves' instead of only 'oneself.'

This shift resonates with emerging theories of 'intersectionality,' that is to say, a multiple sense of identity based on a wide variety of resources – race, gender, sex, ethnicity, sexuality, class and so on. The obvious linkage between intersectionality and anarchism is that an anarchist society must offer greater freedom for the development and flourishing of these diverse identities. Further, unlike traditional forms of anarchism, which focus predominantly on the struggle between employers and employees (see Chapter 2) – it does not ultimately reduce one's essence to social class, to a position in a capitalist economy. Yet there is also a subtler but arguably more profound connection to be found as well. Anarchism's refusal of common sense, of the taken-for-granted, provides an anti-capitalist ethos that intervenes against the marketization of identity as such. Anarchic 'selves-management' could therefore act as a form of resistance to this capitalist takeover of 'ourselves.' It accepts the intersectional and therefore multiple character of selfhood but seeks to 'manage' it in a more progressive and less coercive way. It is an ethical and political commitment to not making identity feel like 'work' – to allow our identities to grow, intersect and develop freely. This radical ideal of anarchic selves-management has quite transformative and revolutionary implications for capitalist economic and social relations generally.

LUCY PARSON, 1851–1942

Lucy Eldine Gonzalez Parsons was a prominent anarchist activist, labour organizer and journalist. Parsons claimed First Nations and Mexican ancestry and may have been born as a slave in the United States. Little of Parsons' work survives today, and most of what we know of her thoughts on anarchism comes from a number of newspaper articles she wrote. Her views on the oppression of women clashed with those of Emma **Goldman** (see box in Chapter 12). While Goldman argued that women face a specific and unique form of oppression under patriarchy – a view that has characterized **anarcha-feminism** (see box in Chapter 4) and intersectional anarchism to this day – Parsons was of the opinion that women's oppression was instead a form of the oppression of the working class under capitalism. For Parsons, then, the oppression working-class women experienced was primarily because of their class rather than because of their womanhood. Parsons took a similar position on racial oppression, writing at one point in her life that the oppression of people of colour and the violence done to them, which included lynching, in the South of the United States was a form of class oppression and that they were oppressed because they were poor workers and not because of their race. This was an opinion that changed over the course of Parsons' life, however, and she later argued that the oppression of people of colour was in fact racial oppression first and foremost. It is important to remember in this that Parsons' key contribution to anarchism was not as a theorist but as an activist and as someone who organized workers, for example through the radical trade union the Industrial Workers of the World. The Chicago Police Department described her as 'more dangerous than a thousand rioters.'

Anarchic selves-growth

Crucial to these efforts is to resist the pull of traditional 'self-management,' avoiding subjecting our multiple different selves to the managerialism which is so central to contemporary capitalism. Much of modern anarchism has sought to combine the twin desires for personal exploration and collective experimentation. The revived commune movements of the 1970s speak to such longings. They are also found in the explicitly anti-capitalist **anarcho-syndicalist** federations (see box in Chapter 8) that emerged internationally – particularly in Latin America. More recently, such efforts have been marked by a shared global commitment to **prefiguratively** transforming the world through and by these radical local alternatives (see box in Chapter 2). I think that central to all these varied projects is the creation of a radical form of 'selves-management' which focuses on challenging one's existing social identities and exploring new ones. 'Who we are' is not a permanent state, something to be asserted now and forever, but instead a starting point for personal and collective experimentation. Anarchism offers the opportunity to create types of organizations that will allow for these novel 'selves' to emerge and thrive.

Anarchism thus offers a novel and quite revolutionary perspective for thinking about ourselves as individuals with different identities. It highlights the possibility that we will not be defined by social categories or ruled by our socially prescribed selves – whether it be as a political citizen, economic employee or cultural subject. It is the exciting potential to craft a new type of social existence based on constantly discovering how we can live differently rather than living up to any externally prescribed and internalized self-expectations.

This puts a fresh anarchist spin on established desires for personal growth. Traditionally, these are linked to efforts at self-improvement. However, longing to be happier and more ethical and even enhance one's personal wellness are all commonly used to discipline us too. They become exacting demands, anxiety-inducing images which make individuals responsible for achieving at all times the very best version of themselves (Cederstrom and Spicer, 2017). Conversely, in the spirit of anarchism, what matters is the free creation and development of our multiple selves, our ability to nourish our diverse identities, drawing on them as opportunities to explore fresh ways of living and being in the world and developing new relations with other people, technologies and tribes. The emancipation associated with selves-growth requires, in turn, a new anarchic relationship between ourselves. Within the contemporary free market, we are tasked with appropriately managing our various identities in which work and non-work selves unite to form an integrated self that knows how to effectively act both professionally and personally. More recently, this has been translated into a desire and a demand that people properly 'balance' their work and life selves. In practice, this puts work at the centre of people's 'healthy' identity and can perversely lead them to invest more time into their professional self at the expense of other ways in which they might flourish as human beings.

Anarchism points instead to the ability to reorient subjectivity away from traditional management ideas in favour of values of curiosity, openness, continual discovery and constant expansion of one's potential selves. The contemporary anarchist thinker Saul Newman (2001) in particular speaks to such a radical subjective emancipation in which identity is rechannelled into desires for liberation and equality. It reflects an alternative model of power prioritizing potentiality over control. Here, the empowered self is not one who can outcompete others in a battle for material resources or social esteem, rather it is discovering and expanding beyond existing limits, exploring possibility through making connections (see Bloom, 2016).

Conclusion

These are hard ideas to grasp, so consider a fictional example. In his widely read science fiction novels, the Scottish author Iain M. Banks sets his stories in an anarcho-communist future society called 'The Culture.' It is defined by the elimination of money and providing people with whatever they materially need or desire – from homes to transportation and even game-playing. This is enabled through the use of technological advances to make the production of goods quicker and more accessible to all members of the population. The inhabitants of 'The Culture' view societies that still use money and capitalist labour as 'underdeveloped' and barbaric. Particularly relevant to notions of anarchic 'selves-management' is that the citizens of this new world use their material security to explore the full range of identities – often changing genders, taking up new passions and pursuing different lifestyles from decade-long research studies to year-long parties. Technology and social organization are subordinated to human desires, however multiple and extraordinary. The idea that something called 'the economy' should determine what we do and who we are would be as strange to them as their world is to us.

This chapter has introduced the concept of anarchic 'selves-management.' It challenges the common fascination with 'self-management' in two ways: first, by suggesting that anarchist ideas of self-management focus much more on ownership and control of workplaces, rather than adopting forms of neo-normative control that encourage people to fit into existing workplaces – anarchists want new forms of organization – and second, by suggesting that postanarchist practice can allow for a freer exploration and experience of identity. The idea of anarchic selves is one that is always seeking out new experiences and ways of being in the world, as well as being based on a commitment to creating a type of society that materially and culturally supports these efforts. It is a transformation of the increasingly 'self-driven' capitalist subject into the 'selves-driven' anarchist, as someone who is not afraid to explore the multiplicity of who they are and who they might become.

Questions for further study

1   How would you describe the concept of identity introduced in this chapter? How does identity relate to the idea of multiple 'selves'?

2   In what ways is self-management exploitative and oppressive in mainstream business and management contexts? Why is anarchist self-management different?
3   Going back to the concept of identity, what is the relationship between self-management and 'selves-management'?
4   In terms of social organization, how might anarchist 'selves-management' work in practice? What examples can you think of that show how 'selves-management' might operate? Think about examples in the workplace and in other organizations, as well as examples from literature or other fiction media, such as films or television.

References

Alvesson, M. (2000). "Social Identity and the Problem of Loyalty in Knowledge-Intensive Companies." *Journal of Management Studies*, 37(8), 1101–1123.
Bloom, P. (2016). *Beyond Power and Resistance: Politics at the Radical Limits*. London: Rowman and Littlefield.
Boje, D. M., and Winsor, R. D. (1993). "The Resurrection of Taylorism: Total Quality Management's Hidden Agenda." *Journal of Organizational Change Management*, 6(4), 57–70.
Breevaart, K., Bakker, A. B., and Demerouti, E. (2014). "Daily Self-Management and Employee Work Engagement." *Journal of Vocational Behavior*, 84(1), 31–38.
Burchell, G., Gordon, C., and Miller, P. (eds.). (1991). *The Foucault Effect: Studies in Governmentality*. Chicago, IL: University of Chicago Press.
Caproni, P. J. (2004). "Work-Life Balance: You Can't Get There From Here." *The Journal of Applied Behavioral Science*, 40(2), 208–218.
Cederstrom, C., and Spicer, A. (2017). *Desperately Seeking Self Improvement*. New York, NY: OR Books.
Cooper, R., and Baird, M. (2015). "Bringing the 'Right to Request' Flexible Working Arrangements to Life: From Policies to Practices." *Employee Relations*, 37(5), 568–581.
Courpasson, D., and Clegg, S. (2006). "Dissolving the Iron Cages? Tocqueville, Michels, Bureaucracy and the Perpetuation of Elite Power." *Organization*, 13(3), 319–343.
Courpasson, D., and Reed, M. (2004). "Introduction: Bureaucracy in the Age of Enterprise." *Organization*, 11(1), 5–12.
De Menezes, L. M., and Kelliher, C. (2017). "Flexible Working, Individual Performance, and Employee Attitudes: Comparing Formal and Informal Arrangements." *Human Resource Management*, 56(6), 1051–1070.
Dolgoff, S. (1974). *The Anarchist Collectives: Workers' Self-Management in the Spanish Revolution, 1936–1939*. Toronto: Black Rose Books Ltd.
Friedman, A. (1977). "Responsible Autonomy Versus Direct Control Over the Labour Process." *Capital & Class*, 1(1), 43–57.
George, D. A. (1993). *Economic Democracy: The Political Economy of Self-Management and Participation*. Basingstoke: Macmillan.
Goldman, E. (1917). "Anarchism: What It Really Stands For." In *Anarchism and Other Essays*. New York, NY: Mother Earth Publishing Association.
Healy, G. (2004). "Work–Life Balance and Family Friendly Policies – In Whose Interest?" *Work, Employment and Society*, 18(1), 219–223.
Holloway, J. (2002). *Change the World Without Taking Power*. London: Pluto Press.

Kanter, R. M. (1972). *Commitment and Community: Communes and Utopias in Sociological Perspective* (Vol. 36). Cambridge, MA: Harvard University Press.

Kropotkin, P. (1896)."Anarchism: Its Philosophy and Ideal."Available at: www.panarchy.org/kropotkin/1896.eng.html (accessed July 19).

Newman, S. (2001). *From Bakunin to Lacan: Anti-Authoritarianism and the Dislocation of Power.* Lanham, MD: Rowman and Littlefield.

Pickerill, J., and Chatterton, P. (2006). "Notes Towards Autonomous Geographies: Creation, Resistance and Self-Management As Survival Tactics." *Progress in Human Geography*, 30(6), 730–746.

Reedy, P. (2014). "Impossible Organisations: Anarchism and Organisational Praxis." *Ephemera: Theory & Politics in Organization*, 14(4), 639.

Rhodes, C. (2014). "Ethical Anarchism, Business Ethics and the Politics of Disturbance." *Ephemera: Theory & Politics in Organization*, 14(4), 725.

Rocker, R. (2004). *Anarcho-Syndicalism: Theory and Practice.* Stirling: AK Press.

Rose, N. (1996). *Inventing Our Selves: Psychology, Power and Personhood.* Cambridge: Cambridge University Press.

Sacks, S. R. (2017). *Self-Management and Efficiency: Large Corporations in Yugoslavia* (Vol. 12). London: Routledge.

Swann, T., and Stoborod, K. (2014). "Did You Hear the One About the Anarchist Manager?" *Ephemera: Theory & Politics in Organization*, 14(4), 591–609.

6

BUSINESS ETHICS

David Bevan

Reading many business ethics books or journal articles, you will find that the subject involves a large number of overlapping academic ideas. In the field of management, these subjects include accounting, law, strategy, marketing and human resources, with references to other fields, such as religious studies and moral philosophy. Philosophy and religion also make significant cultural contributions to arguments in mainstream business ethics because of its necessary concern for what is right and wrong.

So how does anarchism relate to ethics in general and business ethics in particular? Morality is often claimed as an individual characteristic or an inevitable consequence of being human. Each of us is an individual ethical agent capable of choosing to assist another individual or group, or to not do so. But such a position is at odds with the worldview of conventional economics and how it is taught in contemporary business schools. Because ethics and morality are mental phenomena (i.e., they exist as ideas in our heads or in conversations we have with one another and cannot be measured in the way the physical world is measured), they have been excluded from many of the theories used in studying business in order to explain how and why we act (Ghoshal, 2005). If management in general excludes ethics, then 'business ethics' certainly does not sit comfortably in discussions of management, and for many people, it is simply an oxymoron, a contradiction in terms (Collins, 1994).

In this chapter, anarchism will be defined as an unfinished, and unfinishable, practice. It is not something that can be easily defined and hence that could be concluded (Rocker, 1998 (1938)). The notion of unfinishable tasks is not likely to be favoured by managers who prefer to have goals that can be clearly achieved, when they can see whether or not a task has been completed. Anarchism is a continuing process, a theory and a practice of how to live, while management and managers operate in a world of final deliverables and outputs.

This chapter will

- provide an overview of business ethics,
- discuss the existing response of anarchists to business ethics, and
- explore the possible and continuing response of activists to key issues in business ethics.

In this chapter, the words *moral/morality* and *ethical/ethics* will be used interchangeably, even though they are often given slightly different meanings. Similarly, terms like *market, commerce, business,* the *economy/economics* and *trade* are all used to refer to issues of peaceful exchange between individuals in respect of valuable goods and services.

Business ethics: some indicative positions

To reduce a profusion of complex ideas to something bite-sized, this section will adopt the traditional management school technique of using a Venn diagram. To any student of management, this slide should appear immediately familiar in its format. Loosely borrowed from set theory in pure mathematics, such diagrams assist management teachers and authors with the simplification and analysis of any given group of things or actions. In managerial business ethics, it is used by authors to illustrate where and how, for example, law and ethics overlap and are distinct (Crane and Matten, 2016) or the three-part taxonomy of society, economy

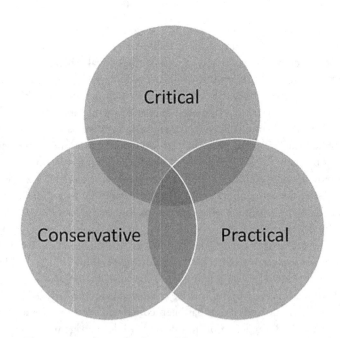

FIGURE 6.1 Three approaches to business ethics

and environment – otherwise known as the triple bottom line (Elkington, 1998). Here, I will use it to describe three broad ways in which business ethics is usually understood.

Conservative

In this category, I summarize commentators who propose that 'business is good.' This is either by understanding it as amoral (or outside any realm of moral values and distinctions) or as entirely and legitimately ethical and beyond the moral reproaches of sceptics. First, the voice of a business school dean,

> Capitalism is undeniably amoral, but it has emerged as a new global theology – a theology without morality, without a bible. It only offers a transaction manual for wealth creation and the efficient allocation of capital and it does that superbly well. No-one should question, in my opinion, the benefits of capitalism.
>
> *(Jackson, 2003, 2005)*

This view is echoed by many classical management thinkers, for example Peter Drucker, who has strong views about mixing social responsibility with commerce.

> If you have a business executive who really wants to take on social responsibilities, get rid of him fast. He doesn't have the right sense of priorities and will do a poor job running the business.
>
> *(Drucker, 2003, 2005)*

The economist Milton Friedman is also commonly cited as someone who has little time for business ethics. He suggests that 'The corporation is amoral but the people who run the corporation are not amoral. I think it's very important to realize that moral distinctions are distinctions about what individual people do' (Friedman, 2003, 2005). Here, Friedman appears to agree that institutional ethics are impossible, or at least that ethics are an individual issue and not one that can be addressed by an entire organization. For Friedman, this makes business 'amoral' and not 'immoral.' It means business can be understood as necessary, while remaining morally neutral in the debates about corporate responsibility and ethics. He leaves little room for doubt:

> A corporation is simply an artificial legal structure. It doesn't have any [*moral responsibility*], it is neither moral, nor immoral. It is simply what it is.
>
> *(Friedman, 2003, 2005)*

In his writings, Friedman's case seems to have three main assertions (see 2002, for example):

1   Only humans have moral responsibility.
2   Managers must act solely in the interests of owners/shareholders.

3 Social issues and problems are not the responsibility of corporate managers but of the state/government.

Moral responsibility is hence not a matter for the firm, and the employee is framed as a role holder who is de-humanized in her duties because they are subject to the owner's financial interests. Broadly ethical responsibilities are placed squarely in the hands of the state (although here we will not explore Friedman's habitual call for minimal regulation and free markets). His maxim is that 'there is one and only one social responsibility of business – to use its resources and engage in activities designed to increase its profits' (Friedman, 2002, p. 112) assumes the context of a supposed 'free society,' that is to say, a society in which economic freedoms are guaranteed.

The implication here is that business and ethics must be separated, 'because it is wrong to judge business conduct by the standards of fields whose objectives are altogether different' (Sternberg, 1999, p. 2). Indeed, 'business organisations that seek anything but long-term owner value are guilty not of socialism, but of theft' (op cit., p. 6).

> The defining purpose of business is maximising owner value over the long term by selling goods and services. This simple statement is the key to understanding business, and consequently the foundations of business ethics.
>
> *(Sternberg, 1999, p. 32)*

If the way that we act in business is somehow different to the way that we act in everyday life, then perhaps business is more like poker than ethics. It is a different sort of game and one that does not require the same assumptions. For Albert Carr, quoting the British statesman Henry Taylor, a 'falsehood ceases to be falsehood when it is understood on all sides that the truth is not expected to be spoken' (Carr, 1968, p. 143). His article has been the basis of considerable discussion among business ethics academics (see for example: Sullivan, 1984).

> Cunning deception and concealment of one's strength and intentions, not kindness and openheartedness, are vital in poker. No one thinks any worse of poker on that account. And no one should think any the worse of the game of business because its standards of right and wrong differ from the prevailing traditions of morality in our society.
>
> *(Carr, 1968, p. 3)*

Critical

The commentators in this part of the Venn diagram fundamentally oppose the suggestion that business is, or can be, ethical. Indeed, business may be inherently unethical or immoral, and the ethical credentials of managerial forms of organization have often been challenged (Parker, 2002). Others have argued that to qualify or vary ethics with the prefix 'business' or 'market' is to overwhelm or pervert its original meaning (Bevan and Corvellec, 2007).

ADAM SMITH, 1723–1790

This thinker is impossible to avoid if you study business, management and economics. He is heralded as a father of economics, a foremost theorist of capitalism and an icon of the 'hidden hand' of the free market. A lot of societies, think-tanks and institutes promoting capitalism bear his name. Born in Scotland, Adam Smith is one of the key figures of the Scottish Enlightenment – an intellectual movement that has contributed to a lot of areas of human knowledge. Not constrained by one field of inquiry, scholars of this period provided nuanced accounts of human activities which encompassed insights of political economy, philosophy and sciences, and Smith, being no exception, has a lot more to offer than merely being a proponent of free-market capitalism. Taking his two most famous books together, he proposes that sympathy with and for others is the human instinct that prevents self-interest from becoming dominant, just as market competition is a mechanism that prevents the self-interest of some becoming dominant over everyone.

Despite his contemporary reputation as being an advocate of the free market, Adam Smith is actually an early critic. He explores, in the course of two extensive volumes, a theory of humanity which insists that the economy and the moral order are dependent on each other. In *The Wealth of Nations*, Smith is in favour of trade as a natural means of exchange: 'it is by treaty, by barter, and by purchase, that we obtain from one another the greater part of those mutual good offices we stand in need of' (Smith, 1998 (1776); Book 1, Chapter 2, Section 2). Yet at the same time, Smith suggests some problems that contemporary economists seem to overlook:

> Wherever there is great property there is great inequality. For one very rich man there must be at least five hundred poor, and the affluence of the few supposes the indigence of the many.
>
> *(Smith, 1998 (1776); Book 5, Chapter 4, Section 2)*

Smith also offers what sound like some rather anarchist sentiments:

> Civil government, so far as it is instituted for the security of property, is in reality instituted for the defence of the rich against the poor, or of those who have some property against those who have none at all.
>
> *(Smith, 1998 (1776); Book 5, Chapter 1, Section 2)*

Of course business ethics is not specifically mentioned because it does not emerge as a specific set of ideas until the 20th century, and when he was writing, the private company was in its infancy, but he certainly characterizes business people in terms that lead to a view that ethics and business are incompatible:

> The interest of the dealers, however, in any particular branch of trade or manufactures, is always in some respects different from, and even opposite to, that of the public . . . The proposal of any new law or regulation of commerce which comes from this order . . . ought never to be adopted, till after having been long and carefully examined . . . with the most suspicious attention. It comes from an order of men, whose interest is never exactly the same with that of the public, who have generally an interest to deceive and even oppress the public, and who accordingly have, upon many occasions, both deceived and oppressed it.
>
> *(Smith, 1998 (1776); Book 1, Chapter 9, Conclusion)*

Despite these consistent suspicions of business and government, and the relations between the two, as well as more than 600 pages on the impossibility of a good life without respect for others (in his work *Moral Sentiments* (1976 (1759)), Smith is still acclaimed as a poster-boy of the unrestrained, free market. In what has become a contemporary cliché, Smith's entirely undeveloped and once-used metaphor of an 'invisible hand' of the market is taken by 20th-century management authorities as the central intellectual pillar of pleas for unrestricted trade.

Much more recently, the philosopher Alain Badiou (2001) has argued that the idea of business ethics is a term with no real content. For Badiou, the economic and managerial arguments that drive trade and seek to capture all intellectual, social and productive activity make the idea of business ethics a practice of empty complacency or 'smug nihilism' (Badiou, 2001, p. 38). Commerce seeks to co-opt ethics so that individuals do not complain or even disrupt the progress of the market system. Edward Herman and Noam Chomsky (2008) make a complementary claim in the field of social marketing, which is to say that capitalism systemically absorbs or pays off any criticism. For John Roberts (2001, 2003), corporate social responsibility is a narcissistic attempt to persuade self and others that your company is being ethical or, worse, mere strategic marketing aimed at cultivating customers or disarming regulators (see also Chapter 15). Elsewhere in organization studies, Carl Rhodes identifies a lack of concern for others as a contributing factor in major corporate ethical failures, such as Volkswagen's emissions scandal of 2015, and asserts that 'corporate business ethics is a form of organizing that acts as a subterfuge to facilitate the expansion of corporate sovereignty' (2016, p. 1501).

More generally, the sociologist Zygmunt Bauman has analyzed the consequences of increasingly ubiquitous bureaucratic processes in all aspects of organizing. For Bauman, at each step and in each stage of the materials and services economy, what he describes as the 'moral impulse' is neutralized.

> This is achieved through a number of complementary arrangements: (1) assuring that there is a distance, not proximity between two poles of action – the

'doing' and the 'suffering' one; by the same token those on the receiving end are held beyond the reach of the actor's moral impulse; (2) exempting some 'others' from the class of potential objects of moral responsibility, of potential 'faces'; (3) dissembling other human objects of action into aggregates of functionally specific traits, and holding such traits separate so that the occasion for reassembling the 'face' out of disparate 'items' does not arise, and the task set for each action can be exempt from moral evaluation.

(1993, p. 125)

These arrangements, with which we are all familiar from daily experiences across school, university and work, produce in workers and customers a fragmented understanding of what any organization actually does. If an individual never sees the big picture, has responsibilities which are specific and is only ever following someone else's orders, then this produces regular scandals, as organizations are discovered to have engaged in unethical practices. Everyone is to blame, and no-one is to blame.

Practical

The contributions from practitioners selected here offer a third set of views. Whereas both critical and conservative thinkers are likely to be more heavily informed by theoretical preferences, the practical voice is that of managers. On the purpose of business, Patrick Le Lay, speaking in his role as CEO of France's national TV channel TF1, commented,

(F)rom a business perspective, let us be realistic: basically, the job of TF1 is to assist Coca Cola, for example, to sell its product. For an advertising message to be successful, the brain of the viewer needs to be available. Our programmes are designed to offer this access: that is to say their purpose is to divert and engage viewers between adverts. What we are selling to Coca Cola is access to people's minds.

(Demey, 2004, p. 92)

Then from a senior pensions' fund chairman, who at the time of making this statement was managing £9 billion of assets: 'trustees would be failing in their primary role if they allow issues of ethics to cloud their investment decisions' (Selby, 2011). In this case, ethics apparently gets in the way of 'good' business, rather than encouraging it.

Robert Jackall, an executive who wrote extensively about his experiences as a manager, gives us an account which echoes what Carr said about poker – what is right in the corporation is not what is right in a man's home or in his church. He reports an interview with a man called Brady, which ends as follows:

'What is right in the corporation is what the guy above wants from you. That's what morality is in the corporation.'

The corporate managers to whom I presented this case see Brady's dilemma as devoid of moral or ethical content. In their view, the issues that Brady raises are, first of all, practical matters. His basic failing was first, that he violated the fundamental rules of bureaucratic life.

(2000, p. 109. Emphasis in original)

Jackall goes on to identify the actual rules in the organization as having little to do with ethics.

1   Never go around your boss.
2   Tell your boss only what he wants to hear, even when your boss claims he wants dissenting views.
3   If your boss wants something 'dropped,' you drop it.
4   Be sensitive to what your boss wants, so that he does not have to 'boss' you.
5   Your job is not to report something that your boss does not want reported, but rather to cover it up. You do what your job requires, and you keep your mouth shut.

(op cit., p. 115)

Jackall concludes that 'bureaucracy erodes internal and even external standards of morality not only in matters of individual success and failure but in all the issues that managers face in their daily work' (op cit.; pp. 191–192). The bureaucratic context shapes the lives of the employee and subordinates any individual morality to a general form of organizational behaviour which is characterized by obedience and submission.

We can see an illustration of this in Dennis Gioia's account of his work as a recall co-ordinator at Ford when the Pinto model was exploding with fatal consequences (see also Chapter 10). The company had done a calculation of how much it would cost to re-engineer the Pinto, or to pay out compensation for a certain likely number of deaths and injuries. They chose the latter course, and Gioia did not halt production, which as a manager he could have done. He concludes that he was thinking like the company, a mind-set that discouraged him from considering ethical questions.

My own schematized (scripted) knowledge influenced me to perceive recall issues [*of the Pinto*] in terms of the prevailing decision environment [*at Ford*] and unconsciously overlook key features of the Pinto case.

(1992, p. 385)

In practical terms, what the voices of these managers, and those who have studied them, show us is that ethics in business means doing what you are told. The idea of ethics as independent thought appears not to be encouraged, being largely irrelevant to everyday management decision making.

The business ethics industry

These three understandings of business ethics are responses to a vast array of text-books, journals, consultants, institutions and so on. This *industry* often comments on the ethical failures that are identifiable in every corporate scandal, whether social, environmental or financial. The problem is that (from a critical perspective) the business ethics business is broadly complicit with the system in which these fail-ures continue to occur. These professional business ethics practitioners – preachers, teachers, activists, advocates, consultants and so on – effectively function as therapists who point to problems but rarely do anything to change the system that produces them. They have careful, well-organized scripts on a range of issues and arguments, including corporate moral agency, corporate governance, corporate social respon-sibility, corporate citizenship and so on. All are seeking to shepherd corporations or industries to comply with various – and sometimes mutually incompatible – ideals of correct behaviour. The idea that there is a correct behaviour that can be written down in a code of ethical conduct is a result of Bauman's bureaucratic thinking applied to personal decision making. Codes of ethics are an attempt to reduce ethi-cal complexity to a set of simple and easily digestible measures; universal norms of business that can be followed without endangering the practice of business.

The United Nations Global Compact (UNGC) can be considered to be one of many international attempts to provide a framework for business ethics. Few con-temporary business ethics textbooks will not include a broadly positive review of it. The UNGC is a set of ten business principles initially articulated in 2000, according to which global commerce can conduct itself fairly and sustainably. So, a 'good' busi-ness will, for example, agree that it seeks to 'abolish child labour.' Most people would agree with the principle that child labour should be prevented. But this principle represents no more than an ideal unless we acknowledge that to achieve it requires a comprehensive global system of education, administration and enforcement which is accessible to any potential victim of the abuse and which would prevent it from arising. This UNGC is an excellent example, in the context of this chapter, of a conventional approach to business ethics. It is easy enough for people in the Global North to agree that we are against abusive child labour, but it is meaningless, unless at the same time we are making schooling available to children until they achieve working age, as well as addressing the global economic inequalities which make child labour desirable and sometimes necessary, for workers, families and business owners.

An anarchist response

The chapter so far has dealt with the problems with thinking about conventional business ethics, so how would anarchists respond? There isn't a great deal writ-ten about this, largely because anarchists are profoundly suspicious of conventional business and would hence be unlikely to be impressed by the idea that hierarchi-cal capitalist organizations could claim to be 'ethical' at all. Carl Rhodes (2014) addresses this issue when he sets out to disrupt the legitimacy which business ethics might claim by thinking through what the philosopher Emmanuel Levinas suggests is a primordial responsibility to other people. Rhodes, like Derrida (1997), suggests that Levinas is an anarchist in terms of the rest of Western philosophy. Levinas places ethics as a 'first philosophy,' suggesting that there is nothing more important or immediate because the relation of any individual to her others is involuntary and absolute. The implication of this is that it takes an effort for any human to avoid ethical engagement. In a careful re-examination of Levinas's book *Otherwise than Being* (Levinas, 2004), Rhodes uncovers Levinas's specific take on anarchy: 'it cannot be sovereign, like an *arche*. It can only disturb the State ... disorder has an irreducible meaning, as refusal of synthesis' (Levinas, 2004, p. 194, footnote #3). Thus, argues Rhodes, ethical anarchism is inherently political. Undermining the rationalizing project of the business of Business Ethics, Rhodes reasons that 'Business ethics is not the responsibility of business, it is the responsibility of the societies in which business operates ... it is "our" responsibility' (Rhodes, 2014, p. 733). He continues by suggesting that ethical business

> does not need moralistic managers or do-gooding CEOs, it needs a civil society that will disturb corporate power in the name of ethical anarchism, and that is in opposition to the imposition of sovereign corporate power justified by neoliberalism.
>
> *(Ibid.)*

Such a business ethics, if we can even call it that, suggests clearly and explicitly an activist mode of social engagement, which we shall consider more fully in the final section.

The anarchist political theorist Benjamin Franks takes an alternate path to connect anarchism and business ethics, reconstituting Friedman's maxim as 'the social responsibility of the anarchist is to destroy business' (Franks, 2014, p. 699). From this potentially sensational framing, Franks develops an outline of anarchism which is based in 'the stable, pervasive but not necessarily universal principles found consistently in the historical and contemporary libertarian socialist or class struggle anarchist groups' (ibid., p. 702). Franks suggests that conventional business ethics offers a 'flawed moral position' (p. 706) and that contemporary CSR concepts, such as corporate citizenship, shared value and corporate virtue, are cynical attempts to provide public relations for business. This is a project centred around the demands and interests of the corporation, a commercial practice of ethics for cash. Franks sees anarchism – or a living practice of democracy – as a force which is generally suppressed by these commercial forces but one which must continue to struggle for 'alternate productive and distributive practices where both internal goods (virtues) and external goods (surplus) can, and are, generated on anti-hierarchical, **prefigurative** principles' (p. 721, see box in Chapter 2). Franks encourages anarchism through critical thinking of the practices and relations of production but also more substantial, anti-corporate activism. This is an ethics against contemporary business, a political analysis of business, not an ethics for business.

Conclusion

For any critical thinker, whether anarchist or otherwise, it is clear that business ethics is in, at best, a morally paradoxical proposition. For anarchist and other activists, there is scope for responding through individual action in keeping with the idea of anarchism as a continuing political practice which assumes that social arrangements do not need to be based on contemporary economic or managerial common sense (Rocker, 1998 (1938)).

This suggests a personal responsibility for action that can also be found in an implausibly simple maxim for action offered by Levinas. He suggests an ethics performed or realized in an action when two people arrive at the same door simultaneously: '(We) say, before an open door, "After you, sir!"' (Levinas, 1985, p. 89). We recognize the other person and make a concrete effort to assist him. To reject as simplistic and pointless the idea of small individual gestures is to miss the point of ethical action. It is not through corporate organization or ideological programmes that ethics is enacted but through a series of particular and specific acts (Bateson, 2000, p. 477). This is more in line with the notion of social change put forward by the philosopher Gabriel Tarde, who suggested that 'great *constant* forces . . . are given direction by *small, accidental, new* forces, which, by being grafted on the first ones, set into motion a new kind of periodic reproduction' (Tarde quoted in Taymans, 1950, p. 616). It is that simple to act ethically as an individual, but ethical action is not as immediately easy for someone holding responsibility in a formal organization, whether as worker or manager. That is the problem that this chapter has engaged with – to what extent do the structures and priorities of formal business and management roles make ethical action impossible?

Ursula le Guin, a science fiction writer who was often described as an anarchist, made an appeal that seems to me to capture a sense of ethics within the terms this chapter has set out: 'We live in capitalism, its power seems inescapable – but then, so did the divine right of kings. Any human power can be resisted and changed by human beings' (Le Guin, 2014). An anarchist ethics would be resistance to that power.

Questions for further study

1 Try and define the critical, conservative and practical approaches to business ethics. How are they different? What examples can you think of for an application of ethics in each of these categories?

2 Think of some examples of recent corporate scandals. You can look in the news or in a mainstream corporate governance textbook to get inspiration. How would the ethical positions discussed in the first sections of the chapter respond to these scandals?

3 What might be the anarchist responses to business ethics discussed in the chapter? How would they approach corporate scandals?

4 Can the ethical anarchist or activist positions outlined in the chapter be applied at an organizational or managerial level?

References

Badiou, A. (2001). *Ethics: An Essay on the Understanding of Evil*. London: Verso.

Bateson, G. (2000). *Steps to an Ecology of Mind: Collected Essays in Anthropology, Psychiatry, Evolution and Epistemology*. Chicago, IL: University of Chicago Press.

Bauman, Z. (1993). *Postmodern Ethics*. Oxford: Blackwell.

Bevan, D., and Corvellec, H. (2007). "The Impossibility of Corporate Ethics: For a Levinasian Approach to Management Ethics." *Business Ethics: A European Review*, 16(3), 208–219.

Carr, A. Z. (1968). "Is Business Bluffing Ethical?" *Harvard Business Review*, (January-February), 143–153.

Collins, J. W. (1994). "Is Business Ethics an Oxymoron." *Business Horizons*, 37(5), 1–8.

Crane, A., and Matten, D. (2016). *Business Ethics: Managing Corporate Citizenship and Sustainability in the Age of Globalization* (3rd Edition). Oxford: Oxford University Press.

Demey, E. (ed.). (2004). *Les Dirigeants Face au Changement: Barometre 2004*. Paris: les editions du huitieme jour.

Derrida, J. (1997). *Adieu à Emmanuel Lévinas*. Paris: Galilée.

Drucker, P. (2003, 2005). "Out-take and Interview Media from 'The Corporation'." In M. Achbar, J. Abbott, and J. Bakan (Eds.), *The Corporation*. Canada: Metrodome; Free Press.

Elkington, J. (1998). *Cannibals With Forks: The Triple Bottom Line of 21st Century Business*. London: Victor Golanz.

Franks, B. (2014). "Anarchism and Business Ethics: The Social Responsibility of the Anarchist Is to Destroy Business." *Ephemera*, 14(4), 699–724.

Friedman, M. (2002). *Capitalism and Freedom (1962)* (Paper Edition). London; Chicago, IL: University of Chicago Press.

Friedman, M. (2003, 2005). "Out-take and Interview Media from 'The Corporation'." In M. Achbar, J. Abbott, and J. Bakan (Eds.), *The Corporation*. Canada: Metrodome; Free Press.

Ghoshal, S. (2005). "Bad Management Theories Are Destroying Good Management Practices." *Academy of Management Learning and Education*, 4(1), 75–91.

Gioia, D. (1992). "Pinto Fires and Personal Ethics: A Script Analysis of Missed Opportunities." *Journal of Business Ethics*, 11(5-6), 379–389.

Herman, E. S., and Chomsky, N. (2008). *Manufacturing Consent: The Political Economy of the Mass Media*. London: The Bodley Head.

Jackall, R. (2000). *Moral Mazes: The World of Corporate Managers*. Oxford: Oxford University Press.

Jackson, I. (2003, 2005). "Out-take and Interview Media from 'The Corporation'." In M. Achbar, J. Abbott, and J. Bakan (Eds.), *The Corporation*. Canada: Metrodome.

Le Guin, U. (2014). Speech at 65th National Book Awards Ceremony. New York City, National Book Foundation Awards Ceremony: National Book Foundation.

Levinas, E. (1985). *Ethics and Infinity – Conversations With Philippe Nemo*. Pittsburgh, PA: Duquesne University Press.

Levinas, E. (2004). *Otherwise Than Being – or Beyond Essence* (A. Lingis, Trans.). Pittsburgh, PA: Duquesne University Press.

Parker, M. (2002). *Against Management*. Oxford: Polity Press.

Rhodes, C. (2014). "Ethical Anarchism, Business Ethics and the Politics of Disturbance." *Ephemera*, 14(4), 725–737.

Rhodes, C. (2016). "Democratic Business Ethics: Volkswagen's Emissions Scandal and the Disruption of Corporate Sovereignty." *Organization Studies*, 37(10), 1501–1518.

Roberts, J. (2001). "Corporate Governance and the Ethics of Narcissus." *Business Ethics Quarterly*, 11(1), 109–127.

Roberts, J. (2003). "The Manufacture of Corporate Social Responsibility: Constructing Corporate Sensibility." *Organization*, 10(2), 249–265.

Rocker, R. (1998 (1938)). *Anarcho-Syndicalism* (R. E. Chase, Trans., and N. Chomsky, Ed., 6th June 2004 Edition). Edinburgh: AK Press Working Classics.

Selby, T. (2011). "Ethical Investment Trustee Priority." *Professional Pensions*. Available at: www. professionalpensions.com/professional-pensions/news/1650649/ethical-investment-trustee-priority.

Smith, A. (1976 (1759)). *The Theory of Moral Sentiments*. Oxford: Oxford University Press.

Smith, A. (1998 (1776)). *The Wealth of Nations*. Oxford: Oxford Paperbacks.

Sternberg, E. (1999). *Just Business: Business Ethics in Action*. Oxford: Oxford University Press.

Sullivan, R. (1984). "A Response to 'Is Business Bluffing Ethical?'" *Business and Professional Ethics Journal*, 3(2), 1–16.

Taymans, A. (1950). "Tarde and Schumpeter: A Similar Vision." *The Quarterly Journal of Economics*, 64(4), 611–622.

PART III
Structure and culture

7

DECISION MAKING AND POWER

Maarit Laihonen

Introduction

Who makes decisions at work? Who should make decisions at work? Contemporary organizations are now said to be freer, more empowering and more equal than ever, and work itself is often described as a path to satisfaction and fulfilment. It seems that old hierarchical and bureaucratic structures are dead and that companies are now flat, smart and decentralized. In spite of this, many people experience feelings of being unhappy, tired and stressed at work (Siltala, 2004).

Decision making, a core activity of any business organization, would be described in textbooks as an activity carried out by a manager or a managerial team. Whether normative (how decisions should be made) or behavioural (what managers actually do), the focus is on individuals who are considered superior in their skills or qualifications to decide the next steps of an organization (see Chapter 9). Although during the last couple of decades, decentralization of decision making and participatory approaches have gained some space in management education, the fundamental role of the manager has rarely been questioned as the final authority in decision making.

Anarchists consider decision making as something that should not be left in the hands of the few but as something that the many should be involved in. This is based on the anarchist ideals of aiming towards organizations without permanent hierarchies and which have flatter forms of organizing that divide power more equally. Power is a perpetual and fundamental feature in organizations, and it is most visible when decisions are made. Although anarchist organizations aim to reject explicitly hierarchical power, other forms of power are still present and may result in hidden hierarchies being recreated and reinforced. Even in organizations guided by anarchist principles of decision making and collective action, hierarchy and control can still emerge because both overt and covert forms of power remain difficult to eradicate. If we want to understand how flatter, less-hierarchical forms of organization might be encouraged, then it is important to understand how and why power exists in all organizations. Combining the understanding of power and anarchist thinking about overcoming it can help us in seeing new possibilities of how to operate our decision making. In the chapter, 'organization' and 'collective action' will be used interchangeably in order to emphasise the goal-oriented and collective nature of organizations.

This chapter will

- review different approaches to the nature of power and how it has been discussed in the context of anarchism,
- look at how power exists in organizations,
- consider a specific collective consensus decision making method,
- discuss the possibilities and limits of anarchist practices of decision making, and
- explore the lessons from anarchist decision making practices for other organizations.

Power and control in organizations

Power manifests itself in different levels of society and personal relationships. Nation-states are the most institutionalized form of societal power and include a variety of sub-institutions enabling those holding the political power to use legislation, material infrastructure, the military and the police force for their purposes. The power of nation-states is the traditional object of anarchist critique. Other formal organizations – business firms, non-governmental organizations, charities – are also structures where power is explicitly organized hierarchically. In other social relations and forms of collective action, such as in friendships, family relations, networks or even momentary assemblies like demonstrations and protests, power relations are there but often much more implicitly. Common to all human associations are social relations, and in the case of organizations with a set goal, such as a company, these are shaped by the specified purpose of the organization. Thus, power always exists, it is never absent, but it takes different forms, especially in hierarchies where other members of the organization have less power because of their structural position.

Organizational structures have been of concern for anarchists and alternative political movements because of how they shape power relations, but hierarchical structures have also been suggested to be one of the causes of social and environmental problems at local and global scales. The link between organizational forms and their connection to the surrounding political organization of society have been raised by some management writers (Parker et al., 2014; Fleming and Spicer, 2014) but have rarely been central to textbooks. Instead, hierarchy is assumed to be a natural state of affairs, an inescapable feature of human life. We will see in this chapter how a wider understanding of power relations is important for understanding the internal power relations of anarchist organizing.

What is power?

Power is a tricky issue to understand, as it is not only explicit but often implicit – built into relations and interactions, already an element of the personal characteristics of group members as well as the cultures that they live in. Power has been theorized in various ways – from its innermost nature (where does it exist) to the forms it takes (explicit hierarchies, violence, other forms of physical power). Here we will mainly look at power as coercion and domination (Hearn, 2012), but first we need to understand the wider nature of power in order to see the different forms that it takes. After that we can proceed to trying to find ways of overcoming power or altering its form.

Let's begin by briefly summarizing some of the views on power. For Max Weber, one of the most important thinkers on organization, power was an ability to control others, to get them to do things that they wouldn't otherwise do. He analyzed power from the perspective of hierarchies, for example in the context of the state and its ability to use physical force, such as by using the military or the police (Weber 1978 (1922)). For Karl **Marx**, however (see box in Chapter 11), the power relation was essentially an issue of social classes not just the individual's position in hierarchies. For Marx, the domination of the capitalist class that owns property, including factories and other means of production, over the working class, who have to sell their labour to the capitalist class in order to survive – is the key issue in understanding how power relates to the organization of capitalist societies (Gartman, 1978). Marx's views have recently become popular again because of radical changes in working life (see also Van Meter, 2017), but they are also echoed in accounts of power that show how ideas about what is considered proper and possible at any given moment is shaped by 'ideology,' by the dominant ways of thinking of any historical period. So, for example, the early 20th-century Italian Marxist Antonio Gramsci concentrated on how particular ideas became dominant, or **hegemonic**, in politics and society (Gramsci, 2012; Lears, 1985, see box in Chapter 15). Probably the most influential recent view of power is Michel **Foucault**'s conception of power as a form of thought, or a 'discourse,' which produces ways of knowing about the world and existing in it (see box in Chapter 4). Power, for Foucault, is the very process of producing human beings in particular ways, shaping them into 'subjects' with particular characteristics and ideas – men and women, managers and workers, management students and anarchist professors. Our social contexts make us who we are, and this means that power is ubiquitous and inescapable (Heiskala, 2001). Power cannot be taken away from social relations.

How does power function?

There have been various attempts at defining and describing the different forms that power takes. For example, a well-known division is presented by Lukes (2005, esp. ch. 3), who divides power in three ways according to how it is exercised. First it could manifest as coercion, a force based on threat; second a capacity to set the agenda and shape what is imagined to be possible; or third, a form of manipulation which involves the intentional prompting of the thoughts and actions of others. In the context of anarchist literature, Uri Gordon (2010) utilizes Starhawk's (1987) classification of power in order to aim to give it some different and maybe even liberating possibilities. Starhawk again identifies three central forms of power: power over others (domination); power from within or power to do things (capacity); power with or power among others (Gordon, 2010, pp. 41–46). As we have seen so far, the first form is the most commonly acknowledged (Gordon, 2010; Kreisberg, 1992) and is also the most common object of resistance. However, the other two forms are equally fundamental in that they provide the capacity to dominate, including by concealing or revealing the power relations in everyday actions, thereby often normalizing inequalities. But power-to and power-with can also be used to reveal and perhaps overcome forms of power that have become naturalized as 'common sense,' such as men's common domination over women. 'Calling out' such hierarchies, making illegitimate power visible, fits well with the view anarchists often have when they criticize power structures and develop methods for overcoming them.

It is also important to understand how power manifests itself. For example, the US futurist Alvin Toffler discussed the use of power in society and how it has changed over time. He suggested that it was initially a matter of the control of violence, then of wealth and finally of knowledge (Toffler, 1990). Although he saw them having developed in this order in history – knowledge being the contemporary form that power takes in a digital economy – anarchists would consider the two former equally important concerns in terms of hierarchical state structures (violence) and sources of inequality (wealth). In the context of an organization, this means that anarchists would concentrate on how to overcome whichever source of hierarchical power seems most relevant at any particular time in order to address its negative coercive and dominating outcomes and promote collective action, equality and **mutualism** (see box in Chapter 17).

This means thinking more deeply about how organizations produce various forms of power, as well as encouraging members to make decisions beyond narrow versions of task-related empowerment or job rotation (Conger and Kanungo, 1988; Honold, 1997). Anarchist principles can help us think about some crucial issues in decision-making processes within an organization and also in the social context that supports and promotes hierarchical structures. This means thinking about who can communicate and how, because we do not all have equal capacity to intervene and be listened to. For example, Grubačić (2013) criticizes the idea of pure reason and dialogue, suggesting that such assumptions are limited to the privileged in the Global North and are of less use in contexts in which class, gender or ethnicity (for example) already shape the way in which discussions can happen. Relying too heavily on an ideal of rationality in communication assumes that everyone has equal access to a conversation which could lead to rational outcomes through deliberation. The expectation of a specific kind of capacity to engage can shut out different people from different backgrounds and with different abilities to participate.

Anarchist principles and power

Most formal organizations are managed through central authority which is built into the official hierarchies, such as management structures and policies. The main anarchist critique of these arrangements is based on the idea that they are repressive structures which act against the principles of autonomy, cooperation, voluntary association, mutual aid, direct action and decentralized decision making which encourages participation and creativity (cf. Gelderloos, 2014, pp. 8–9). So seeing power as something that can be shared with others offers a fruitful starting point for challenging these assumptions (e.g. Kreisberg, 1992, ch. 3; Gordon, 2010). This principle of **cooperation**, not competition, is important for anarchist or anarchically organized communities all over the world (see box in Chapter 8). Although shared values might not be constantly discussed, they are brought up and made visible whenever necessary by all those involved, unlike in traditional organizations, where values and other fundamental issues are normally outlined and communicated from 'above' by the management.

The strength of anarchism is in its deep connection between theory and practice. It is 'a moral conviction, an ethical disposition that finds expression in practice and as practice' (Critchley, 2013, p. 4). For anarchists, theory and practice 'are two sides to the same coin' that cannot be separated (Springer, 2016, p. 12). Hence, for an anarchist approach, we need to concentrate on what gets done, not just theory. How is an ethical or political disposition turned into action, concentrating on the aim of making domination visible and then organizing differently (Grubačić, 2013)? It must be remembered that the positive side of power is responsibility, or the acceptance of duties (Morriss, 2002, p. 39). This means that as power takes many visible forms, so can responsibility be rearranged in visible ways. Sharing power and responsibility equally is one of the central goals of the consensus method of making decisions.

Anarchist decision making

> I believe that the social ideas of anarchism: autonomous groups, spontaneous order, workers' control, the federative principle, add up to a coherent theory of social organisation which is a valid and realistic alternative to the authoritarian, hierarchical and institutional social philosophy which we see in application all around us. Man will be compelled, Kropotkin declared, 'to find new forms of organisation for the social functions which the State fulfils through the bureaucracy' and he insisted that 'as long as this is not done nothing will be done.' I think we have discovered what these new forms of organisation should be. We have now to make the opportunities for putting them into practice.
>
> (Ward, 1966, p. 7)

As Ward describes in the preceding quote, there is a connection between the ideal of a desirable society and the way that organizations are structured and people make decisions within them. This connection is built on shared values. For anarchists, the values of the contemporary state and large corporations are oppressive and go against their egalitarian ideals. This means that it makes sense to study how social movements and other alternative organizations do things differently. These are organizations which are positioned against dominant political, technical and economic structures and offer a distinctive understanding of practical sense making, reasoning and experience. They go beyond a narrow analysis of organizing to **prefigure** (see box in Chapter 2) changes in the way that people relate to one another. This is based on the idea that human beings are shaped by the social orders that they find themselves in, which is to say that their attitudes and practices are socially constructed. Anarchists do not consider the innermost nature of humans to be selfish and competitive. Against such a version of 'human nature,' many anarchists would argue that people are normally generous, co-operative and oriented towards collective projects. This means that any advocacy of the inevitability of hierarchy is also to assume that people are not equal and that they must compete to find their place in some sort of structure of dominance.

As we have seen, power can take many forms, and it is practiced through a variety of means. This can be through social institutions such as the law and the police, formal managers and leaders, and implicit norms in human interaction which dictate who gets listened to and who does not. Power cannot be eradicated, but it can be made more visible. If its structures and effects maintain systems that create inequalities or make decisions which harm members of the organization or if the decision-making processes are considered unfair, then this power over others can be seen to be illegitimate. This is clearly the case for anarchists, a group who are committed to the idea that no one person or group should have privilege over another person or group. More recent, **postanarchist** thought (see box in Chapter 5) is strongly in line with **Foucault**'s (see box in Chapter 4) idea of power being an everyday practice, a mundane and often unnoticed way of controlling others and ourselves (1991, and see boxes in Chapter 4). For example, a law, institution or custom becomes a form of domination when we internalize its demands and then repeat that control over others in everyday actions. Anarchist communities are clearly not free of this either. It is a partly unconscious activity, a policeman inside us, but anarchists have been very concerned to create forms of organizing within which these forms of oppression can be named and made visible.

Classical anarchist approaches for liberating people from the repressive hierarchical systems of state and economy generally involve proposals for whole societies but do also discuss the self-organization of work and industry. This stream of anarchist thought and action is often referred to as collectivism, or **anarcho-syndicalism** (see box in Chapter 8), and is often located as originating in the work of Mikhail Bakunin on organizing collective grassroots workplace organization in the 19th century (see Chapter 2). But despite talk of liberation at work, unequal power relations and repression have not vanished from workplaces or society. Especially if we think on a global scale, both humans and nature are continuously subordinated within the global economy.

MIKHAIL BAKUNIN, 1814–1876

Mikhail Bakunin was a Russian collectivist anarchist who developed the idea of a revolution from below. Born into the Russian aristocracy, he took up a commission with the Russian Imperial Guard and served in Lithuania, resigning three years later in disgust at the repression of the local people. Bakunin accepted Marx's analysis of capitalism and the need for its overthrow by revolution but strongly disagreed with Marx's insistence on the need for a transitional worker's state, believing that it would simply lead to new forms of repression and authoritarianism. He believed that workers should organize their own institutions from the ground up, achieving more complex forms by voluntary federalism, joining together to produce larger federations of worker-controlled organizations. Bakunin rejected all forms of government and illegitimate external authority, believing that human nature was essentially benign. It was the distorting effects of external restraint, inequality and privilege that were responsible for the ills of society. Although he is sometimes held to be more of an activist and charismatic leader than theoretician, his contribution to anarchist and libertarian thinking is significant. Most would also see his predictions concerning the authoritarian tendencies of state socialism as prophetic. More recently, the resurgence in anarchist thinking and politics that began in the 1960s has led to his becoming an influential thinker within contemporary communitarian movements.

Anarchist alternatives in practice

Anarchism is not about being against organizations or organizing. Anarchism is against authority but not against organization (Ward, 1966). In fact, it is very much about organizing – for example, the anarchists often have well-developed ideas about how to better organize relationships between workers and the local arrangement of work. Similarly, a stream of anarchism called 'social ecology' has proposed a form of social organization that would work against the exploitation of the non-human environment. Social ecologists such as Murray **Bookchin** argue that there is no necessary contradiction between the well-being of humans and non-human nature and that modern environmental destruction is a result of the oppressive organization of globalizing capitalism (e.g. Bookchin, 1982, see box in Chapter 10).

> Perhaps the greatest crime of the industrial system is the way in which it systematically thwarts the inventive genius of the majority of its workers. . . . Most people in fact are 'educated' beyond their level in the industrial pyramid. Their capacity for invention and innovation is not wanted by the system. 'You're not paid to think, just get on with it,' says the foreman. 'We are happy

that we have re-established the most fundamental principle – management's right to manage: said Sir Alick Dick when he took over as chairman of the Standard Motor Company.

(Ward, 2008, pp. 54–55; see Kropotkin, 1985)

In mainstream management literature, the word *anarchy* is used to describe a situation where 'the management' has lost its power (e.g. Mullins, 2010, p. 691). This is partly true, but a more accurate description from an anarchist perspective would be to specify that the power has been removed from managers themselves. Although empowerment, delegation, dialogue and similar buzz words have been popular in the management literature, the fundamental function of a manager has not been questioned in practice. There is talk of so-called self-management of employees but not of the idea that this means that these employees no longer need managers (see Chapter 9). The freedom to organize work is still almost entirely vested in a class of people who establish working hours, wages and organizational structures which are based on explicit structures of hierarchy, command and control. In the global economy, through international supply chains which echo older colonial power relations, poorer countries and less powerful actors are often subordinated to Western multinationals. This is not merely a question of organization or management theory but a way of understanding power relations that is built into the global economic system. So is another way of organizing the world possible?

Consensus decision making

Achieving **consensus** (see box in Chapter 9) means discussing a topic until a solution acceptable to all is found. For many decisions, this is not that hard, but it is also possible that consensus cannot be reached. In such a situation, the decision is deferred for a future discussion or if a decision must be made, then how to proceed is negotiated between the differing parties. The consensus method reflects the idea of power as something that is collective – power-with or power-among (Kreisberg, 1992; Starhawk, 1987). The fundamental idea of consensus is to overcome the problems of structural power or the tyranny of the majority and return the control of self and other to the people who will be the objects and subjects of this control. Thus, traditional dialogue is only one part of the method that is presented in the following; it is not an end in itself. The ultimate goal is to find solutions to problems in which the expressed interests of different groups of people are in balance with each other.

Crucially, this also means that the particular processes of decision making in any given instance should be decided amongst those who are affected by the decisions. How to make the decision is part of the decision making too, and there should be no assumption that the same method will always be used. Rules and processes based on past events cannot regulate current and future actions. This would be to let tradition determine the present. Flexibility of processes in decision making is essential and should run through all levels of the organization. If a process is not suitable for the specific needs of the people and problem presented, it can be renegotiated by the members. Sharing concrete tasks equally, including decisions about how to make decisions, is essential for the experience and integrity of the process.

To give a concrete and personal example, in the case of a protest camp organization that I participated in, it was clear that there were a variety of different types of tasks that needed to be equally shared among members. Everyday tasks such as cooking, doing dishes and carrying water might not be as tempting to many as tasks related to activities directly related to the protest itself, but they needed to be taken care of and they concerned the well-being of all. Without performing these functions well, the camp would not have been able to continue, so using time for good decisions pays for itself compared to using time for fixing bad decisions. The protest camp was small, but a larger organization could be arranged in committees or councils responsible for particular activities, and if there were 'higher' committees, then the 'lower' committees would have a veto and could not be overruled by the higher decision. This would be based on their better local knowledge of that specific activity if it was felt that decisions of the higher council would harm those activities. Finally, it is common that the committee members' terms of office would be limited to ensure that a certain cadre of people didn't continue to monopolize decision making.

There are various guidelines that draw together examples of practices, as well as possible problems and solutions that aim towards diminishing the negative effects of creating majorities and minorities that are the central problem of traditional voting systems. The anarchist group Seeds for Change (2010, p. 12) suggest that

> Consensus isn't about everybody thinking the same thing. Differences of opinion are natural and to be expected. Disagreements can help a group's decision, because with a wide range of information and opinions, there is a greater chance the group will find suitable solutions. Easily reached consensus may cover up the fact that some people don't feel safe, or confident enough to express their disagreements.

An emphasis on clear process is important to ensure that, particularly in large groups, decision making is visible and not hidden behind closed doors (Freeman, 1972).

The following table summarizes some ideal features and practical issues of consensus process (based on Butler and Rothstein, 1987; and Seeds for Change, 2010).

Of course, consensus can be criticized for its inefficiency. In addition, if there is already a difficult atmosphere in the organization, then it can make the process so tense that reasonable discussion becomes impossible. However, when thinking further about these problems, it is clear that they are present in traditional hierarchical systems too. Inefficient decisions are made because those at the top haven't consulted those at the bottom or because employees don't trust managers to make decisions in the employees' interests. So how does this consensus process differ from talk about empowered workers and employee engagement? Firstly, the ideal of consensus openly states background assumptions and prerequisites, and this is not something that commonly happens in contemporary management, if at all. Also,

TABLE 7.1 Central features of consensus process

Fundamentals and conditions for consensus	Unity of purpose/goal
	Commitment to reach consensus
	Trust and openness
	Sufficient time
	Clear process
	Active participation and listening
	Delegation of implementation (in large groups)
	Committees or councils (in large groups)
Process	Introduction
	Opening out
	Discussion
	Clarifications
	Synthesis
	Implementation
	(The central parts of this process might need to be repeated a few times.)
Possible problems	Participants not understanding the process
	Lack of information
	Hostile atmosphere (which prevents people from participating openly)
	Domination of certain individuals (intended or unintended)
	Concentration of responsibilities in implementation
	Consensus not reached
	The goal of consensus preventing necessary measures from being taken, such as guaranteeing everybody's safety

discussion until consensus is very rare, largely because management would assume that when 'consultation' ends, they make the decisions. However, it is really important to recognize that none of the preceding is definitive and that a group might decide to move forward without consensus. The point is that it is up to the group. Thus, we need to return to the original idea, which is to give the members of the organization their autonomy, and then they can negotiate what kind of processes they wish to employ.

Conclusion

These practices are not timeless, and they differ depending on context. Nonetheless, they are influenced strongly by revolts and revolutions in the past in which people organized themselves against oppressive forces. In his book *Anarchy Works* (2014), Peter Gelderloos collected almost 100 real-life examples of anarchist, antiauthoritarian and autonomous forms of collective action on all levels from one organization to a whole society. Some of these are clearly examples which were functioning at large scale too. For example, during Lenin's terror after the Russian revolution, an insurrectionary anarchist army

> developed a more formal structure to allow for strategic coordination along several fronts, but it remained a volunteer militia, based on peasant support. Guiding questions of policy and strategy were decided in general meetings of peasants and workers. Aided rather than hindered by their flexible, participatory structure and strong support from the peasants, they liberated an area roughly 300 by 500 miles across, containing 7 million inhabitants, centered around the town of Gulyai-Polye. At times, the cities surrounding this anarchist zone – Alexandrovsk and Ekaterinoslav (now named Zaporizhye and Dnipropetrovsk, respectively) as well as Melitopol, Mariupol and Berdyansk, were freed from the control of the state, though they changed hands several times throughout the war. Self-organization along anarchist lines was deployed more consistently in the rural areas in these tumultuous years. In Gulyai-Polye, the anarchists set up three secondary schools and gave money expropriated from banks to orphanages. Throughout the area, literacy increased among the peasants.
>
> *(Gelderloos, 2014, p. 139)*

So what can we learn from this example? If people have a reason and a sense of possibility, they will organize for their common good, and they can do it at scale. This is also why protest camps, social movement organizations like Occupy and Extinction Rebellion and anarchist forms of organization exist. People see that there is a need to organize and that they can make the organization function without giving away their power to hierarchical structures. Perhaps from such unorthodox organizations like these, we can also find answers to pressing issues in traditional business organizations. People have acted collectively throughout human history, which suggests that they are capable of overcoming or working within the colossal powers of emperors, kings and feudal lords. In principle, business organizations have the freedom to organize themselves in whatever way they wish, so perhaps they are an easier place to begin.

There are a variety of problems in using these practices, and sometimes consensus is close to impossible to achieve. There are also sometimes complicated issues where nuanced background knowledge is needed and the role of expertise becomes a problem if power and decision making is completely decentralized (see Chapter 9). The process has to be able, therefore, to take into consideration how to include the different knowledges and skills of different people. However, unlike mainstream decision-making systems, anarchist practices are designed to deal with these issues, and not ignore them, as most managed organizations routinely do. Anarchists aim to avoid the concentration of power by making it explicit, openly discussing processes, rotating roles and naming power when it appears. It is obvious that power does not 'vanish' in these circumstances but instead tends to be distributed more equally between different members of communities and organizations. Despite the impossibility of having a perfectly fair and open organization, there is an intrinsic value in aiming to think through these problems on the basis of a fundamental and equal right to speak out. The decentralization of power has its own prefigurative effects. Means and ends become inseparable, and the motivations of workers become entwined with the successes and failures of their own organizations.

Questions for further study

- Are hierarchical forms of organization 'natural' for human society? What would it mean for a form of organization to be 'natural'?
- What would it be like to work in an organization that valued autonomy, cooperation and voluntary association, mutual aid, direct action, and decentralized decision making? How would it differ from organizations you have worked in? How would your day-to-day work change? Would your life as a student be different if your university was run in this way?
- Can there be rules for consensus decision making? What would there need to be in an organization to make consensus decision making work? How would the structure, the relationships and the practices be different from what we might normally find in an organization?
- What would it mean for an organization if the consensus was to elect a manager?
- Could an economy function if it was populated by anarchist organizations with workers making their own decisions? Who else would need to have a say in how the economy was organized? How could this be organized?

References

Bookchin, M. (1982). *The Ecology of Freedom: The Emergence and Dissolution of Hierarchy*. Palo Alto, CA: Cheshire Books.
Butler, C. T., and Rothstein, A. (1987). *On Conflict and Consensus: A Handbook on Formal Consensus Decisionmaking*. Portland: Food Not Bombs Publishing. Available at: the anarchistlibrary.org/library/c-t-butler-and-amy-rothstein-on-conflict-and-consensus-a-handbook-on-formal-consensus-decisionm.
Conger, J. A., and Kanungo, R. N. (1988). "The Empowerment Process: Integrating Theory and Practice." *Academy of Management Review*, 13(3), 471–482.
Critchley, S. (2013). "Introduction." In J. Blumendfeld, C. Bottici, and S. Critchley (Eds.), *The Anarchist Turn*, pp. 1–6. London: Pluto Press.
Fleming, P., and Spicer, A. (2014). "Power in Management and Organization Science." *The Academy of Management Annals*, 8(1), 237–298.
Foucault, M. (1991). *Discipline and Punish: The Birth of a Prison*. London: Penguin Books.
Freeman, J. (1972). "The Tyranny of Structurelessness." *Berkeley Journal of Sociology*, 17, 151–165.
Gartman, D. (1978). "Marx and the Labor Process: An Interpretation." *Insurgent Sociologist*, 8(2–3), 97–108. (See also, Marx, Karl: *Capital I*.)
Gelderloos, P. (2014). *Anarchy Works: Examples of Anarchist Ideas in Practice* (2nd Edition). London/Zagreb: Što čitaš?

Gordon, U. (2010). "Power and Anarchy: In/equality+ In/visibility in Autonomous Politics." In N. J. Jun and S. Wahl (Eds.), *New Perspectives on Anarchism*. London: Rowman and Littlefield.

Gramsci, A. (2012). *Selections From the Prison Notebooks*. New York, NY: International Publishers.

Grubačić, A. (2013). "The Anarchist Moment." In J. Blumendfeld, C. Bottici, and S. Critchley (Eds.), *The Anarchist Turn*, pp. 187–201. London: Pluto Press.

Hearn, J. (2012). *Theorizing Power*. Houndsmills; New York, NY: Palgrave Macmillan.

Heiskala, R. (2001). "Theorizing Power: Weber, Parsons, Foucault and Neostructuralism." *Social Science Information*, 40(2), 241–264.

Honold, L. (1997). "A Review of the Literature on Employee Empowerment." *Empowerment in Organizations*, 5(4), 202–212.

Kreisberg, S. (1992). *Transforming Power: Domination, Empowerment, and Education*. New York, NY: State University of New York Press.

Kropotkin, P. (1985, orig. 1898). *Fields, Factories and Workshops Tomorrow* (C. Ward, Ed.). London: Freedom Press.

Lears, T. J. J. (1985). "The Concept of Cultural Hegemony: Problems and Possibilities." *The American Historical Review*, 567–593.

Lukes, S. (2005). *Power: A Radical View* (2nd Expanded Edition). Houndmills: Palgrave Macmillan.

Morriss, P. (2002). *Power: A Philosophical Analysis* (2nd Edition). Manchester: Manchester University Press; New York, NY: Palgrave.

Mullin, L. J. (2010). *Management and Organizational Behavior* (9th Edition). Upper Saddle River, NJ: Prentice Hall.

Parker, M., Cheney, G., Fournier, V., and Land, C. (2014). "The Question of Organization: A Manifesto for Alternatives." *Ephemera: Theory & Politics in Organization*, 14(4), 623–638.

Seeds for Change. (2010). "Consensus Decision Making." Available at: www.seedsforchange.org.uk/consensus.pdf.

Siltala, J. (2004). *Työelämän huonontumisen lyhyt historia: Muutokset hyvinvointivaltioiden ajasta globaaliin hyperkilpailuun*. Helsinki: Otava.

Springer, S. (2016). *Anarchist Roots of Geography: Toward Special Emancipation*. London; Minneapolis, MN: University of Minnesota Press.

Starhawk. (1987). *Truth or Dare: Encounters With Power, Authority, and Mystery*. New York, NY: Harper and Row.

Toffler, A. (1990). *Powershift: Knowledge, Wealth and Violence at the Edge of the 21st Century*. New York, NY: Bantam Books.

Van Meter, K. (2017). *Guerrillas of Desire: Notes on Everyday Resistance and Organizing to Make a Revolution Possible*. Oakland, CA: AK Press.

Ward, C. (1966). "Anarchism as a Theory of Organization." *Anarchy*, 62, 97–109.

Ward, C. (2008, orig. 1973). *Anarchy in Action*. London: Freedom Press.

Weber, M. (1978, orig. 1922). *Economy and Society: An Outline of Interpretative Sociology* (G. Roth and C. Wittich, Eds.). Berkeley, CA: University of California Press.

8

ORGANIZATIONAL CULTURE

Elen Riot and Martin Parker

Introduction

Over the past few decades, it has become common for management thinkers to talk about the importance of 'organizational culture.' This refers to the idea that people aren't motivated by command and control structures, by being ordered to do things, but by beliefs and values, by the symbols and rituals that give meaning to working lives. If managers can shape culture, then they have ways of ensuring that behaviours follow an organization's mission statement. There is an echo here of anarchist ideas of **prefigurative** organization, an arrangement in which means and ends are necessarily interrelated because how you do something is just as important as why you do it (see box in Chapter 2). Anarchists, it could be said, take organizational culture very seriously indeed. If you believe that what you do may possibly transform the world, then all the steps matter. Such a frame of action is a problem for management because it involves questioning some central assumptions about knowledge. You are experimenting with what you know and what you are about to discover.

In this chapter, we describe two cooperatives (organizations that are run democratically by those who work in them) associated with the French anarchist trade union, the Confédération Nationale du Travail (hereafter CNT). In the chapter, the founders, a baker and an architect, will talk about culture as a source of inspiration but also as an obstacle to their everyday cooperation within the team of workers. After describing the two cooperatives, *La Conquête du Pain* (The Conquest of Bread, the bakery) and *La Belle Equipe* (The Beautiful Team, the construction group), we will outline different ways of thinking about culture as something that reflects the interests and histories of people involved in organizing. The kind of culture which is described in management textbooks is one in which the 'values,' 'vision' or 'mission' are described by management. This is the imposition of culture from above, in which employees are told what their beliefs should be. But what if culture were treated as something which was produced by everyone at work? What if the shared memories of a group of people helped them understand what they were doing and why they were doing it?

This chapter will

- highlight the difference between how management theory and anarchism think about culture in organizations;
- discuss the examples of two cooperatives, a bakery and a construction firm, and show through the words of two of their founders how they have tried to foster a particular anarchist culture;
- based on the stories the baker and the architect tell, question how conflict and contradiction are part of organizational culture; and
- suggest how an anarchist organizational culture works differently from a mainstream management one with regards to conflict and contradiction.

Culture and anarchism

In mainstream management books, you will find organizational culture described as a tool that helps to explain individuals' behaviour. According to this approach, a manager is supposed to identify desirable or undesirable cultural characteristics and manage them to fit with the goals of the firm. It is essential to control culture when it proves problematic and threatens the interests of those who own and control the firm (Willmott, 1993). In anarchist organizations, culture is seen quite differently. If culture matters to anarchists, it is because they declare that they are against any form of official authority and so wish to create social orders and cultures that allow people to realize their freedom. Culture should not be about top-down control but the expression of collective memories – events experienced by a group of people, shared through their lifetime and afterwards in memory (Halbwachs, 1992). As long as it exists and can be debated as it changes over time, it is alive. Managerial cultures create and enforce ideas and images so as to create a collective identity and impose it on others, not through a process of nurturing collective memory but by imposing ideas, language and imagery from above. No wonder that so many workers in conventional organizations are sceptical about their corporate culture (Parker, 2000).

Anarchists have devised different forms of collective action so that their common knowledge, based on memory, does not freeze and die. The main one is to insist on forms of organizations which are cooperative, so that everyone can speak and what is done and said is based on common decisions and representations (Swann and Stoborod, 2014). Anarchists insist on cooperative practices because they argue that any enforced common culture (such as those imposed by managers in mainstream organizations) makes it difficult for sharing with others to work properly. This problem is identified in many studies of corporate cultures. In tech, a large IT company, Kunda (2009) described an organization that makes it "business as usual" for engineers to "burn out" on projects because the future of the firm depends on complying with a "culture of excellence" (Peters and Waterman, 1982). Weeks (2004) describes a British bank, where a "ritual of complaint" unites employees faced with the unpopularity of their organization. They need to deal with clients who hate their bank on an everyday basis because of management decisions. As a result, they take responsibility, but they also hate the bank they work for and their job. Most of their work consists in learning how to lie and become an effective hypocrite when talking about their organizations 'values.'

CO-OPERATIVES

Co-operatives are organizations where ownership and control rest with members rather than outside owners. According to the International Co-operative Alliance, a co-operative is an autonomous association of persons united voluntarily to meet their common economic, social and cultural needs and aspirations through a jointly owned and democratically controlled enterprise (see box on **Suma** in Chapter 1). In 2019, there were three million cooperatives on earth, providing jobs or work opportunities to 10% of the employed population. The 300 top cooperatives generated 2.1 trillion US dollars. Workers' co-ops developed in response to industrial capitalism and its disempowering effects on workers. Skilled workers created co-op workshops by drawing on their savings and mutual credits in order to maintain their autonomy from factory owners. These co-ops gradually developed welfare services for members and effectively formed the start of the labour and trade union movement. Workers' co-ops are businesses owned and controlled democratically by those who work in them, with membership restricted to employees. Worker ownership has been heralded as providing a way in which people can self-manage and enjoy a supportive working environment. Workers' co-ops have also been seen as an instrument of social change: through the egalitarian and democratic principles they promote, they potentially offer an alternative to neoliberal capitalism.

To avoid this enforced culture at work, anarchists place much more stress on collective learning rather than reproducing knowledge, partly because it avoids the more skilled and educated taking a position of authority over others. 'Autodidacticism,' a term meaning 'self-education' or 'self-directed' learning, is often associated with radical working-class organizations and movements at the end of the 18th and in the first half of the 19th century.

For instance, as Chapter 2 on the 'prehistory' of management suggests, in their use of new techniques in such industries as textile and print (Rebérioux, 1982), anarchists were always keen on perfecting and inventing specific practices to organize work in a fair and equal way. This ideal is quite different from the celebration of individual entrepreneurship, with its 'winner takes all' ethos or obedience to shared values in the name of a corporate culture. While such a culture might require enforcement from above, anarchist understandings of the fair and egalitarian organization of work belong to a collective, shared memory. Forcing a certain culture on people means disguising what really happened, replacing lived memories with engineered narratives. On the contrary, anarchists believe in 'propaganda by deed' or 'direct action,' that acts should speak for themselves without the need for imposition by managers: direct action embodies anarchists' objectives of creating a free society where people can govern themselves democratically without domination or hierarchy. For example, the labour and trade union movements have developed out of various forms of worker action and also building new forms of organization with their own values and histories. Being aware of the weight of culture can help the process of building organizations 'against management' (Parker, 2002). As we shall see, culture, when authentic, is not easy to manage.

Two co-ops

The two organizations presented in this chapter are both production co-ops, one in the food industry, the other in construction. Both are located in the Paris area. They are presented here through the words of two men who were pivotal in each of the organizations. Both organizations are closely tied to the anarchist union, the CNT (Confédération Nationale du Travail, translated as National Confederation of Labour), as part of a network of cooperatives, and they have strong relationships with various social movements. All members pay a great deal of attention to the origin of the products, from the raw material throughout all the steps of the production process, and of course to the working conditions of their members.

Pierre, who is in his thirties, introduces his organization, a bakery:

> In the Conquest of Bread, our team is currently about eight employees and two apprentices, we specialize in such breads as spelt flour and gluten free.... Our practice of workers' self-management consists in specific choices such as viaticum (union money collected to support various international worker's movements), social tariff and 'baguette suspended' (a system when one pays a surplus in advance for whoever comes later and cannot afford to pay), the free distribution of unsold products after eight at night. We were inspired by a bakery which was created in the 1900s in Paris, la Fraternelle, and closed in the 1990s. We work closely with other structures in the web of the union: small farmers, associations of smallholders, consumers' cooperatives as well as nurseries, schools, restaurants.

Jean-Pierre, an architect in his sixties, presents his organization, a construction cooperative called The Beautiful Team.

> We are part of the CNT, the public buildings and work sector, our members are between 60 and 80, they are mostly not qualified, but we also have people trained

as architects or with a PhD. Workers struggle to speak out during meetings. They do not imagine that they could, one day, create a workers self-managed firm because of the down payment. So, we wanted to experiment and create a production coop, in complement to our union meetings, literacy courses, training onsite, as well as our employment agency and trades union council. This is because we observed most production coops rely on professional and social skills acquired with experience. So, workers must be able to experiment and formalize their own tools which they need for productive autonomy.

Both stories illustrate the choices and dilemmas involved in anarchist organizations. The two industries, food and construction, are also emblematic of sectors where work conditions are harsh and exploitation frequent. Both testimonies deal with power, tools, standards of action and collective memories.

Culture at work

In both the baker's and the architect's interviews, they explore how their common culture acted as a frame to define their structure, as well as how their relation to the organization's culture depends on what they try to invent and share in the present and build for a desirable future. Even the name of their organization is important, because it refers to a rich and complex anarchist culture and history.

The name of the bakery is borrowed from anarchist Peter **Kropotkin**'s (see box in Chapter 3) book *The Conquest of Bread* (1906), an exploration of how it would be possible to end poverty for the masses. The implications of the name go much further than just the reference to baking. Kropotkin was especially keen on defending barter between farmers and workers, with no money involved and no intermediaries. He predicted it would replace wage-labour and build a strong system of cooperation. His system was soon implemented in Ukraine with Nestor Mahkno's peasant revolt, which succeeded in liberating large areas of Ukraine between 1917 and 1920. Such was its success, and hence its challenge to the state, that the newly existing Soviet Union took military action to crush the revolt (Scott, 1998, p. 208).

The name 'La Belle Equipe' is borrowed from the title of a 1936 movie by Julien Duvivier in which some unemployed workers win the lottery. One of them buys an old wash-house, and they transform it into an open-air café. They meet with a string of bad luck, and in the original version, one kills the other in a fight for the love of a woman. The cooperative of friends is confronted with external events that break their collective harmony. The film acts as quite an ominous warning for cooperators about outbound allegiances and social pressures.

Both stories mix hope, chance and defeat. It may explain why when the architect is wary about 'success,' the baker smiles and nods: 'I agree, if a network of workers' self-managed organizations would succeed, it would be perceived as a threat by capitalism and immediately destroyed.' Facing obstacles and overcoming defeat is what they are here to talk about.

Fighting your own culture

Both the baker and the architect are not satisfied with their own society. They resist a culture of success and competition for money, power and status. Wanting to succeed and rule over others is just a way to benefit individually but does nothing to develop collective skills and **identity** (see box in Chapter 4). The architect comments that

> I know our comrades. When we need to plan, having someone tell them about this plan, they won't accept it, they are stubborn. In construction, people have a loud mouth but they do not necessarily have the knowledge to put things in perspective. . . . At present, the main challenge is to convince all union members that the Belle Equipe cooperative is their business too, because for most of them, it is the story of the two people who started it.

The other limit of the work culture in the food and construction industries is that they tend to hire men with a low level of education. The baker struggles to get more diverse employees and, more specifically, to fight sexist attitudes among male employees.

> My partner said let's hire girl apprentices but when I was in training, there was one girl out of two hundred and fifty trainees. It just is a sexist job. Once a comrade was pregnant, her boss forbade her to access the kitchen, he said her baby would suffer.

The architect echoes that view: 'In construction, we have one union member out of 80 who is a woman, however, there are more and more women, they may be preferred to migrants because they have a higher education.' He jokes that a sociologist who came to analyze their practices left appalled by their 'macho' language during meetings: 'She thought we had no understanding of race and gender prejudices because "we were obsessed by class." In particular, she pointed at the 'masculinist' way we talked to each other.'

Women have a real influence in the anarchist movement, but in the experience of the baker and the architect, women also protect their family's interests and that may conflict with the commitments to the collective work project and the demands of the union in terms of extra time to make collective decisions.

> We argue it is easy to work hard, until you are exhausted, this is not our approach, we also organize a cinema club, we insist on the role of culture, but family is the first enemy, we had a super guy for the cooperative and his wife just told him not to do it because of their children, she thought the risk was too high.

The desire to protect one's family, the feeling that other commitments might matter too, creates a fear of risk and an avoidance of responsibility. However, talking about these problems also makes clear the conflicting choices members of the cooperatives have to make, choices about which management biographies of successful business leaders tell us very little. For example, one of the founders of the bakery left for a year to raise his baby daughter.

The architect says that workers can easily claim to be anarchist, but their deeds should reflect their words.

> Most of our workforce is unqualified, they learn by doing, but not the right way. Our comrades' lack of skills limit the ability to make profits, so we have union workshops for that, so they can share know-how, but despite a lot of goodwill, the quality of work is deficient, self-criticism is not common.

The problem is that wider French culture – of individual success, patriarchal understandings of power and lack of shared responsibility – does not always help the organizational culture of these co-operatives.

Struggling with difference

Throughout the history of the anarchist political movement, anarchists have perhaps been more open than many to other cultures. The movement and the groups that make it up have always involved minorities with an internationalist approach, looking beyond borders and across cultures. In the case of the cooperatives discussed in this chapter, because they operate in industries where work is hard and low paid, the labour force often comes from the most recent waves of immigration to France. The architect hired workers from Mali on his construction site, and he had them join the union. The principles of the union impose that decisions are reached by **consensus** (see box in Chapter 9), often after long deliberations where everyone can express his or her opinion. This system proved difficult to accommodate with Malians because they often speak very little French and because they live in workers' hostels far away from the construction sites, where they have a collective life of their own. The union organized training sessions for language and skills, but these efforts have proved unsuccessful so far. The architect comments on the difficulties posed by trying to bridge gaps between cultures in the case of the workers from Mali:

> For instance, we accept that union members do not attend all meetings, or we organize football games instead of the movie club, only we change the rules of the football game, to show that this is still a union practice. . . . We also discussed a prayer room for Ramadan. Once, one of the Malian workers, who was already married, had to marry his brother's wife in Africa after he died. We understood when a worker, who was sleeping in the corridor of the hostel, would always get back there to sleep even after we worked hard to find him a room of his own, this was because he did not want to lose touch with his village.

In trying to be faithful to the cooperative ideal of sharing and **mutual** support, the union and the architect decided to invest in and design housing for the Malian workers (see box in Chapter 17). This met with external opposition and hostility from the Malian families:

> we were generous with Malian families, the union was helping them get out of hostels. But we still had their village lifestyle in mind, we thought they shared kitchen and wash houses, but their wives said no. We thought it was better that they no longer had to go to the launderette, but the women wondered why they could not have the French lifestyle, five rooms, with an individual fridge and washing machine. Experimentation involves facing the facts, so you can change reality, today, in front of the bourgeois ideal, there seems to be no attractive alternative.

The baker experienced a similar reaction when he tried to reach out to the children and youth from the public housing blocks in the area. He believes in using the organization to educate people about food and work but is also aware of the contradiction involved in selling his whole-wheat bread to the middle class first, even though most of the workers have different tastes. The baker recognizes how problematic it is to build a cooperative around political principles but then to have to sell products in ways that do not support those principles:

> We live in a middle-class milieu, people have a great deal of cultural capital, as we open new shops in districts of Paris, we support their gentrification. Although we have special social rates, the limit of our social work is that the youth from the council flats prefer McDonald's at the corner . . . we worked for four years to change this image, now the kids come on Friday nights for free 'pains au chocolat.' We are also part of national and international baker federations, we supported the strike of automobile workers in Aulnay by supplying bread, yet I know we are still in a closed, small circle.

Neither the baker nor the architect are afraid of addressing cultural difference, but they are also well aware that their organizational culture can be exclusive, particularly insofar as it reflects the differences between the culture of the nation and that of more recent migrants.

Co-creating organizational culture

One of the key issues that anarchist cooperatives like the ones discussed in this chapter have to deal with is the fact that the specific rhythms and requirements of the organization and a wider anarchist project do not always align. Because they are also anarchist activists, the members of the cooperatives tend to insist on the need to find common goals through open debates, something which is central to how anarchists operate. A lot of the time spent together is related to union activities, supporting workers in defending their legal and social rights. This is one of the goals of the anarchist movement as a whole, particularly anarcho-syndicalist activists. This means that participation in social movements and activities, such as large strikes and demonstrations, is fairly routine and expected. However, the main aim of a strike, where workers refuse to work, is to stop the organization from functioning, even if only for a short period of time. In 2016, after a series of long strikes, the bakery was trying to raise €35,000 by subscription to avoid having to file for bankruptcy. Yet on 12 November 2015, it posted a message on its website saying,

> Because we are an experiment in worker self management, we are both employer and employee. The general assembly voted for the strike to continue at the occasion of the inter-branch mobilisation day. We will demonstrate at 2 P.M. Place de la République.

Paradoxically, the cooperative is at the same time calling for the strike to continue and for donations to help support the cooperative as a result of the loss caused by the strike. Raising this amount to support the cooperative was a success, and, at the time of writing, the bakery is still a working business. One of the reasons why people were ready to contribute is that they were interested in supporting the strike movement. Rather than suppressing contradictions or conflicts, they are made into a lived experience that people can learn from, although there is no denying the risk that the bakery may have gone bankrupt as a result.

SYNDICALISM

Syndicalism is the term given to the aim of transforming capitalist society through working-class direct action, particularly through working-class industrial organizations. It contrasts with the other major strategy of working-class movements, political action through party organization. Clearly the two strategies are not incompatible, though some anarchist syndicalists do reject political parties entirely. Anarcho-syndicalism shares the principles of solidarity and worker self-management but with the aim of revolutionary transformation towards an anarchist society. Its main instruments have been trade unions, and the main weapons have been the various forms of industrial action including work-to-rules, control over the labour process, industrial sabotage and the strike. Most syndicalists argue that all participants in a trade or workplace should share equal ownership of production and therefore deserve equal earnings, benefits and control. Syndicalism, though essentially a form of socialism, does not necessarily imply communism, however, as earnings may be privately retained, though equally shared, within a syndicate. A syndicalist society would be based on worker self-managed syndicates federating to other syndicates, and the exchange of goods and services would be negotiated between them.

The translation of anarchist theory into organizational practice is by no means simple and is a constant source of contradictions and problems. The architect says, 'The anarchist mythology does not deal well with practical problems and very few models work. We could believe in them twenty years ago but not now, besides, we can see a gap between local experiments and their generalization.' The baker agrees, accepting the fact that he still needs people who are part of a system he is attempting to transform:

> Not everyone can do everything, one cannot train a baker in three months, it takes at least three years, in fact, seven or eight. Personally, I would not go to see a self-proclaimed doctor. Our problem is to prevent any form of specialisation becoming a source of power and let others access it.

One of the important dimensions of anarchism generally is the belief that equality between all is important and necessary to their freedom. This should mean that all responsibility is shared, but the architect insists it is also important to be able to take responsibility and be in charge when the problems appear:

> We devised a cooperative because workers in construction always have had a very fragmented view of their work. Our firm would involve all dimensions . . . we worked for six months, training our colleagues to prepare estimates, site maintenance, orders.

The problem for the construction cooperative is that they realized too late that the collective of members did not want to be a boss – or at least be in charge – if the two founders failed to take responsibility. Anarchists might believe that all their companions should be trusted as friends but what if things go wrong? This principle requires a lot of effort to become a sustainable practice because all members in a cooperative need to be aware of each other's contribution:

> It goes against the grain, because once a guy invested in the firm, and took all the risks; dealt with family pressures, then when new people arrive, he is supposed to accept that these guys are his equal. Since it is difficult to swallow, our cooperatives tend to go the mainstream way.

Finally, consider the belief that all anarchists should be free to do as they wish. Most of the time, if a member is identified as being a problem, he or she just ends up leaving the cooperative. The idea of a boss who can sack people or use discipline to shape behaviour is against the culture of the organization. The baker admits this reluctance to intervene in problematic situations and find solutions that avoid people leaving is true for his own organization:

> We had the problem of someone who was stealing, it cost us thousands of euros, and it took us three years to reimburse, it was very hard for us to give

an ultimatum to that person, it lasted for a very long time because we left all options open.

Perhaps even more alarmingly, this sort of highly libertarian culture can end up being based on nothing more than the power of violence.

> We are incapable of saying no, we find reasons for all actions and finally, to put an end to it, we cornered the guy and we beat him, he does it again, we beat him again, until he leaves. In the autonomous movement and in political organizations, it is who wins the fight, the rule of the strongest.

This is certainly not a solution which could be regarded as acceptable, and it raises the question of how anarchists could collectively reinvent their organizational culture in order to deal with these sort of power issues. Building collective memories, and hence understandings of what sorts of action are permissible and which aren't, requires more than a one-way transmission (Riot, 2014). Indeed, collective memories can turn out to be quite exclusive when you want to include newcomers who may find the people who were there before them 'know it all' and take themselves very seriously.

Indeed, a student who was present at one of our meetings with the baker suggested that the collective memory of the cooperative was a possible source of groupthink. He told the baker: 'Very nice. You just offered us a worker's self-management version of *L'Etabli*, only with less workers and more "bobos."' This refers to a classic of French left-wing culture which would be known to all the people involved in the conversation. Robert Linhart's book *The Workbench* is the diary of a leader of the 1968 student protests in France who decides to become a worker in a factory. The second expression 'bobo' is a compression of 'bourgeois bohemian,' a social group who claim to be radical and revolutionary through fashionable lifestyle and consumption patterns. In this context, it refers to the growing gentrification of the area around the bakery and the appeal of healthy products to wealthier people who can afford them.

At this point, the baker might have felt insulted by being described as more than a cause and effect of the gentrification of a formerly working-class area. Yet, judging by his broad smile, it was clear that he works hard to be free and he feels fine with trying to convince others that the bakery is something to be proud of.

> We go bankrupt if we make no profit, and we lost money during the first few years, but still, the baguettes were cheap and we accepted the consequences of this choice. Meanwhile, we set up the 'baguette suspended' system, we also took time to visit schools, district meetings and my work conditions are worse than when I was a simple worker, because of my legal responsibility. I am the one in charge. I have no back up, but I gained more autonomy. If I want to change the rules of what I do in my seven hours working as a baker,

I can, I can change my craft, for instance, I want to try a new bread, Fonio, a Malian worker recipe, or a Chiapas bread, I can. There no longer is a boss in my team, putting me in competition with my fellow workers.

Conclusion

In this chapter, the stories told by the baker and the architect showed how important collective beliefs were for their co-operatives. The choice of the names of their organizations corresponded to a political mission and an act of allegiance to the history of anarchism. They tried to live anarchist lives by resisting the dominant assumptions of French business culture and also by engaging with other cultures than the one they were familiar with. In the process, their effort was concerned both with defending their traditions and also looking for situations where they could reinvent themselves as a group. Throughout this period, they had to face assumptions about gender, family and caring; providing workers with skills that were useful for the business; and persuading people that they were not employees with a boss, as well as near-bankruptcy because of their support for a strike and a whole host of other problems that any organization would face. It is not easy being an anarchist business, building a living sense of solidarity and equity, while taking responsibility for paying wages, making bread and designing buildings.

Anarchism is a way of being openly critical about market managerialism's claim to provide universal solutions to complex problems (Parker, 2002). Textbook common sense is that organizational culture needs to be engineered from above, providing stories, scripts and values which are intended to shape employees' behaviour. In these two cases, we can see people dealing with everyday life situations, building their worlds from below. Their relation to 'culture' proves quite complex, because they are dealing with French culture and immigrant culture, as well as the continually emerging culture of their organization, rooted in anarchism but always changing to cope with new demands and circumstances. They don't try to downplay or overlook their contradictions and doubts or pretend that they know the answers. Because there are no ready-made solutions, they have to be creative with the present, at the same time that they honour their collective memory.

True to their vision, both the baker and the architect believe that their failures are part of the necessary trial-and-error process. They even argue that if their path had proven too easy, the forces of capitalism would have absorbed or broken them. It is difficult to be precise about what the organizations have done for the workers' welfare, or that of their customers or wider society, since they have not followed recipes or methods that could be measured and benchmarked against other similar organizations. However, the experience of both provides examples of how anarchists might think about collective history as an authentic organizational culture, as they attempt to build a new world in the shell of the old.

Questions for further study

1 Imagine you are a consultant hired to make the two cooperatives more productive. What would be your advice, and what do you think it would change?
2 Take any organizational problem and examine what changes when you decide to ignore or take account of the past. Now take the case of our two cooperatives. What would be different in their collective organization?
3 As Etienne de la Boétie, a French author of the Renaissance, argued a long time ago in his 'Discourse of Voluntary Servitude': 'From all [the] indignities, such as the very beasts of the field would not endure, you can deliver yourselves if you try, not by taking action, but merely by willing to be free. Resolve to serve no more, and you are at once freed.' Can change ever be this simple? Can we simply decide to be free and as a result be free? Think of moments in history when people have not been free. What would have happened if they had 'resolved to serve no more'?
4 Some management consultants appear to believe that organizational cultures can be engineered by managers. Is culture therefore a form of social control?

References

Halbwachs, M. (1992). *On Collective Memory*. Chicago, IL: University of Chicago Press.
Kropotkin, P. (1906/1995). *The Conquest of Bread and Other Writings*. Cambridge: Cambridge University Press.
Kunda, G. (2009). *Engineering Culture: Control and Commitment in a High-Tech Corporation*. Philadelphia, PA: Temple University Press.
Parker, M. (2000). *Organizational Culture and Identity*. London: Sage Publications.
Parker, M. (2002). *Against Management: Organization in the Age of Managerialism*. London: Polity Press; Blackwell.
Peters, T. J., and Waterman, R. H. (1982). *In Search of Excellence: Lessons from America's Best-Run Companies*. New York, NY: Warner Books.
Rebérioux, M. (1982). *Les ouvriers du Livre et leur Fédération*. Paris: Editions Temps Actuels.
Riot, E. (2014). "'Anarchy by the Book? Forget About It!' The Role of Collective Memory in Shaping Workers' Relations to Anarchism and Work Today." *Ephemera: Theory & Politics in Organization*, 14(4), 811–833.
Scott, J. C. (1998). *Seeing Like a State: How Certain Schemes to Improve the Human Condition Have Failed*. New Haven, CT: Yale University Press.
Swann, T., and Stoborod, K. (2014). "Did You Hear the One About the Anarchist Manager?" *Ephemera: Theory & Politics in Organization*, 14(4), 591–609.
Weeks, J. (2004). *Unpopular Culture: The Ritual of Complaint in a British Bank*. Chicago, IL: University of Chicago Press.
Willmott, H. (1993). "Strength Is Ignorance; Slavery Is Freedom: Managing Culture in Modern Organizations." *Journal of Management Studies*, 30(4), 515–552.

9

LEADERSHIP AND AUTHORITY

Lucas Casagrande and Guillermo Rivera

The topic of leadership is one of the most popular issues in the field of management. It is a common belief that it is impossible to organize without a leader and that all successful businesses and organizations must have leaders in order to function effectively. Leadership is a concept that starts from an assumption of authority, that there must be some people in organizations who give orders, make decisions and expect obedience. Without the acceptance of authority, there is no way to ensure that orders are taken seriously or that people will be persuaded to do anything.

Frequently, leaders are described as those who energize people to do extraordinary things, including things that followers might not want to do themselves or indeed might be unable to do themselves without some sort of inspiration. Leaders are often described as being charismatic and being capable of making people feel they are important to a company or other type of organization. In mainstream management literature, leadership is seen as a way to shape or capture the **identity** of the worker, to make him or her work harder without solely relying on a financial reward or something similar (see box in Chapter 4). If people are led well and inspired by their leaders, their commitment and effort will be guaranteed to a degree not possible if rewarded solely in terms of gains of status or money.

But if we only think about leaders, we don't think very hard about what it means to be led. After all, for every leader, there is at least one person who is being led, at least one follower. Is it possible to see ourselves as free when we admit that we need leadership? Is it possible to assume that each individual has his or her own will and that this freedom should be exercised in the world if most of us are destined to be followers? Is it possible to live in a world without authorities, in organizations without leaders? Anarchist thinkers believe in a collective form of organization that does not depend on assumptions about authority, about the need to be led and to have leaders (Walter, 2016). In this chapter, we discuss how authority is created and how it is possible to challenge it. We will explore what it might mean to have an organization run in a way that does not require leadership. To do this, we will look at some examples of alternative organizations from Brazil and Chile.

This chapter will

- make an important distinction between three types of authority – (1) temporary, situational authorization, (2) enunciative authority and (3) institutional authority;
- show how throughout our history authority has advanced from one definition to the next, ending up in the institutional authority of contemporary management;
- introduce anarchist ideas of horizontality and self-management; and
- explore how organizations can be structured to avoid authority and discuss some of the problems these organizations might run into.

The origins of authority and leadership

The freedom of man, says **Bakunin** (1871, see box in Chapter 7), 'consists solely in this: that he obeys natural laws because he has himself recognised them as such, and not because they have been externally imposed upon him by any extrinsic will whatsoever, divine or human, collective or individual.' Authority is thus a means of operating power over others, whether through persuasion (as in the use of the concept of leadership) or through hierarchical power as in the idea of the boss or manager. In both cases, human beings are seen as human resources, entities which are useful for the organization and its purposes. In an attempt to satisfy our material needs, we submit to an authority and resign ourselves to its will.

The French philosopher Paul Ricoeur (2003) questioned authority and where it comes from. As he says, if we question someone about where authority comes from, this person will tend to stutter because it's not an easy question to answer. In the end, he or she will probably quote some law or some rule that will enable him or her to answer the question, but all that does is to push the question back. Where did that law or rule come from? In this way, a 'tricky question comes to mind without malice: where does authority ultimately come from?' (Ricoeur, 2003, p. 101).

We could say that it can be seen as a nonsensical question: authority legitimates itself in its own legitimation. I am the boss because I say I am the boss. This is because, conceptually, authority is a kind of power that makes it possible to command, being asymmetric and hierarchical in its nature. Power is a capacity of the one who possesses such authority, which could supposedly come from the people who are governed but that when questioned by the people themselves takes refuge in a paradox. If power comes from the people, how acceptable is it to be exercised over the same people? It is as if we create a mediation between us and our goal. The authority is whoever mediate this. We abandon ourselves to authority in the name of achieving ourselves.

Ricoeur concludes that we don't really know what authority is. In order to understand it, he divides it into two types:

1) **Enunciative authority** is constituted as symbolic power through the production of beliefs. The word 'enunciate' refers to making a statement. This gives language a central place. Sacred texts produce enunciative authorities, so the wise man is produced as a wise man because texts and rituals say that he is one. In enunciative authority, the authority is assumed because of a statement in a text or in discursive forms.

2) **Institutional authority** is constituted by an organization or institution. Think, for example, of a police officer or judge who has authority from the state itself or a manager who occupies a particular position in an organization. Authority here is assumed because of a certain institution or organization that the person with authority acts on behalf of or with the approval of.

The teacher, for example, is a mixture of these two authorities. She possesses her authority because of the school she works in but also produces belief in authority (her own authority and that of others) through her words in the belief system that she knows better.

While anarchists are skeptical of authority in all its forms, it is clear that some specific situations require specific expertise. As Bakunin (1871) says, no permanent form of leadership will be acceptable to anarchists, but certain situations make us resort to people who better understand what's going on. As in Ricoeur (2003), authority (noun) comes from the authorization (verb) we give to someone. Bakunin insists that legitimate authority comes from authorization. We authorize a third party to do or speak on our behalf. This is because we cannot understand everything. We authorize the cobbler to repair our shoe, but that doesn't mean that they become the enunciative authority on everything else in our lives. In contrast, clerics become the enunciative authorities of the world as a whole. They supposedly understand what the gods want, which is substantially more complex and relevant to more situations than the quality of our shoes.

So the problem is not authorization in specific circumstances but the generalization of a specific circumstance to everything, making what should be a cooperative process of having and recognizing expertise into a hierarchical process in which some have expertise and others don't. This arrangement, this form of organizing, assumes that knowledge is always and permanently ranked and that some will always submit to others. In this way, a circumstantial authorization of something that we do not know how to do (such as making shoes) becomes an assumption about the way that life must be lived (we should authorize certain groups to lead us no matter what), depriving the majority of individuals of their power, creativity and autonomy. So when people say that a leader is a person who motivates us and convinces us to do something, they express leadership as an enunciative authority. This authority is the crystallization of the authorization process, making a noun out of a verb. And, in turn, the authority can become institutionalized, producing the formal hierarchy and the formally named boss. At the very moment that the individual ceases to have the will to do something and delegates his or her goals to another, authority is born.

In a historical sense, considering the authority of religion, the will exercised by the individual initially gave way to the will of god. That, in turn, gave way to the will of the interpreter, representative, or messenger of god – the priest, church, and monarch. For many people now, this interpreter is a member of a secular organization – a scientist, engineer or manager. Max Weber (2002) calls this the 'disenchantment' of the world, a process in which the mysterious authority of the spiritual gives way to secular rationality. Such disenchantment comes from the different constitution of authorities – enunciative authority being primarily associated with religion whereas institutional authority is associated with scientific expertise, rationality and bureaucracy.

Imagine a world filled with magic and rituals: people seeking rain, heat or food. They want to understand the spirits of the world, which are present everywhere, and encourage them to do what human beings want them to. It is possible that particular individuals would sometimes take the lead in these rituals. These would be the sorcerers, people who had so much self-belief that they could imagine that they could convince even the gods and the spirits to satisfy our desires. But soon enough, the wizards would have failed: the rain did not come, and the crops did not grow. It seems likely that they would have then tried to convince others that the spirits were actually at work but in a somewhat mysterious way that still required their intervention. Implicit here would be the idea that the gods had intentions that

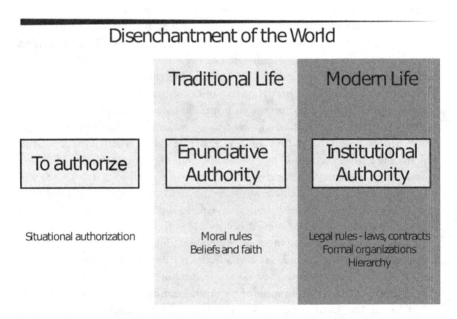

FIGURE 9.1   Disenchantment of the world

were not accessible to ordinary people but also that a sorcerer was the only one who could access and influence their purposes. Enunciative authority was born.

From this sorcerer to an institutionalized religion and then on to management and leadership, there is certainly a long chain of translations. But this path is born there: at the moment when someone was promoted from an equal to being someone who understands spiritual or divine wills. Authority, in this sense, arises from a change in worldview. It begins with an understanding of the world in which all things are attributed motives to a view of the self in which the human bows to other humans who claim to know better how to understand and intervene in the human and non-human world. Interpreting and understanding these external forces is something that is, without a doubt, difficult. That is why those who achieve it, or who make other people believe that they can do it, are raised to a new level above the rest: they are authorities.

Leadership in managed organizations

According to Collinson (2011), the mainstream understanding of leadership is based on hierarchical top-down relations. Traditionally, those theories are based on the understanding of an 'effective leader.' This sort of leader can change the way that followers see him or her and also how leaders and followers see themselves. In these theories, leadership is usually seen as a virtue, as something which everybody agrees is intrinsically good. Being a 'leader' is a good thing, both morally and practically, though examples of bad leaders, such as Adolf Hitler or Idi Amin, are sometimes used as warnings. In doing this, the logic is to accept that it is possible to have good and bad leaders, good and bad authorities, but almost never to question hierarchy itself. The basic assumption is that hierarchy and authority are always necessary in order to organize, even though they can sometimes be abused.

Ideas about hierarchy go back to the origins of mainstream business management. It was born as an applied social science which could be used to increase efficiency without necessarily sharing its benefits. Over a century ago, the French mining engineer Henri Fayol in his 1916 book on industrial administration (1949) understood authority as the core issue. Eight of his fourteen management principles are directly linked to the creation of a central authority which can control workers and head off resistance. Two decades later, the management thinker Chester Barnard (1968; originally published in 1938) understood the organization as a form of co-operation. He assumed that people work because they want to, because they gain various satisfactions from being part of an organization. Thus he could understand the authority of the organization as something legitimate by default. Within this context, he imagined the leader as someone who combines formal authority ('authority of position') with charismatic authority ('authority of leadership'). When both authorities are concentrated in a single person, the workers will accept orders which they would normally begin to question or resist.

We think that even these seemingly benign ideas of leadership commonly used in the management literature are limiting the understanding of other forms of organization, such as non-profit groups, cooperatives and social movements (Reyes, 2014). Leadership in management studies is based on a hierarchical model of business structures, on the common sense which says that most of us must be led, that we want to be led. Indeed, this way of thinking suggests that alternative arrangements are disorganized, since organizations that do not have hierarchical structures are often defined as chaotic, 'non-competitive' and 'unprofitable' (Kokkinidis, 2014). Consider instead that when you read about 'leadership', it should raise suspicion and make you wonder about its 'dark side' (Hanlon, 2016). Whose interests are being advanced here, and what are the dangers of accepting the inevitability of the word? Perhaps leadership, as a form of authority and domination, is a way of naturalizing the inequality of social classes, gender, sexualities and ethnicities. So if we assume that inequality is something that should be worked against, then we should ask questions and not simply assume that what the textbook tells us is correct.

How to do otherwise – anarchist alternatives

Of course, this understanding of leadership has been questioned from the beginnings of anarchism, even before the formalization of management theory a century ago. The broad line of argument is that we should think about and design organizations based on other principles, such as democracy, autonomy and authenticity (Parker et al., 2014; Western, 2014). In this section, we will discuss two examples of how different ways of challenging authority happen in the organizational practices of horizontal collectives in Brazil and Chile. Anarchism as a theory of organization allow us to approach forms of organization based on horizontality or transversality, the assumption that we make decisions as equals and that we do not always need leaders.

HORIZONTALITY

Horizontal, or transversal, organizing is a general term that describes any kind of organization without authority and hierarchy. In such organizations, there is no 'manager' or any kind of boss. People who work in such places are equals, dividing the labour among them without a central authority, using tools like consensus (see Chapter 7) or voting in order to make decisions. If an authority arises on the basis of some sort of expertise, the idea behind horizontal organizations is that we should always put the burden of legitimacy on whoever is in such position, keeping any sort of hierarchy in a constant state of questioning.

Another term often used by anarchists to refer to workplace-level horizontality is 'self-management.' Two scholars working in this area, Maurizio Azteni and Marcello Vieta, suggest that 'Ideologically, self-management has also been associated with libertarian streams of certain anarchist and communist traditions' (2014, p. 49). Those scholars point out that self-management is a common practice with examples in many different parts of the world. For example, during the late 1960s and '70s, it happened in Argentina's 'workplace takeovers' (1964, 1975), Chile's 'coordinadoras industriales' (1970–1973), Portugal's 'self-managed factories and farms' (1970), Algeria's 'movement of autogestión' (1962), Iran's 'self-management experiment around the revolution' (1979), Spain's 'worker takeover of failing firms' (1970's) and Italy's 'worked-recuperated enterprises' (1970s), amongst others. Before that, it stretches back to Catalonia's 'self-managed industrial and agricultural sectors' (1936–1939) and Russia's 'workers control on shop floors' (1917–1918). Recuperated enterprises are 'formerly privately owned firms in trouble that were converted to worker cooperatives by their employees' (Azteni and Vieta, 2014, p. 48). In other words, the workers took over after the managers and owners walked away. These organizations could also often be described as co-operatives:

> an autonomous association of persons united voluntarily to meet their common economic, social, and cultural needs and aspirations through a jointly-owned and democratically controlled enterprise. **Co-operatives** are based on the values of self-help, self-responsibility, democracy, equality, equity and solidarity.
>
> *(ICA, 2013 in Webb and Cheney, 2014, p. 65, see box in Chapter 8)*

The two examples we discuss in the following are based on the experiences of companies taken over by workers in Brazil (Bittencourt, 2014) and a self-organized community centre in Chile (Nova et al., 2018). It should be noted that even though these organizations are based on autonomous principles, horizontality and self-management, as we have seen in the previous chapters in this section, they are not exempt from difficulty.

Brazil: companies taken over by workers

In Brazil in 2018, there were 6,600 co-operatives with a total of 13.4 million members (Wörner, 2018). One of the measures that the government has implemented for supporting this type of organization comes from funds aimed at generating a 'solidarity economy' – that is to say, an economy based on common values of equity and sustainability. In the year 2000, 31 employees decided to take over the Omega boiler manufacturer and start a worker cooperative (Bittencourt, 2014). These workers had no professional education. They had been factory workers all their lives. At the beginning, they reported a bigger debt and found it difficult to obtain loans. According to the workers' testimonies, the first six months were very hard. They went through conditions of precariousness and poverty. As a consequence the workers formed a comradeship of equals who struggled to survive together.

The new kind of organization was initially considered as a cooperative; however, in 2005, and mainly because the clients were hesitant to believe that a cooperative could work, it became a company. Since then, the company has been growing; by 2010, they reported having created a limited liability company with almost 100 workers. The growth of this company over the years has created an organizational structure which can be divided into two groups. The initial cooperative managed by the company is maintained and is composed of the founding partners, while the other workers who have been hired in recent years are employed by the limited company. This difference between the original partners and the new workers has generated tensions within the organization. Thus, according to Bittencourt (2014), the need to balance equity with the possibility of offering work generates an oscillation between different understandings of the organization. In Omega's case, the growth of the organization has generated a hierarchical structure in which it expresses a great internal dilemma between the 'fraternity' that emerged in the process of scarcity and the current company, which has since grown and been successful.

While the Omega experience arose from an alternative organization created as an initiative from its members in a context of crisis, elements of its structure are now repeating standard management practices. This experience shows us the creativity of people committed from the beginning of this project. However, it is also possible to note how, as the authorization process becomes more and more routine, it creates its own hierarchy. In the beginning, the company was a cooperative without any kind of authority, with decisions made by the collective. But once people started to accept the idea that they could mediate the decisions, that other people could decide for them, the direct democracy became a classic company structure and the autonomy of the cooperative became the hierarchy in the company.

Chile: self-management in community centre

Created in 2011, Patio Volantín is an alternative organization that seeks to establish social relations for and with the residents of Cerro Panteón in Valparaiso, the second largest city in Chile. It offers a meeting space where artistic and cultural practices can be developed and is open to anyone who wishes to use it for a personal or collective initiative. According to its members, it could be defined as a self-sustaining organization, which through autonomous and collective management hopes to generate instances of social and economic development in the community, working from the local level and also with the ecological, personal and political environment as a method of social transformation (Goldberg, 2016). One of Patio Volantín's central methods for supporting themselves is *talleres por trueque* (barter workshops). These activities are exchanges of assets, products, ideas or knowledge between participants but without any money changing hands.

To achieve its objectives, Patio Volantín needs volunteers, people it can count on to deliver time and enthusiasm to collaborate with the different activities they do – delivering courses, baking bread, organizing concerts and so on. As the organization has become bigger and more complex, it has had to establish a way to distribute tasks and functions fairly. However, this became more challenging than previously expected. In this uncertain context, the idea of a charismatic leader remained important. This emerged from the way that the different members of the community see the founder of the organization and reflects the manner in which he invites people to be part of the project. It was because of the vital and committed work that he performs that his own identity was so closely tied to that of the centre.

Yet despite this sense of there being a leader, self-management is the lived practice of the place. The participants identify a horizontal organization from their experiences. They see Patio Volantín as an alternative to the dominant model of top-down management, suggesting that their decision-making practices oppose the neoliberal capitalist model of hierarchical structure. Patio Volantín rethinks how self-management is carried out in alternative organizations and what responsibilities it owes to the environment in which it finds itself. Members assume values based on solidarity, equity and direct democratic decision making. Of course, struggles continue to arise, because organizing is never easy. Mostly, they relate to how to keep the community centre going, given its costs. This particular problem also has consequences in the reinforcement of authority. In order to pay the bills, they sometimes fall back on hierarchical modes of decision making – most of the time relying on the founders of the organization. In this case, and perhaps the opposite of Omega, scarcity seems to catalyze the process of authority creation.

CONSENSUS DECISION MAKING

Consensus decision making (CDM) is a democratic procedure in which a group of people discuss a particular issue and try to reach consensus (or full agreement) on a decision. CDM has a rich history across the world. For example, five of the First Nations in what we today call North America formed the Haudenosaunee Confederation, which operated based on a version of CDM. More recently, CDM has appeared in the Occupy movement, where it was used by assemblies of hundreds of people to make decisions. CDM involves the group first discussing a topic to ensure that all members have had a chance to share their views and learn about the views of others and for any relevant information to be distributed. If consensus is already achieved at that stage, then the decision is made; if not, further discussion takes place to identify why there is disagreement and see where consensus might be possible. Depending on the version of CDM used, individuals in the group may be able to block a decision, meaning they disagree so strongly that they cannot accept the decision, or stand aside, where they do not agree with the decision but are willing for the group to go ahead with it. Blocking will often be a sign that more discussion is needed rather than a point at which the whole process is abandoned. Some groups will also operate a form of modified CDM. This can mean that if consensus is not possible, then the group might put the decision to a vote with a high majority of 75% or even 90% approval required. This gets around blocking as the end of the process but avoids the problems associated with simple majority decision making, where potentially just less than 50% of the people involved are not happy with the decision taken. Consensus also helps avoid the competitive nature of simple majority decision making because the point is not to win the contest but to find a solution everyone is happy with.

Conclusion

In this chapter, we have discussed ideas of authority and leadership and have illustrated this discussion with two cases from organizations in South America that allow us to understand other ways of organizing. The experiences from Omega and Patio Volatín are based on the ideas of economic solidarity, cooperativism, horizontality and autonomy. They avoid the creation of fixed authorities, keeping the organization subject to the wills and desires of those who work within it. However, as we can see, this is always a challenging situation, and there is a constant struggle between a hierarchical organization and self-management.

As Atzeni and Vieta (2014, p. 49) have noted, 'the emergence of self-management . . . has often coincided with periods of economic and political turmoil.' As capitalist societies have experienced successive and increasingly frequent crises, self-managed, leaderless organizations have often emerged in response, providing products, services and incomes. In this sense, as well as being ways of avoiding hierarchical authority, horizontal organizations can also be flexible and agile arrangements that can come into existence depending on the circumstances and be continually updated to deal with an uncertain environment.

The struggle between hierarchical and horizontal organization is also a battle of ideas. Business schools want their students to believe in leaders, in gifted individuals with the capacity to shape their worlds. But as we have noted, for every leader, you have people who are willing to be led. Rather like a fraudulent pyramid scheme, students are told that they should accept chains of command and leaders because they themselves might be such leaders in the future. In this sense, there is an exchange of real current power for future imaginary power: 'If I behave obediently now, and accept commands without questioning I will, perhaps, be able to command other people someday.'

This promise seems to us largely false and damaging. Instead, we should work on how to create organizations that can be fair and that respect the autonomy of those who work within them. As we have seen, values such as solidarity and cooperation offer possibilities for social transformation, though they are of course not exempt from difficulty. The problem of leadership is symmetrically the problem of how much freedom we expect ourselves to have. If people are subjected to any kind of authority, any restriction on their freedom, then a barrier is created between them and what they want to achieve for themselves and others. This often means that we substitute the goals of an organization for our own, based on the false common sense of the necessity of hierarchy and the efficiency of market managerialism.

Following leaders means that we work too hard at the expense of our own lives, sacrificing our freedom to the authority of others.

Questions for further study

1   What are your experiences of leading or of being led? How has it felt to have someone tell you to do something you don't want to do? How has it felt to tell someone to do something you know the person doesn't want to do?
2   In your city or neighbourhood, can you identify organizations without leaders, such as cooperatives, community organizations or political groups?
3   In a more informal way, do you see this sort of organization in your daily life? Such as a group of friends with a common purpose or a sports team? Do people need leaders whenever they come together to do something?
4   Given that there are examples of organizations without leaders, such as those discussed in this chapter and elsewhere in this book, do you think it would be a good thing to expand this form of organization? Why?

References

Azteni, M., and Vieta, M. (2014). "Between Class and the Market: Self-Management in Theory and in the Practice of Worker-Recuperated Enterprises in Argentina." In M. Parker, G. Cheney, V. Fournier, and C. Land (Eds.), *The Routledge Companion to Alternative Organization*, pp. 47–63. London: Routledge.

Bakunin, M. (1871). "What Is Authority?" Available at: www. panarchy.org/bakunin/authority.

Barnard, C. (1968). *The Functions of the Executive*. Cambridge, MA: Harvard University Press.

Bittencourt, F. (2014). "Liminal Organization: Organizational Emergence Within Solidary Economy in Brazil." *Organization*, 21(5), 713–729.

Collinson, D. (2011). "Critical Leadership Studies." In D. Collinson, A. Bryman, K. Grint, B. Jackson, and M. Uhl Bien (Eds.), *Handbook of Leadership Studies*, pp. 181–194. London: Sage Publications.

Fayol, H. (1949). *General and Industrial Management*. London: Pitman.

Goldberg, K. (2016). "ISA Pay It Forward." *ISA Student Blog*. Available at: https://isastudentblog.wordpress.com/2016/04/04/a-conversation-with-benjamin-briones-director-of-patio-volantin.

Hanlon, G. (2016). *The Dark Side of Management: A Secret History of Management Theory*. Abingdon-on-Thames: Routledge.

Kokkinidis, G. (2014). "Spaces of Possibilities: Workers' Self-Management in Greece." *Organization*, 22(6), 847–871.

Nova, C., Herrada, C., Peréz, F., Tapia, R., Rivera, G. (2018). *Autogestión en Organizaciones Alternativas: Un estudio de caso en Valparaíso*. Chile: Revista Brasileira de Estudos Organizacionais (RBEO).

Parker, M., Cheney, G., Fournier, V., and Land, C. (2014). "The Question of Organization: A Manifesto for Alternatives." *Ephemera*, 14(4), 623.

Reyes, M. I. (2014). *Liderazgo comunitario y capital social: Una mirada desde el campo biográfico*. Santiago, Chile: Editorial Universidad Santo Tomás.

Ricoeur, P. (2003). *The Just*. Chicago, IL: University of Chicago Press.

Walter, N. (2016). *Sobre Anarquismo*. Santiago, Chile: Editorial Eleuterio.

Webb, T., and Cheney, G. (2014). "Worker-Owned-and Governed Cooperatives and the Wider Cooperative Movement: Challenges and Opportunities Within and Beyond the Global Economic Crisis." In M. Parker, G. Cheney, V. Fournier et al. (Eds.), *The Routledge Companion to Alternative Organizations*, pp. 64–88. London: Routledge.

Weber, M. (2002). *The Protestant Ethic and the Spirit of Capitalism and Other Writings*. London: Penguin Books.

Western, S. (2014). "Autonomist Leadership in Leaderless Movements: Anarchists Leading the Way." *Ephemera*, 14(4), 673–698.

Wörner, B. (2018). "Co-operatives – Still a Success Story in 2050?" Available at: www.rural21. com/english/news/detail/article/co-operatives-still-a-success-story-in-2050-00003007.

PART IV

Markets, finance and accounting

10

FINANCE AND VALUE

Kenneth Weir and Christopher Land

Think about how an everyday product is made. What kinds of work go into creating it, where is that work done, and how is the resulting value distributed? Some people might be surprised when they realize just how little of the value of a phone or pair of jeans goes to the people actually making them. But what is 'value'? Most managers, and most business students, are concerned with producing 'value' and 'maximizing shareholder value,' even though very few management textbooks ever define what value is or how to create it.

Behind this question of strictly economic value is a deeper question of what we actually value: what we consider important and take into account when deciding how to organize things. When examining global production networks, for example, it seems obvious that they are structured around a process that values money and profit above all else. In 1776, Adam **Smith** claimed that 'It is not from the benevolence of the butcher, the brewer, or the baker that we expect our dinner, but from their regard to their own interest' (see box in Chapter 6). And by 'interest,' he meant financial profit. Mainstream management theory, like economics, assumes that people are motivated by monetary interest, but can all interests – all that we value and hold dear – be reduced to economic, monetary equivalence?

Value is one of the central concepts of modern-day economics and business, but it is usually defined in terms of monetary or financial measurement. Yet the word also has another meaning, in terms of ethical or political values, that is to say, the sort of people, actions and things that we care about, that we value. Understood in this broader way, not only in an economic sense, values can help us determine what we consider worthy and valuable and how we make decisions based on those assumptions. There are numerous things that we value but that cannot be measured in monetary terms. Friendship or memories as well as freedom or justice have unquestionable value and significance for us all, yet to get your head around their value is far from straightforward.

This chapter will

- provide an overview of how value is understood in mainstream management and accounting,
- discuss the difference between use value and exchange value,
- present the case study of the Ford Pinto car scandal to highlight the value of human life in mainstream management and accounting, and
- introduce some anarchist perspectives on how we understand value and how we can build a social and economic system with a convivial notion of value at its heart.

Use and exchange

Think about your phone. Did you buy this as a financial investment? Given that a new phone will lose a large part of its value as soon as it leaves the shop, this is unlikely. You may, of course, have bought it to run an online business, in which case, it could be a capital investment. Most of us, however, buy phones so that we can keep in touch with friends on social media, find our way around and play games. We might even use them as phones. Whatever we use our phone for, we value it for its utility, or 'use value.' This is very different from the value that the manufacturers, or management theorists, place on the phone. They are concerned first and foremost with its price and how much money they can make by selling it to you.

Economists understand value in terms of supply and demand, resulting in the idea that the value of a thing is determined by what people are prepared to pay for it. Examination of the topics covered in an introduction to management textbook will show that this is just one small topic – exchange – that is usually covered in a chapter on 'economics for management' or 'markets.' The main concern in management textbooks is with organizing *work*. These textbooks share the same basic interest in work and organization that Karl **Marx** did when he examined the industrial factory system of 19th-century Europe (see box in Chapter 11). Marx's thinking followed political economists like Adam Smith and David Ricardo, who understood that value was produced by work, or *labour*. After all, if you didn't need to work to get something – like air to breathe – then it would have no economic value and there would be no need to pay for it. In *The Wealth of Nations* (1776) Smith argued that value of a good or service could be determined by how long it took to produce. If a man could knit himself a sweater in a week but could earn enough money in just a day to buy one, he would be a fool to waste his time knitting. This idea, that working time determines value, lies behind both managerial and Marxist thinking about value. But this comes at a cost. As Marx recognized, the value system underlying this approach is really a way of valuing *people*. More accurately, it values our *lives*, weighed out in working days, hours or even minutes and seconds. We literally *spend* our lives doing work. Economic value is the time we have given up from our lives to earn money so that we can keep living and then our employers can profit.

Behind economic value, then, is the question of how we value human lives. Most management theory subordinates life to work, valuing it only insofar as it can turn someone else a profit. Anarchist theory has offered a wider conception of value, also asking what it is that we value *in* life. How should we value, for example time spent not working or earning but 'time for politics, contemplation, conviviality and spontaneous enjoyment, which have been displaced by capitalism's narrow focus on commercial production and consumption' (Frayne, 2015, p. 2)? Drawing on ideas from anarchist theory, and particularly from Ivan Illich, we can contrast this capitalist conception of value with an idea of value grounded in *conviviality*, which means the quality of friendliness and enjoyment in spending time together. When thinking about how we work, organize and produce, anarchism offers a more vibrant, more social and richer conception of value. Rather than reducing value to price, an anarchist theory of value asks how we want to live together.

Value in management theory

If you open the pages of most management textbooks, they assume that the ultimate goal of business is the maximization of the price at which goods and services can be exchanged, or 'exchange value.' Indeed, the primary function of marketing, according to such texts, is to maximize the demand for goods and services (see Chapter 15), and the main function of finance and accounting is to keep track of costs on the supply side (see Chapter 11). Together, these should enable a firm to ensure that sales prices balance supply and demand to maximize profitability.

Behind the balancing of supply and demand, however, lies another set of problems. What ultimately determines the price that a customer is prepared to pay for a good, or the price at which a producer is prepared to sell it? For the consumer, value is assumed to be subjective, albeit subject to manipulation by marketing. For the producer, the determinant factor should be the marginal cost of production: how much does the good cost to produce, and will the sale cover the costs of production? Whilst producers would only make something that costs them less to make than to sell, consumers should only purchase what it would cost them more to make for themselves. Smith followed the dominant political economic wisdom of the time in embracing the labour theory of value. A product's value – what it is *worth* and what a consumer is prepared to pay for it – is determined by how long it would take that consumer to produce it for him- or herself. If it is cheaper to make something for oneself than to buy it, then make it. If it costs more to make it, then buying is rational.

But consider this example. One of us has a partner who knits socks for our family at Christmas. It takes the person approximately eight hours to knit a pair of socks. They are lovely socks, but in the person's job, he or she earns £25 per hour, so the opportunity cost incurred by knitting is £200 per pair. Given that woollen socks are £10–12 a pair, the person is not acting in accordance with economic rationality. Unless the person could make a pair in less than 30 minutes, Smith would struggle to understand why he or she knits, when he or she could be earning more by working those hours. This example opens up a key distinction we want to draw in this chapter. Clearly, the reason why our knitter makes socks has nothing to do with economic rationality. He or she finds it relaxing and enjoys knitting whilst listening to music after a long day at work. The recipients also appreciate them more than bought socks, because they see the care that goes into them: their value has a different *quality* and cannot simply be measured in terms of quantitative equivalence with bought socks, even though both keep our feet warm.

Another line of analysis follows from this example. Think of some other knitters halfway around the world in Bangladesh. Here, the workers are standing at their machines as socks are knitted with a speed and regularity that could never be matched by even the most skilful of hands. These workers are not knitting for pleasure or relaxation; they are working for a wage. Their motivation is instrumental, rather than intrinsic; they work for financial reward. It is for these factory workers that our management textbooks are written – or rather, for their bosses. It is these workers who must be motivated (because there is no inherent motivation in their work), who need leaders to shape a strong corporate culture (because they have been thrown together by the labour market, rather than belonging to an organic community of shared values) and who need to have the quality of their work measured and managed (because it is structured by impersonal 'standards' and regulations, rather than years of skill and a sensitivity to the quality of their materials).

Like most textbook topics – leadership, culture management, creativity and innovation – motivation is only an issue if it is lacking. Marx would have called such a situation *alienation*. Alienated work is cut off from a wider connection with friends, family and community: a separation that we implicitly recognize when we talk about work-life balance. In such an alienated context, the intrinsic values of work are missing. They have to be replaced by a more coercive exercise of power – what we usually call 'management' – to motivate people to do work which has been stripped of its intrinsic meaning and value.

Let us again return to our sock-makers. Our first example is working in an unalienated context. This sock-maker is producing for people he or she knows, with skills he or she has control of, that were handed down to him or her by his or her grandmother and that the person mastered over a period of years. The sock-maker can choose the materials he or she works with, the pace of work, what he or she makes, and for whom. These decisions are grounded in the relationships of family, community and tradition. In contrast, commercial textile workers are likely to be young, female migrants, uprooted from their friends, family and community relationships to work in a factory (Jenkins, 2015). These disembedded workers, like the slaves forcibly taken from Africa to work in the cotton plantations of North America, whose products enabled the Industrial Revolution to take place in the UK (Beckert, 2015; Olusoga, 2016), are easier to control and less likely to be able to coordinate collective resistance to change their working conditions. At the heart of capitalism, therefore, is a process of taking value from life. It is by separating work and production, workers and products, from social relationships that they become transferable and saleable commodities. Workers are themselves transformed into commodities: bundles of labour-power measured in hours of quantifiable output that can be exchanged for a wage. Such measurement of the value of production and labour is the main concern of accounting.

VOLTAIRINE DE CLEYRE, 1866–1912

Voltairine de Cleyre was raised in a radical, abolitionist household, her parents naming her after the French Enlightenment thinker Voltaire. She turned to anarchism following the trial of eight anarchists in Chicago and the execution of four of the eight (including the husband of Lucy **Parsons**, see box in Chapter 5). She expanded her thinking on authority and domination to include a focus on slavery and the anarchist idea of employment as a form of waged slavery. Former slaves in the United States continued, she argued, to be bound in a relationship of domination as they were still dependent on employers for their survival, being forced to accept working conditions that were little better than those they had endured as slaves. Liberation from slavery was only a shift to a new form of enslaved domination. Working people were free in the eyes of the law but in practice still chained to property owners, who often resorted to violence to control their workers just as slave owners had their slaves. De Cleyre's analysis of slavery and the idea of human beings as property also led her to a critique of racism and colonialism as well as of women's position under patriarchy as a form of slavery, reflecting concerns mirrored today in **intersectional** anarchism (see box in Chapter 5). In conventional, patriarchal relationships, women were the property of men. Women also faced domination in employment through unequal pay. For De Cleyre, the only way individuals could be genuinely free was to take direct action to liberate themselves from dominating and exploitative conditions and relationships.

Value in accounting theory

Adam Smith's image of value determined by the 'invisible hand' of the market shapes the business disciplines. It lies behind the business school's promotion of self-interest and ideology over social science (Parker, 2018). Yet value theory influenced by the work of Karl Marx, mostly explicitly purged from business and management curricula, surprisingly underpins even that most technical business discipline: accounting. The accounting techniques and theories of the early 1900s replicated Marx's idea of surplus value by entrenching the antagonism between capital and labour in the search for efficiency and growth. Consider, for example, the idea of return on capital employed (ROCE).

ROCE is a measure of operational efficiency and company profitability and is presented as a key ratio for analyzing business performance, often as a 'fundamental measure' (McLaney and Atril, 2014, p. 236). ROCE expresses the relationship between profits and investment, generating a relative measure of returns achieved in a defined trading period against the long-term capital invested in the business. It thus compares profit (as an output) with capital (as an input) in order to determine the effectiveness of profit or wealth creation. This emphasis on capital employed marked the shift from a feudal or early-capitalist stage to full capitalism. Feudal landlords or the mercantile class utilized accounting measures to measure income and expenditure, which ensures constant and direct appropriation of surplus labour, but the capitalist draws upon indirect appropriation by grounding return as a rate of capital employed. This moves the focus from surplus labour to surplus value and gains are made by extracting surplus value from commodities produced by wage labour. The desire to 'improve' rates of return on capital is one that squeezes value from workers in order to generate higher returns. The concern for property owners moves from the absolute income a landowner can derive from his or her assets, to the relative rate of return on investments. As capital can more easily be redeployed and reinvested than land, this understanding of value leads the emerging capitalist class to seek ever higher rates of return.

Wages need to be set at a level that will allow workers to pay their rent, eat, clothe themselves, get to work each day and have the kind of socially acceptable standard of living that will keep them at least turning up for work. This means that wage levels are pretty much set within an industry or sector, but the amount of actual effort that can be extracted for that wage is variable. For example, working a 60-hour week will produce more than a 40-hour week, but the weekly wage may be kept the same. Similarly management can squeeze breaks or set productivity targets so that staff work harder during the same number of hours. Both of these will increase productivity and returns on investment, but at the cost of the energy and time of employees. Time that could be given over to life and energy that could be deployed in more enjoyable, intrinsically meaningful activities are both sacrificed for the sake of profit. This is what Marx (1976) means when he refers to capital as 'dead labour': it is the life force of workers, expended for the sake of profit and transformed into wealth for someone else, rather than on something that enhances that life.

Valuing human life

Think again of the Bangladeshi knitters. They have created value for their employers by working raw wool and cotton into clothing, but that value is not theirs any longer. They owned their labour power, but the products of that work belong to their employer. Without this living labour, there is no production and no profit, so capitalism is dependent on the continued use of living labour to grow and create more value, more capital. They receive a wage for this, but regardless of that, part of their life has been given up to produce a commodity. In this way, accounting practices enable employers to place a financial value on what their employees' lives are worth. This practice is also extended to the value of their customers' lives, as is illustrated by the example of the Ford Pinto.

The 1960s saw Ford facing increased competition from Japanese car manufacturers, threatening their global and domestic market share. In an attempt to fend off this threat, Lee Iacocca, in 1968 the president of the Ford Motor Company, authorized production of a new car: the Pinto. Production of the Pinto was to be completed within two years – shorter than the normal three-and-a-half-year development cycle – and be ready for launch in 1971. The Pinto was to weigh no more than 2,000 pounds and cost no more than $2,000. During 1970 and 1971, the prototype model failed several industry safety standards. Standards proposed by the National Highway Traffic Safety Administration (NHTSA) suggested that by 1972, all new models should withstand rear-end collisions of 20 mph without fuel loss, rising to 30 mph by 1973. Early testing in 1970 revealed that the Pinto failed the 20 mph test. The result was often damaged fuel lines, leaks and ruptured fuel tanks. Nonetheless, Ford released the Pinto to the market as planned.

In May 1972, Lily Gray and Richard Grimshaw were travelling in a Pinto and involved in a rear-end impact of approximately 30 mph. Lily Gray was killed in the accident, and Richard Grimshaw was left with significant and life-altering injuries as the impact started a large fire in the Pinto. The Grimshaw family pursued Ford for damages, eventually winning $3.5 million and exposing the company to further legal action, including a criminal case arising from a devastating crash in 1978 that involved a 1973 model.

What emerged during subsequent investigations of Ford's practices was a series of documents and decisions that highlighted the costs and benefits of resolving the fuel leak that would then meet with NHTSA standards. An internal document identified that the design flaw could be fixed for $11 per car. Employees at Ford then conducted a cost-benefit analysis to evaluate a total product recall and repair. While the cost per car was relatively low, the cost-benefit analysis placed the cost of rectifying all affected vehicles at $137.5 million. The costs of inaction, however, would be far less at $49.5 million. This figure was reached by using legal standards and precedents to cost loss-of-life payouts. The NHSTA, for instance, valued the cost to society of a life lost through a car accident to be $200,725. The calculation hinged on 'productivity losses' to society and the economy. This was broken down as follows (Birsch and Fielder, 1994, p. 26).

Future productivity losses	
Direct	$132,000
Indirect	$41,300
Medical costs	
Hospital	$700
Other	$425
Property damage	$1,500
Insurance administration	$4,700
Legal and court expenses	$3,000
Employer losses	$1,000
Victim's pain and suffering	$10,000

(Continued)

Medical costs	
Funeral	$900
Assets (lost consumption)	$5,000
Miscellaneous accident costs	$200
Total per fatality	**$200,725**

Using the NHSTA figure and internal crash data, Ford estimated that 180 deaths were likely, coupled with 180 serious injuries and a total of 2,100 burned vehicles. This then yielded the expected legal costs to Ford.

Unit Cost	$200,000 per death; $67,000 per injury; $700 per vehicle
Total Cost	(180 x $200,000) + (180 x $67,000) + (2,100 x $700)
	= $49.5m

This figure of $49.5 million represented a lower cost to Ford than halting production, redesigning the cars and rectifying the flaw in those cars already sold. In short, it was cheaper to let a few hundred people be killed or seriously injured than it was to stop them dying. The cost of a life had been calculated, weighed against future profits and found wanting.

What the Pinto case shows is that human life, under capitalism, is often valued in terms of money, profits and 'future productivity.' It renders the value of life in terms of a person's potential to work and thereby contribute to profit. In crude terms, life is the value of your human capital, and the death of an individual is valued in terms of the death of an abstract, average employee: the death of potential labour.

Value and non-human life

So far, we have focussed on human life, valued solely according to the logic of profit maximization. However, these arguments can extend to all of natural life, including plants and animals. For example, in order to support an economy that makes and sells hamburgers, mass deforestation and the mass slaughter of animals is required, which has implications for climate change that risk changing the very conditions of possibility for life on earth. Even if such an economy attempts to 'price in' the environment, a logic is constructed which accounts for the value of life through abstract metrics like 'ecological services' or the value of a species, for example, bees to agriculture. Measures of eco-efficiency, for instance, reflect a monetary conception of value that values nature in much the same way that capitalist accounting values labour. Consider the view of nature as a source of 'value' (Tinker and Gray, 2003; Milne and Gray, 2013) from which ecological indicators measure nature through money rather than the value of species and ecosystems in maintaining harmony and sustainability in the local and global environment. This encourages a cash-equivalent view of different non-human species, reducing them all to the same kind of measure as economic value, which is evident when organizations pursue cost-saving approaches to conserving or protecting non-human species.

In biodiversity planning and schemes of species protection, the simplistic economic type of value given to nature allows for different species to be 'traded' against each other. If one particular species offers greater ecological efficiencies, then it becomes possible to allow the abundance rates of a particular low-value species in a given region to decline (Sullivan and Hannis, 2015; Weir, 2018). The death of a low-value species is compensated for by the growth in a higher-value species. We see this, for example, through the plantation of trees with higher carbon sequestration rates to replace low-absorbing trees in situations where countries have a desire to reduce their total carbon emission rates. This promotes a narrow engagement with goals of ecological sustainability that promotes the view that nature is best of use to humanity as a service provider (Sullivan, 2009) and that non-human species are only of use as efficient value creators, suggesting an optimal economics that permits the death of inefficient (and so unvalued) species.

This is a phenomenon already noted by anarchist theorists such as Murray Bookchin (1971, 1982), who criticized the dualism that encourages a sense of domination by humans over nature that is rooted in market exchanges and relationships. This results in an instrumental view of the environment, reducing complex social and ecological relationships to hierarchical forms of social organizing. The way that we measure society makes phenomena and relationships into commodities. This raises two questions. First, why is such a system so widespread, and how is it perpetuated? Second, what are the alternatives? Answers to both can be found in anarchist writings, the first in Proudhon and the second in Scott, Illich and Bookchin. It is to these writers that we now turn in an attempt to articulate some elements of an anarchist theory of value that suggests an alternative to capitalist accounting practices.

An anarchist theory of value

What the various forms of anarchism share is a focus on everyday life and a rejection of hierarchical rule. First and foremost, then, our anarchist theory of value is a refusal of a logic of capitalism that values everything according to the maximization of profit. Instead, we wish to celebrate a broad range of living values. As Colin Ward puts it,

> far from being a speculative vision of a future society, [anarchism] is a description of a mode of human experience of *everyday life*, which operates side-by-side with, and in spite of, the dominant authoritarian trends of our society.
>
> *(Ward, 1973, p. 18, italics added)*

Unlike the grand plans of managers and accountants, anarchism starts from the everyday, from the practices which produce the 'life' side of the work/life boundary.

Capitalist accounting and management, however, increasingly forces all of life into processes geared towards a single form of value: maximizing profit.

> Many anarchists want to insist on the sheer shittiness of most work and the way in which life's routines become subordinated to the demands of work. So-called leisure time becomes increasingly occupied by preparing for work, shopping for it, dressing for it, travelling to and from it and, most of all, recuperating from it in order to be able to get through the next day, the next week.
>
> *(Sheehan, 2003, p. 69)*

If capitalist values ignore all of those things we value outside narrow economic value, then why would we willingly give up our lives to this profit motive? At the most basic level, we can answer this question with one word: force. As Pierre-Joseph **Proudhon** (2011, see box in Chapter 2) argued, the very concept of 'property' contradicts a fundamental assumption of the right to life. The existence of private property denies people the right to water, to somewhere to live and to access to land on which to hunt or farm unless they can establish property rights. Such property rights are backed up by the state, which claims the right to enforce property rights through violence, for example, by imprisonment or punishment. Without access to the necessities of life, there is no freedom. Under a system of private property, you are forced to pay for access to the necessities for staying alive through money gained by selling your labour to the same people who have denied you access in the first place. Most of us have to work in order to eat and drink, secure a home, and clothe ourselves. In order to maintain our existence, we surrender control over our labour to an employer. As Proudhon (2011, p. 106) argues, this fundamentally breaches the very condition that makes us human.

From this, we can derive our first principle of an anarchist theory of value: it is concerned with maximizing equality, freedom and the unconditional right to life. In this sense, anarchism is concerned with the maintenance and development of **commons**, or collective property (see box in Chapter 17). We can capture this with the slogan *Omnia Sunt Communia* or 'everything for everyone' (De Angelis, 2017), but this does not mean that everyone is an individualized consumer, maximizing his or her utility. 'Commoning' is focussed on organizing according to principles of equality and liberty, so that it is possible for us all to live together in conviviality. Whilst managerial economics and accounting focus on private profit from others' labour, anarchistic value theory is concerned with maximizing the collective good and ensuring equality of access to what is shared and held in common. In this vision, private property is abolished and, with it, private profit and interest, which is premised upon exclusionary access rights, guaranteed by state violence.

This shift of attention from private profit, measured as money, to value as something that is lived, requires a different understanding of value than our current accounting practices offer. One approach to this is through closer attention to the local, everyday nature of use-value and how value-in-use is seen in everyday practice. In *Two Cheers for Anarchism*, James Scott (2012) considers the relationship between 'vernacular' (i.e. what people use in everyday language) and 'official' practices of naming and measurement. The seemingly neutral value practices of accounting are only useful from the perspective of an investor or a manager. By claiming to be objective, however, they are able to dominate other value practices, making local, lived realities difficult to see and limiting our understanding to an abstract universalism based on the death of all that is unique and particular.

Numbers and quantification play a special role here. The appearance of precision and objectivity that numbers present stands in contrast to the vernacular, which is localized and specific, rather than global or comparable.

> Vernacular measurement is only as precise as it needs to be for the purposes at hand. It is symbolized in such expressions as a 'pinch of salt,' 'a stone's throw,' 'a book of hay,' 'within shouting distance.' And for many purposes vernacular rules may prove more accurate than apparently more exact systems.
>
> *(Scott, 2012, p. 33)*

Rather than offering more 'universal' modes of measurement, such as those deployed by a state or capitalist enterprise, vernacular forms can be more effective in concrete settings. Scott offers the example of a piece of Native American advice to sow corn when the oak leaves are 'the size of a squirrel's ear' (2012, p. 33). Whilst less precise than giving a specific date, it is better suited to the local conditions. Because oak leaves develop in line with ground temperature, following this advice minimizes the chance that corn will be damaged by a late frost, whereas a fixed planting date would be unable to account for local climatic variations or changes year on year. Central to the idea of vernacular measurement is valuation based on concrete use-value and situated practice, rather than a more abstract form of context-independent exchange value, determined by a distant centre of control. For the latter, value needs to be abstract, transferable and comparable. In contrast, the anarchist vernacular is concerned with living, value-in-use. Exchange value is dependent upon the uprooting of the vernacular, destroying its value to actual, living individuals in concrete settings. This shift from use value to exchange lies behind many of the problems that arise from managerialism. We would suggest that the vernacular offers a more vibrant and life-affirming form of value, albeit something that resists simple translation into accounting calculations.

This gives us another principle of an anarchist theory of value: value should be accounted for in terms that are grounded in concrete, lived experience and use, rather than in abstract exchange. This may mean quantification in some cases but not necessarily all. Qualitative valuation (where value is judged by those involved based on the shared impressions and opinions of their community) may suit some contexts and practices better than quantification, as in the example of planting corn or knitting socks.

Bookchin (1971, 1982) attempts to depart from capitalist and market-led assumptions about value by emphasizing diversity and communal forms of social life. He argues that convivial solutions can be posed if integrated into social structures and outcomes that avoid centralized control. His focus is on 'living well' paired with a social-ecological outlook that recognizes the limits to economic growth and insists on the measures of living well as social outcomes and not economic ones. For example, he stresses the values found in pre-capitalist societies, such as face-to-face association and **mutual** aid, and proposes these as principles of a society which emphasizes social life (Bookchin, 1982, and box in Chapter 17). This would flatten social hierarchies and align human relationships to nature, with value becoming concerned with what activities benefit the broader human and non-human ecology.

MURRAY BOOKCHIN, 1921–2006

Bookchin's work contributed to philosophy, ecological economics, social theory and history – to name a few. In anarchist terms, his work is perhaps most closely associated with ecological anarchist movements and a view of anarcho-communism that advocates common ownership of the means of production over the protection of private property and waged labour. He proposed a new vision of society made possible by the expansion of technology. On the one hand, these developments were made in order to generate more profit for wealth holders; on the other, a series of social, cultural and political contradictions were also produced. The technological changes of the late 1950–60s, however, meant that young people could easily see the value in not working, as technology had created materially abundant societies. Scarcity – the compelling motivation for social organizing – had now been overcome. Bookchin also promoted ecological concerns above profit by focusing on the impact that capitalist production and organizing had on local ecologies. He developed a 'social ecological' vision of what society could be, based on a rejection of dominant capitalist values. He brought this to the core of his challenge to hierarchical society and viewed technological advancements as key to eliminating the domination and repression, the toil and authority, that is crucial to hierarchical society.

Another anarchist thinker, Ivan Illich (1973), draws upon conviviality as a 'value' that resists the social organization of the industrial mode of production. The position Illich takes is much the same as Bookchin's: put less emphasis on technology and economic growth and encourage the sharing of tools and ideas in order to make people creative and autonomous. The problem is that decisions made according to economic measurements of value have come to dominate the development of technology and related systems, with perverse outcomes. Illich gives the example of transport, which has gone from a situation where a few could travel further and faster (e.g. on steam trains) to the contemporary situation in which many, in the

USA at least, are completely dependent on cars for their everyday lives (Wilson, 2014, p. 133). Rather than improving our lives, cars have become a necessity for existence and something we have to work to pay for, so that we can get to work. Whilst an automobile society is good for economic indicators, it is destroying the planet and sacrificing lives.

Against this illogical outcome, Illich (1973, p. 91) suggests that we should encourage 'modern technologies that serve politically interrelated individuals rather than managers.'

> I choose the term 'conviviality' to designate the opposite of industrial pro-
> ductivity. I intend it to mean autonomous and creative intercourse among
> persons, and the intercourse of persons with their environment; and this in
> contrast with the conditioned response of persons to the demands made
> upon them by others, and by a man–made environment.
>
> *(Illich, 1973, p. l, pp. 263–265)*

Like Scott's vernacular value practices, conviviality is structured around living with others collectively. This would mean collective decision making about what is valuable, with actions, technologies and decisions judged in relation to what is a good life for the community and the environment. It is a value that starts from human interdependence (on each other and on the environment) instead of individual consumers maximizing their utility.

IVAN ILLICH, 1924–2002

A Catholic priest turned philosopher, Illich is famous for his contributions to education, economic development and ecology, all of which found reflection in his anarchist writings. Radically criticizing the functioning of schools in contemporary capitalist countries, he suggests that schools are the only place where learning counts because knowledge learned outside of the classroom is ignored by society. This means that students learn what capitalism needs and are taught through the development of skills to meet those needs. Education replicates an industrial mode of production. He proposes an alternative model of learning and education based on 'conviviality' aimed at escaping the grip of capitalist technologies in order to enjoy a happy collective co-existence. He emphasized how humans are working for machines and becoming enslaved into a machinic social order that reduces us to mere consumers and transfers power to a specific professional elite. Instead, he wishes people to resist the demands placed upon them by such a social order and to become creative and autonomous. This, he hopes, would lead to a social order in which people have free and equal access to community tools and giving people freedom to exercise individual autonomy to create the conditions of their own future.

Collective discussions over ethical values, what is a good life and what is sustainable, are complex, but does that mean that we should not try? Given the overwhelming evidence of the damage caused by over-simplistic economic metrics, anarchist valuation practices, rooted in collective responsibility, present a clear alternative. The machineries of value that dominate in society have become oppressive, and all too often are not questioned. Failing to be critical leads to our everyday life being captured and administered in ways that do not reflect our everyday experience.

Conclusion

Against the value practices of capitalism, we have argued that anarchism offers four elements of a theory of value that would positively affirm a different life. These principles are

1   A collective right to life is more important than property rights or other abstract rights that require the violence of the state to enforce them. This right to life is not necessarily restricted to humans.
2   How we determine value is local, context specific and grounded in lived experience, even when it claims to be universal and objective. Saying that something is universal and objective is the result of some interests dominating others and appearing to be natural.
3   The expression of value is the result of political dialogue between equals. Anything else is domination.
4   The ultimate goal of valuation is conviviality: a life enjoyed together with others.

Using the ideas of anarchists like Scott, Illich, Bookchin and Proudhon, it is possible to lay out these basic principles and consider some of their implications for management and organization. In each case, an attempt is made to reconfigure organizations around a value logic that rejects the imperative of maximizing profiting. We have argued that the dominant tools of organizing found in business schools and textbooks, such as motivation theory and accounting, are based on a labour theory of value that permits and rewards exploitation of the many for the benefit of a few. Against this, anarchism offers an alternative set of practices, orientated towards conviviality and located in a vernacular context. This represents a fundamental challenge to the dominant logic of management and accounting. It replaces economic imperative and control with localized, democratic discussion.

Beginning again with everyday life, with use-value as the foundation of value, means that there are no simple, universalizing equations, like ROCE for instance, that can measure value for everyone. Instead, we need to have informed, open dialogue. We have to recognize that *any* discussion of value is, at the root, a discussion of our collective flourishing and how we can live together, with others on a planet of finite resources.

Questions for further study

1 How would you define use value and exchange value? What examples can you think of to help illustrate these definitions? Why do you think it is important to differentiate between use value and exchange value?
2 Consider the case of the Ford Pinto. What is given value in this example, and how is that value decided? Could this process of giving things value be done differently? What would this mean in this particular case?
3 How have the authors of this chapter defined an anarchist approach to value? What is involved, and how does this differ from the mainstream management and accounting practice when it comes to value?
4 Try to imagine what an anarchist process of deciding on value might look like? Who would be involved in making that decision? What would they need to take into account?

References

Beckert, S. (2015). *Empire of Cotton: A New History of Global Capitalism*. London: Penguin Books.
Birsch, D., and Fielder, J. H. (1994). *The Ford Pinto Case: A Study in Applied Ethics, Business, and Technology*. Albany, NY: State University of New York Press.
Bookchin, M. (1971). *Post-Scarcity Anarchism*. San Francisco, CA: Ramparts.
Bookchin, M. (1982). *The Ecology of Freedom: The Emergence and Dissolution of Hierarchy*. New York, NY: Black Rose Books.
De Angelis, M. (2017). *Omnia Sunt Communia: On the Commons and the Transformation to Postcapitalism*. London: Zed Books.
Frayne, D. (2015). *The Refusal of Work: Rethinking Post-Work Theory and Practice*. London: Zed Books.
Illich, I. (1973). *Tools for Conviviality*. London: Marion Boyars. References to the Kindle edition, published 2011.
Jenkins, J. (2015). "The Significance of Grass-Roots Organizing in the Garment and Electrical Value Chains of Southern India." In K. Newsome, P. Taylor, J. Bair, and A. Rainnie (Eds.), *Putting Labour in Its Place: Labour Process Analysis and Global Value Chains*. London: Palgrave.
Marx, K. (1976). *Capital: A Critique of Political Economy* (Vol. 1). Harmondsworth: Penguin Books.
McLaney, E., and Atrill, P. (2014). *Accounting & Finance: An Introduction* (7th Edition). Harlow: Pearson.
Milne, M. J., and Gray, R. H. (2013). "W(h)ither Ecology? The Triple Bottom Line, the Global Reporting Initiative, and Corporate Sustainability Reporting." *Journal of Business Ethics*, 118, 13–29.
Olusoga, D. (2016). *Black and British: A Forgotten History*. London: Macmillan.
Parker, M. (2018). *Shut Down the Business School: What's Wrong With Management Education*. London: Pluto Press.
Proudhon, P.-J. (2011). *Property Is Theft! A Pierre-Joseph Proudhon Anthology* (I. McKay, Ed.). Edinburgh: AK Press.
Scott, J. C. (2012). *Two Cheers for Anarchism*. Princeton, NJ: Princeton University Press.

Sheehan, S. (2003). *Anarchism*. London: Reaktion Books.

Smith, A. (1776). "An Inquiry Into the Causes and Nature of the Wealth of Nations." Full-text available at: www.marxists.org/reference/archive/smith-adam/works/wealth-of-nations/index.htm (accessed 11 June 2018).

Sullivan, S. (2009). "Green Capitalism and the Cultural Poverty of Constructing Nature as Service Provider." *Radical Anthropology*, 3, 18–27.

Sullivan, S., and Hannis, M. (2015). "Nets and Frames, Losses and Gains: Value Struggles in Engagements With Biodiversity Offsetting Policy in England." *Ecosystem Services*, 15, 162–173.

Tinker, T., and Gray, R. (2003). "Beyond a Critique of Pure Reason: From Policy to Politics to Praxis in Environmental and Social Research." *Accounting, Auditing & Accountability Journal*, 16(5), 727–761.

Ward, C. (1973). *Anarchy in Action*. London: Freedom Press.

Weir, K. (2018). "The Purposes, Promises and Compromises of Extinction Accounting in the UK Public Sector." *Accounting, Auditing & Accountability Journal*, 31(3), 875–899.

Wilson, M. (2014). *Rules Without Rulers*. Winchester: Zed Books.

11

ACCOUNTING IN ORGANIZATIONS AND SOCIETY

Anders Sandström

If one looks up 'accounting' in the *Swedish National Encyclopaedia* (1990), the definition translates as the 'collection, registration, aggregation and reporting of financial transactions in companies or organisations.' Classic textbooks on accounting usually make a distinction between financial accounting and management or internal accounting. Financial accounting focuses on providing information to existing and potential investors and parties external to the organization such as creditors and regulatory agencies. This is today governed by 'generally accepted' accounting principles, which are a combination of rules set by authorities and longstanding traditions. Management accounting primarily focuses on the information that directors and managers need to establish, the objectives of the organization and the strategies to fulfil those objectives. Consequently, accounting in a capitalist context is primarily a tool for investors and owners of capital in their efforts to monitor, manage and control credit and the trade and production of goods and services and to maximize profit and return on investments (Roslender, 2017).

It is therefore perhaps not surprising that the radical left, including anarchists, have had a strong negative attitude towards accounting from as early as the late 19th century, considering it to be an integral part of the system they wanted to abolish. 'From each according to his ability, to each according to his needs' was a slogan popularized by Karl Marx in his 1875 *Critique of the Gotha Program* (2008). The long-term visions of anarchists, communists and others on the radical left are often of a future utopian society without money in which ideas about credit and debit have no place and where society's commonly owned resources and labour could satisfy everyone's needs without having to make difficult decisions about what to produce and consume. In such a future, accounting would of course have little use: there would be no investors or managers for whom accounting records would be useful and no private enterprise that would require regulation or indeed a centralized authority to perform that regulation. Both financial and management accounting would be unnecessary. A quote from the French anarchist Ravachol in the late 1800s sums up the sentiment: 'There currently exist many useless things; many occupations are useless as well, for example, accounting. With anarchy there is no more need for money, no further need for bookkeeping and the other forms of employment that derive from this' (in Abidor, 2016).

***

KARL MARX, 1818–1883

Arguably one of the most famous radical thinkers, Marx even got a school of thought named after him – Marxism – since his intellectual heritage is so vast that it would be impossible to attribute it to any particular area of knowledge. He is a subject of thousands of books and essays, and no doubt you either already have encountered his name in your studies or will study him at some later stage. For the purposes of this chapter and book more generally, it is enough to say that Marx is one of the most important analysts and critics of capitalism. He suggested that our society is shaped by a struggle between those who own and control and those who sell their labour and that we can see the effects of this within all capitalist organizations and societies. It is often argued, and not without reason, that Marx borrowed extensively from Pierre-Joseph **Proudhon** (see box in Chapter 2). However, if you want to further explore issues like value, exchange, production, alienation and others – Marx is a must-read.

***

Not all anarchists, however, agreed with this, with some, such as Proudhon and **Bakunin** (see box in Chapter 7), thinking that there would probably need to be something like money, at least for a long transitional period before we reach the 'society of abundance' in which everyone's needs are easily met. In a capitalist economy based on privately owned businesses competing against each other in markets, accounting information is generated for the goal of maximizing shareholder returns. However, in an anarchist economy, organized around self-governing democratic workplaces and neighbourhoods cooperating together, the accounting information needed will have to be aimed at quite different goals of facilitating democratic decision making, equity and solidarity.

In this chapter, we will

- briefly summarize the history of accounting;
- argue for the necessity of accounting in any economy, including an economy based on anarchist values and institutions, as long as resources are scarce;
- provide an overview of the arguments against markets; and
- broadly describe how an economy based on anarchist values might look and what accounting challenges such an economy would encounter.

The history of accounting

The cradle of financial accounting is usually placed in Mesopotamia, in the area around the Tigris and Euphrates Rivers in present-day Iraq over 5,000 years ago. However, it was not until the late 15th century that what is referred to as modern accounting, i.e. double-entry book-keeping, was first described in written text. In 1494, the Venice-based Franciscan monk Luca Pacioli created the first known description of double-entry accounting in the mathematical dissertation *Summa de Arithmetica Geometria Proportioni et Proportionalita* (Overview of Arithmetic, Geometry, Rule of Three and Proportionality).

Before the Industrial Revolution, the purpose of bookkeeping was mainly to register transactions between independent producers of goods and their customers or traders who bought goods for resale or lenders and borrowers. During the 17th and 18th centuries, large mercantile companies were created, such as the East India Company, which ran extensive trade in colonies around the world, where the focus was on importing goods to and from different parts of the world. Profits were the result of buying 'exotic' goods cheap in the colonies and selling them dear in the home country, combined with buying manufactured goods cheap in the home country and selling them dear in the colonies. The actual production of goods in both colonies and home countries was carried out largely independently by peasants and artisans who controlled the actual production process. The pricing of goods and assets from an accounting perspective was simple and followed naturally as a result of market transactions between independent parties. With the Industrial Revolution, an entirely different scenario came into play.

In the early 19th century, technical progress had made it possible and profitable to mass produce goods. It became profitable for the owners of capital to invest much larger sums in production than before. Workers were contracted for longer times, and it became important to control production processes. A hierarchical division of labour and organization grew rapidly, with groups of workers whose only job was to manage and control other workers. The production units grew ever larger as a result of better forms of communication and economies of scale, and it became important for investors to evaluate and compare different units based on the most profitable use of scarce resources. A large number of economic indicators and analytical tools were developed to evaluate and compare the efficiency of different units with respect to hours worked, resources used, and so on. This trend was intensified by Taylorism (named after the American engineer Frederick Taylor, 1856–1915), which, in the early 20th century, attempted to scientifically manage the optimal use of materials and labour in any given production process. At roughly the same time, as the proportion of financial transactions that were internal within large organizations and between different organizational units belonging to the same group grew, senior officials in the multinational chemical company Du Pont Group developed a set of key indicators or key ratios in order to facilitate the allocation of capital to the most profitable units within the group – the so-called 'return on investment' (ROI) ratios. Different versions of ROI ratios are still widely used today.

After the Second World War and especially in the period after 1970, the world economy has been characterized by two strong trends: an increasing concentration of capital and ownership in most industries and an expanding financial sector. Many industries today are dominated by a small number of global business groups that are often interlinked and whose revenues in many cases exceed the GDPs of smaller countries. According to the activist group Global Justice Now, in 2016, 69 of the largest economies on the planet were corporations, with the rest being states. These business groups often control and own firms in several stages in the production and distribution chain. One instance with far-reaching implications, not only for the economy but also for the functioning of democracy, is the development of the media and entertainment industry in which today just a handful of huge actors control how and what news will be reported and what values movies and TV shows will convey. Another striking example is the retail industry in the US, where Walmart and Amazon control their market segments to a degree that gives them the power to dictate the terms and prices for both vendors and customers.

At the same time, speculative financial transactions make up an overwhelming majority of all monetary transactions in today's economy. According to the Global Policy Forum, in 1975, roughly 80% of foreign exchange transactions involved real trading of a product or a service; the remaining 20% were speculative. In 2011, less than 1% could be traced to genuine international trade in goods and services. Many companies nowadays make significantly more money by speculating in currencies and securities than by producing goods and services and providing them to consumers. In the US, financial profits as percentage of total corporate profits of domestic industries have gone from roughly 13% in 1980 to well above 35% in the early 2000s. This trend came to an end with the crisis of 2007–09 after which levels have declined a little but still remain very high (Lapavitsas and Mendieta, 2016).

This history means that today's accounting principles were shaped by the interests of private capital owners in controlling and managing the use of their capital, by nation-states' interest in taxing corporations profits' and assets and by demands from accountants who in their daily work prepare financial information in income statements, balance sheets, cash flow reports, financial analyses and so on. The design of accounting procedures, in turn, has helped create favourable conditions for capital accumulation by certain groups, return on investment and control of resources at the expense of other groups and in that way affected how and how quickly different economic systems and ideologies have evolved. The increasing complexity of accounting systems has also meant that accountants throughout history, and especially in recent years, have been able to monopolize accounting knowledge and form themselves as an independent group with its own aspirations for power and influence in relation to the capital-owning class. For example, the overall financialization of the economy and the creation of complex securities and financial assets and the focus on very short-term returns have increased the bargaining power of top management accountants, especially in the financial and banking sector, resulting in ever increasing salaries and bonuses.

The need for accounting

Most economists would agree that any economy has at least three tasks to accomplish: the organization of production, the organization of consumption and, because humans abandoned individual economic self-sufficiency long ago in order to take advantage of the efficiency gains from a division of labour, the allocation of goods, services and resources among different producers, users and consumers. For instance, the radical economist Robin Hahnel defines an economy as a system for organizing production and consumption of goods and services and the disposal of waste (2012). He suggests that, since we are rarely self-sufficient, then an economic system must coordinate how people produce different things, and everyone consumes things made by others.

Anarchists like **Kropotkin** had a vision of an economy of abundance where labour would produce more than enough for all and where our needs for goods and services would be satisfied without much effort and without having to rely on accounting or money to prioritize and choose between different economic alternatives (Kropotkin, 1906, see box in Chapter 3). This old idea has gained some traction lately with the rapid technological developments in such areas as artificial intelligence, 3-D printers, robotics and a huge amount of services and information that are now spread over the Internet basically free of charge (Bastani, 2019). Indeed, the increase in productivity since the Industrial Revolution and especially in the last decades has been exceptional. Compared with 1950, the US in 2000 produced five times more with the same work effort. In other words, a US citizen in 2000 could have enjoyed the same material standard as in 1950 by working only eight hours a week. However, increased productivity has not led to fewer hours worked. Instead, the development has primarily resulted in dramatically increased consumption, which has, among other things, led to great negative impacts on the environment and the climate, and together with neoliberal policies such as deregulation, tax reductions and the dismantling of welfare systems, it has also created enormous inequality and wealth asymmetry.

Members of a non-capitalist democratic economy in which profit maximization and growth are not primary goals would presumably be inclined to prioritize leisure in terms of fewer working hours at the expense of more consumption of goods that we don't really need. A reduction in working hours can of course be implemented in several different ways, for example through a lower retirement age, a reduction in annually worked hours with more time for vacation leave, shorter working days or specifically targeted policies such as parental leave. Such an economy would also encourage the production of sustainable high-quality products instead of products designed to break and be replaced at short intervals. One can also expect that collective consumption would increase at the expense of private consumption, through various collective solutions for housing and transport and the establishment of pools of certain capital goods for shared use. Such a development would not only have positive effects on personal quality of life and health but also mitigate the environmental disaster of climate change. The earth's assets, such as clean air and a protective atmosphere, and natural resources, such as different minerals and ecosystems, are not infinite and are currently being used up at a rapid pace because of profit seeking.

A modern economy based on anarchist institutions and values, such as having decision-making input to the degree one is affected by the outcome of a decision, economic justice and equity, solidarity and freedom to express one's creative needs and potentials would allocate the benefits and burdens resulting from our collective economic activity more equally. However, within the foreseeable future, we will not be able to meet all our needs and desires and produce all the goods and services we demand without work and consuming non-renewable natural resources and manufactured productive resources. In other words, we will have to prioritize what is to be produced and consumed and decide how to deal with the profits and problems we create.

As long as productive resources are scarce and the production of goods and services consumes resources, all economies – whether they call themselves capitalist, socialist, anarchist or something else – must make choices about what to produce and consume and decide how they want to allocate resources and consumption rights between individual producers and consumers. Different economies will make different decisions depending on their values and goals, and they will organize decision making differently and allocate decision-making power and influence to different actors, but they must all inevitably choose some options over others.

Since resources are finite, there will be an opportunity cost associated with every use of a resource. An opportunity cost is the potential benefit or revenue that is sacrificed when a resource is used in a certain way and not another. Every use of a resource means sacrificing other possible uses. For example, if an economy chooses to use part of its productive resources to produce cars, that means that those same resources – labour, machines, tools, land and so on – cannot be used to produce other items, such as computers, wind turbines, trains, fridges and so on. In order to make fair and efficient decisions when choosing between different possible alternatives, including decisions about the trade-off between leisure and work and what technological innovations to implement and how, decision makers will need to have access to information about opportunity costs for different available options. In an anarchist economy, the decision makers would be all the affected parties and not just the individual buyers and sellers, as in a capitalist or socialist market economy, or a central planning board, as in a centrally planned economy. This means that all productive resources, intermediate and final goods and services should be priced in a way that reflects opportunity and *social* costs (as opposed to only the cost for the individual producer and consumer). Without such information, there is no way for decision makers to make fair and efficient decisions, regardless of how well intended they may be.

There will always be someone making these decisions. If affected consumers and producers are not allowed to influence production and consumption plans, someone else will decide what to produce and consume. Either, as in market economies, the *individual* buyers and sellers who are directly involved in the transactions will make decisions based on their individual bargaining power and regardless of the social effects, or, alternatively, as in centrally planned command economies, some government department will try to estimate consumer preferences and costs and prepare production plans. Costs and benefits for goods and services will not necessarily look the same in different types of economies. In a private market economy, the prices that individual buyers and sellers negotiate will not include costs that other affected parties will be burdened with, for instance, the damage to society caused by pollution. However, in a planned economy that aims for prices to reflect true social costs, these costs can be included in the price.

Anarchist communists, such as Peter Kropotkin and Errico Malatesta have argued that it will be necessary to abolish money to create a truly fair and democratic society. However, as we have seen, a developed economy aiming at fair, democratic and efficient decisions will need information about opportunity costs and social costs conveyed via a price system, and any type of price system presupposes the use of some kind of currency, though not necessarily in the form of physical banknotes and coins that can be hoarded. Today, an immaterial currency with units that are recorded in and circulate between different actors' accounts based on rules decided and planned outside of a market is quite conceivable (see Chapter 14).

The purpose of accounting is to enable and facilitate the registration, organization and distribution of the essential information needed to make financial decisions. An anarchist economy will obviously have different values and institutions than a capitalist or state socialist economy regarding decision making, income distribution and ecological sustainability. If such an economy is to be democratic, ecologically sustainable and efficient, it *must* implement an accounting system that summarises and presents the required information to all affected parties in a transparent and accessible way. If it fails to do so, it will eventually revert into some version of the authoritarian economic systems that it aims to escape.

The problem with markets

In capitalist and market socialist economies, the accounting system is indeed very much part and parcel of the market system. The financial transactions that the accounting system registers, aggregates and reports to decision makers take place and are valued with the help of markets. The market system, defined as a system of competitive bidding between individual buyers and sellers, is unacceptable to an anarchist economy for many reasons. Robin Hahnel, co-creator of the economic model of participatory economics and a key economist and thinker in the development of decentralized forms of democratic planning, repeatedly emphasizes four of them when assessing markets (2012).

- ### *Markets are unfair*

In a private market economy, capital owners receive profit without doing any work. And when labour is hired through a labour market – regardless of ownership – those who make a greater contribution to the companies' revenues or otherwise have a stronger bargaining position will get a higher income than those who contribute to a lesser extent or have less bargaining power regardless of their effort and sacrifices.

- ## *Markets undermine solidarity and promote selfishness*

Markets encourage forms of human interaction that are characterized by pettiness and enmity while cooperation based on respect and empathy are discouraged. Those who most effectively exploit human beings (and nature for that matter) are rewarded, and those who treat others fairly and with respect are punished. The way in which we regulate and coordinate our trade and economic activities affects the type of people we become, and markets are social environments that nurture selfishness while punishing solidarity.

- ## *Markets are undemocratic*

Markets undermine the character traits and abilities that are necessary for the democratic process, such as the ability to manage and communicate complex and often contradictory information, to take collective decisions and to feel empathy and solidarity with others. Furthermore, market transactions favour those with more wealth over those with less. Capital owners always receive most of the efficiency gain that market exchanges may create, and economic liberalism leads to greater concentration of wealth; in a political system where money influences electoral prospects, this means concentration of political power as well.

- ## *Markets are inefficient*

Economists use two definitions of efficiency. The narrower definition means that an outcome is efficient if there is no other possible outcome where at least one person is better off without someone else being worse off. This is called a Pareto optimal outcome. The broader definition says that a result is efficient if it maximizes the net social benefit (i.e. the difference between the total benefit to society and the total cost to society). Based on either of these definitions, even most liberal economists acknowledge that markets allocate resources inefficiently when there are externalities, competition is weak and markets are out of equilibrium. Their argument, however, is that these situations are exceptions and rare and basically can be disregarded because, in the long run, markets are the best mechanism we have.

But how true is this? Let's take a quick look at how common these situations are in a market economy. First, what about 'externalities'? These are costs that are borne by others than the individual buyer and seller, and manipulations to 'externalise' costs and let others bear the costs of production and to 'internalize' benefits without paying for them are standard behaviour for companies in a market economy. Today, the most obvious example must be CO_2 emissions causing climate change with potentially catastrophic results for the whole planet. When one thinks of it, *most of* our acts of production and consumption involve externalities. As a result, markets usually overproduce goods and services when there are negative externalities associated with their production or consumption and underproduce goods and services when there are positive externalities. This means that the same aspect that makes market transactions convenient for the individual buyer and seller – excluding all other affected parties from the negotiations – is also a *major* source of inefficiency.

Second, if it is true that markets with weak competition lead to inefficient allocation of resources, then it needs to be observed that the trend is towards less competition, not more. Markets that require large investments in fixed assets or research and development have an inherent tendency to concentrate due to economy of scale by which a company's per-unit costs decrease as a result of the possibility to spread large up-front expenses to more units. Another type of market with an inherent tendency to concentrate are markets that involve networks, such as air travel, electric power or Internet services, since the value of a network is increased the larger it gets. Examples of companies with huge market power in network markets are Apple and Microsoft in the software market and Google in the search engine market.

Finally, equilibrium is not a default state, and markets often fail to balance supply and demand because of speculation. When buyers and sellers speculate, they often create a large excess demand that drives up prices, eventually leading to a 'market bubble' or excess supply driving prices down, leading to a 'market crash.' As the history of the last few hundred years shows very clearly, market bubbles and crashes are recurring events. The most recent example of a market bubble with pervasive consequences for the whole capitalist system was, of course, the 2007–2009 financial crisis, the effects of which are still reverberating.

In summary then, markets are not as stable or efficient as many people like to think. This means that any economy which seeks to be fairer, more inclusive and more sustainable can't simply assume that markets will do the work for us.

An anarchist economy

Ever since the days of Proudhon, anarchists have agreed that private ownership of productive resources is not compatible with a fair and democratic society since it gives the decisions about what to produce and invest, how to organize production and how to allocate the results of production to the owners of capital, who are separated from the people who actually do all the work. An anarchist economy will have different decision makers compared to capitalist or state socialist economies, and the overall challenge for an anarchist economy is to allocate power and influence to workers and consumers and at the same time protect the interests of other groups in the economy that are affected by their actions.

The accounting system of an anarchist economy must facilitate the creation and distribution of the information that these new decision makers need in order to make efficient and fair decisions and, as far as possible, simplify such decisions. To understand the new challenges that such an accounting system will meet, we need to take a closer look at how a developed anarchist economy could organize its decisions about production, consumption and allocation of resources.

While anarchism is a theory of organization which questions top-down decision making, hierarchy, markets and so on, many anarchists have been hesitant to describe alternative social structures and decision-making procedures, especially with regard to decisions about investments, what to produce and how to allocate consumption rights. One of the best known exceptions is participatory economics, which is a model for how we can organize a modern economy around anarchist values and was first presented in 1991 in two books by Michael Albert and Robin Hahnel. Since then, it has been discussed and further developed in numerous books and articles.

A participatory economy aims at maximizing economic democracy or self-management, which means that influence over a decision is determined by how much a person is affected by the decision. Decision making must therefore take place in democratic worker and consumer councils and their respective federations, where members discuss and vote on decisions regarding their own affairs. All members have equal rights, and all members have one vote. The worker council would be the highest decision-making body of the workplace and is the equivalent to the general meeting in a limited liability company, where only shareholders are represented. The worker councils may form federations at different industry levels to deal with issues affecting multiple workplaces and wider issues affecting the industry; they can also delegate decision making to smaller teams of workers inside their workplaces and implement various majority rules for different types of decisions, in order to promote self-management.

However, democratic influence in a workplace where each member has one vote does not necessarily mean that all members have the same skills for participation in the decision-making process. Workers whose daily tasks mostly involve planning, analyzing, negotiating and so on necessarily develop a greater ability, knowledge and self-confidence to present, evaluate and argue for or against proposals in meetings compared to members whose daily activities mainly consist of performing tasks that others have designed. Therefore, in a participatory economy, the workplaces are expected, to the extent possible, to bundle together the necessary work tasks into so called *balanced jobs*, which each on average contain a similar set of both empowering and more menial and tedious tasks. To the extent that each job is balanced in this way, members get reasonably similar opportunities to participate in the workplace decision making.

A participatory economy also aims at maximizing economic justice, that is to say, how access to society's produced goods and services should be shared among citizens. Today, many people accept or even aim for income inequality, which in theory is based on one's contribution to production, with some complementary need-based consumption. The more productive one's work and/or capital is, the greater the income one is entitled to according to this principle, though some on the left question whether owners of capital should be paid a 'rent' on the money that they already have. Wages that are set and determined in labour markets are expected, at least in theory, to comply with this 'productivity principle.' In reality, however, the distribution of income primarily depends on the relative bargaining power of workers and not solely on their productivity, though the latter may certainly affect bargaining power.

Advocates of the participatory economics model believe that income, to be fair, should be based only on factors that one can affect. This would mean the effort and sacrifice in the form of longer working hours, higher work intensity or more socially useful tasks. The worker councils in a participatory economy are therefore expected to design and establish procedures to assess different sorts of work. These assessments would then form the basis for the distribution of the members' income among themselves.

The wider coordination of economic relations between producers and consumers would be done via a decentralized democratic planning procedure called 'participatory planning' that replaces markets. The self-managed worker and consumer councils and federations propose and revise their own production and consumption plans regarding both individual and collective goods and services, over a number of iterations. The steps in the annual participatory planning procedure are simple. Workers suggest through their worker councils and industry federations what they want to produce; consumers suggest through their neighbourhood councils and consumer federations what they want to consume. Then indicative prices for all final and intermediate goods and services, categories of labour and productive resources are updated based on excess supply or demand, and the steps are repeated in a number of iterations until a feasible plan is achieved (i.e. until there no longer exists any excess supply or demand for any product or service in the economy).

The proposals would also require approval by other councils and federations, who simply vote on whether to approve them or not. Worker councils decide if production proposals made by other worker councils are making use of scarce resources responsibly by comparing the estimated benefits to society of the goods and services they propose to produce with the opportunity cost of using the capital goods, natural resources and labour, as well as the social cost of producing the intermediate goods they are asking for. On the consumer side, consumer councils compare the total social cost of the proposed consumption of other councils with the consumers' income. There is no central planning board that approves the plans because they have been developed in a bottom-up, participatory manner.

Accounting challenges

A long-term anarchist alternative to the market system must be genuinely democratic and enable those affected by the decisions to influence them through a bottom-up structure of industrial and geographic federations. It must also be decentralized without any central planning bureaucracy, generate the necessary information and reveal real social benefits and costs for different alternative economic actions, including effects on other people as well as on the environment. Finally, it must encourage participation without being too time-consuming or boring. The 'economy' must become something that everyone controls, not something that is used as an explanation for inequality within and between states and an excuse for not decarbonizing our businesses.

The goal of an accounting system for an anarchist economy would be to enable affected parties and decision makers to quickly form an opinion about the effects of economic activities and investments and to understand who will be burdened with costs, who will enjoy benefits and whether the allocation of burdens and benefits is fair. One important task when designing such a system is to think about how the classification and categorization of goods, services, labour and productive resources should be done for the planning procedure to result in prices that reflect social costs and opportunity costs as accurately as possible.

There are four accounting issues or problems that will be essential for an accounting system in an anarchist economy organized along the lines of participatory economics to solve in order to enable decision makers to make fair and efficient decisions (Sandström, 2018).

First, consumers and producers have different interests regarding the categorization of goods and services. In a participatory economy, both consumers and producers are expected to participate in the annual planning procedure by proposing their planned consumption and production in the coming year. In a developed economy, there is normally a very large variety of available goods and services, and consumers and producers will have very different desires and requirements regarding the categorization of these goods and services for democratic planning of production and consumption to be possible. Consumers presumably want categories with as few details as possible to consider when planning their consumption. Producers, in contrast, need to consider potential differences in resource utilization for the production of different varieties of goods and services when preparing their production proposals and therefore need to work with more detailed information. And both consumers and producers will need to be able to adjust their proposals as time progresses.

Secondly, the costs charged to worker councils for their use of labour will not correspond with the workers' individual remuneration, as in a capitalist or socialist market economy. The worker councils' costs for using different categories of labour should reflect opportunity costs, while members' incomes should be based on effort and sacrifice.

Thirdly, in a participatory economy, productive assets, such as land, factories, machines and tools, belong to all the citizens in society, and the worker councils' costs for getting access to these resources do not necessarily correspond to their historical acquisition costs but should reflect the assets' current opportunity costs.

Finally, in a participatory economy, society's costs in terms of negative environmental or social effects resulting from activities of producers and consumers are borne by those who cause them and not by other people in society. Those who suffer from the effects of particular forms of production or consumption must be compensated.

An accounting system for a participatory economy must handle all of these challenges, as well as facilitating longer-term investment and strategic planning procedures. It must identify the accounting entities (worker and consumer councils and their federations) whose economic activities and transactions need to be recorded and monitored in order to facilitate effective and fair decisions based on the values of the economy. It must also define, categorize and quantify all different varieties of goods, services, capital, resources and emissions of polluting substances so that consumers and workers can understand them in an efficient and accurate way. And finally, it needs to facilitate the allocation of pay, costs and benefits to the accounting entities in ways that, to the extent possible, correctly reflect workers' actual effort and sacrifice in their workplaces and worker councils' contributions to and utilization of the economy's resources. These are big issues, but what is at stake here is the future of our economy and even our planet.

Conclusion

In a democratic economy in which giving people control over decisions that affect their lives is a goal, there can be no investors or owners of capital who own factories and other means of production and thus control what is produced or how production is organized. This sort of power results in continual attempts to seek maximum return on investment without regard to adverse effects on other groups in society or to the environment. Nor can there be groups of workers – managers or accountants – whose sole task is to obey orders or to perform monotonous and repetitive tasks while others make all the decisions and monopolize tasks that provide access to information and power. Any differences in income must be relatively small and based only on differences in the choices people make regarding levels of effort or sacrifice and not on differences that are beyond individual or collective control, such as being born in a position to access education or some of sort of opportunity which is denied to others.

These practical ideas about how we could obtain, sort and present financial information to promote democratic decision-making and economic cooperation will have a positive and beneficial impact on how our lives are organized. The ideas of participatory economics will assist and improve the development of new alternative economic institutions, such as self-managed workplaces or consumer associations. This means that any future accounting system will have to constantly change, developing to mirror but also affect the design of the key institutions of the economy, such as the ownership of productive capital, how capital and resources are allocated, new technologies and new understandings of value (see Chapter 10). An anarchist economy, organized around self-governing democratic workplaces and neighbourhoods cooperating together, will need accounting information. The difference between this and accounting in a capitalist system is that the information will be used to help produce democratic decision making, equity and solidarity. Accounting could give power to the people.

Questions for further study

1   Some people argue that capitalism is the only system that is compatible with human nature. What needs and potentials are part of our human nature and what needs and potentials are produced by the kinds of institutions we work in and the different spheres of social life we live in?
2   Climate change is one obvious devastating externality, but what are some other examples of negative *and positive* externalities? Are there any economic activities that don't have any external effects?
3   How would including externalities in price formation affect prices of different goods and services, such as food, public transport, cars and housing? What goods and services would be more expensive, and what goods and services would be cheaper when externalities are included?
4   If an anarchist economy would decide to prioritize free time instead of work and consumption, how could this be implemented, and what are the pros and cons of different ways to do this?
5   How would the performing of accounting tasks on different levels (i.e. the role of accountants) in an anarchist economy differ from today? Who would be involved in accounting tasks, and what kind of status would they have?

References

Abidor, M. (ed.). (2016). *Death to Bourgeois Society: The Propagandists of the Deed.* San Francisco, CA: PM Press.

Albert, M., and Hahnel, R. (1991a). *Looking Forward: Participatory Economics for the Twenty First Century.* Boston, MA: South End Press.

Albert, M., and Hahnel, R. (1991b). *The Political Economy of Participatory Economics.* Princeton, NJ: Princeton University Press.

Bastani, A. (2019). *Fully Automated Luxury Communism.* London: Verso.

Global Justice Now. (2016). Available at: www.globaljustice.org.uk/news/2016/sep/12/10-biggest-corporations-make-more-money-most-countries-world-combined (accessed July 2019).

Hahnel, R. (2012). *Of the People, by the People: The Case for a Participatory Economy.* Oakland, CA: AK Press.

Kropotkin, P. (1906/1995). *The Conquest of Bread and Other Writings.* Cambridge: Cambridge University Press.

Lapavitsas, C., and Mendieta-Muñoz, I. (2016). "The Profits of Financialization." *Monthly Review,* 68(3).

Marx, K. (2008). *Critique of the Gotha Programme.* Rockville, MD: Wildside Press.

Roslender, R. (ed.). (2017). *The Companion to Critical Accounting.* London: Routledge.

Sandström, A. (2018). *Anarchist Accounting: Accounting Principles for a Participatory Economy.* London: Glowbox Design Co-op.

PART V

New technology and new economy

12

THE COLLABORATIVE AND SHARING ECONOMY

Ozan Ağlargöz and Feyza Ağlargöz

Open any management textbook and you will see technology mentioned as one of the most important factors influencing organizational design. Technology supposedly even determines how societies are organized, with the Fordist production line and McDonaldized fast food being just two very well-known examples of how developments in technology have been seen to shape the wider world and how we behave in it. So what about collaboration – the 'sharing economy' or 'gig economy' of Lyft, Airbnb, LiftShare, P2P lending, crowdsourcing and so on? Mobile developers at Upwork (www.upwork.com), transcribers at Mechanical Turk (www.mturk.com/mturk/welcome), assembly workers hired from TaskRabbit (www.taskrabbit.com) for your newly bought IKEA bookshelf and an Uber driver who drives you back from an all-night party are all examples of workers working in the gig economy. How has technology played a role in making these forms of work possible? And have these technological developments also played a role in redefining how society operates? Do we (as some **techno-optimists** might claim, see box in Chapter 13) now live in a collaborative, sharing or gig society?

In this chapter, we will explore both the darkest and the brightest visions of collaboration using anarchist ideas as our guide. It has been suggested that the importance of collaborative technology means we are witnessing a shift from one economic era to another (e.g. Barley and Kunda, 2006). Are we? Or is this just a new version of technologically enabled capitalism? The nature of work and employment has certainly changed and will likely continue changing during the 21st century, but to what extent does this justify talk of a new form of economy? Whether this is a consequence of an explicit strategy or the unintentional consequence of technological development (Barley, Bechky, and Milliken, 2017), it is clear that some sort of change is real and here to stay. If we take a pessimistic stance and suggest that modern management and organizational practices have not served our society well (Cunliffe, 2014, pp. 136–137), does this then mean that new forms of technologically assisted management and organizational practices should be contemplated? And what is the role of collaboration and sharing in this change, either in the work itself or in collective resistance to its damaging consequences? After all, it might be that we find anarchist ideas of **mutualism** to be stimulated by the individualization of the contemporary gig worker (see box in Chapter 17). The issue for this chapter is whether we can use these ideas to help us change work and society for the better or whether we will be unable to solve our contemporary problems with the same kinds of thinking that we have used to create them.

This chapter will

- review what various authors have said about collaboration and sharing in consumption and work,
- describe the recent transformations related to the gig economy and their consequences in the labour market, and
- discuss some alternative options for contemporary collaborative processes.

Collaboration in consumption and work

Collaborative consumption and work are not new. *Minga* in Latin, *dugnad* in Nordic and *imece* in Turkish are the actions denoting not only voluntary efforts put together in collaboration for social usefulness but also traditional ways of organizing work within these language communities. And yes, these everyday arrangements are anarchist (see Chapter 17). Recalling the etymological root of the term *anarchy*, these are examples of some of the many ways of working and consuming without centralized and hierarchical authority. As we have seen in the rest of this book, the abolition of private property and of monetary exchange, barter, self-management and voluntary participation are all inherent both in collaborative movements and in anarchism.

Since the rise of consumer capitalism two centuries ago, we have been encouraged to think of buying for private consumption as the dominant model for the acquisition of goods and services (Buczynski, 2013), but it has never been the only model. Considering all the contemporary excitement around collaboration, Sundararajan (2016) asks what is new and interesting about borrowing someone's home, 'getting a ride,' borrowing a car, sharing a meal, lending money or getting help with your home improvements? Given the historical precedents, be it a business model, consumer identity or a political movement, one might easily envisage the sharing economy becoming central to a new way of producing and consuming. Indeed, the existence of many collaborative practices, combined with the problems of neo-capitalist ideals due to ongoing crises and the pursuit of more sustainable ways of organizing, seem to suggest that it is the logical alternative for our era (Atsushi, 2014; Botsman and Rogers, 2011; Gansky, 2010). Consuming and working collaboratively promises the worker emancipation from a permanent career within a large corporation and hence provides an opportunity to become a micro-entrepreneur selling whatever goods and services one is interested in. However, consumers can carry on buying whatever they want, be it a queuing service for their favourite brunch place by using the LaborMe app or someone to look after their pet while they are away (White and Koltrowitz, 2017). For both workers and consumers, all these services are available on-demand through their connected devices. It seems like a utopian future, but is it an anarchist one?

Although complementing consumption and work with collaborative ideals often seems well-intentioned, the recent rise of collaboration is not uncomplicated. When capitalism goes through a period of crisis, such as in the case of the Great Depression in the 1930s or the financial crash of 2007–8, it regenerates itself by employing new technologies, new organizational forms, new modes of exploitation, new types of jobs and new markets (Srnicek, 2017, p. 32). Collaborative technologies and forms of work may be a part of this, but the process has not gone without resistance. Uber has had many problems and scandals, with its service being suspended in some cities partly because of protests from taxi drivers and suggestions that its drivers were not properly vetted, as well as being badly paid. Airbnb's micro-entrepreneurs were being heavily criticized in cities like Barcelona, Berlin and New York for their effect on local housing markets. In addition, the sharing economy appears to be becoming the conventional economy. EasyCar club is owned by EasyJet, General Motors has invested in Lyft, Zipcar was bought by the conventional capitalist firm Avis Group for $500 million in 2013 and TaskRabbit was acquired by IKEA in 2017.

In their mainstream management textbook, Ebert and Griffin (2017) define entrepreneurship as the process of seeking business opportunities under conditions of risk. For the same authors, entrepreneurs are said to be people who accept both the risks and the opportunities involved in creating and operating a new business venture. Entrepreneurship and innovation are said to be the greatest engines of growth and market disruption (see Chapter 16). Readers have most probably come across Tom Goodwin's highly circulated quote: 'Uber, the world's largest taxi company, owns no vehicles. Facebook, the world's most popular media owner, creates no content. Alibaba, the most valuable retailer, has no inventory. And Airbnb, the world's largest accommodation provider, owns no real estate. Something interesting is happening' (2015). But is something *really* interesting happening, or is this just a new capitalist strategy for maximizing profit? And does this having something to do with anarchist ideas about different forms of organization?

Today, whenever we are surprised by something new, we quickly begin to come across the same thing again and again, wearing out its newness. With new technologies and forms of organizing work spreading so fast, it is perhaps a feeling of sameness rather than newness that characterizes the current period, as whatever is new quickly becomes commonplace and unremarkable. How the new becomes widespread is the subject matter of the diffusion process tradition (Greenwood et al., 2008) within what is generally called neo-institutional theory (DiMaggio and Powell, 1991). We might believe that the diffusion of collaborative consumption and work would be rapid and uncontested, but the evidence suggests that problems, like the ones stated earlier, are obvious. This means that the future of 'post-industrial' or 'post-capitalist' organizing is still far from clear. We believe that scrutinizing the institutional cracks and clashes that occur during the diffusion process of collaborative consumption and work might allow us to understand the merits of collaborative ideals and perhaps protect them from the interests of big corporations. Otherwise, the result will be nothing but more of the same.

The sharing economy

Although there is no strict definition, we will consider the sharing economy as the consumption side of the collaboration coin. What do people claim is new about the sharing economy? First, by using technology, the new version extends the limits of collaboration beyond family and friends to much more expansive spaces and times. Secondly, the digital marketplace, powered by technology, shifted power from traditional corporations to crowd entrepreneurs. The sharing economy is market-based and puts underutilized labour and resources to productive use, allowing people's time and technology to be allocated where it can be of use. It relies on crowd-based networks and complicates not only what we know as employment and work but also the boundary between the personal and the professional (Sundararajan, 2016). Gansky (2010) labels the typical business model in the sharing economy as a 'mesh' business. Mesh businesses offer something shareable (i.e. less frequently used, relatively expensive physical products), supported by advanced web and mobile technology, and connects users both via word of mouth and through social networks. Stephany (2015, p. 9) suggests that there is 'value in taking underutilized assets and making them accessible online to a community which leads to a reduced need for ownership of those assets' as the desirable outcome of the sharing economy.

In an ideal sharing economy, it is expected that there will be more options for its participants, a better future in terms of sustainable production and consumption and increased and denser forms of social interaction. Sharing emancipates and provides autonomy for its participants. It seems that we can easily argue that the pure sharing economy overlaps with the ideas of anarcho-communists like **Bakunin, Kropotkin** (see boxes in Chapters 7 and 3) and Goldman in many ways, particularly with reference to the collective use of property. But is this sort of diagnosis justified? The reality of our times produces diversified hybrid forms in which collaborative and commercial logics collide. Sundararajan (2016) raises a series of important questions about the sharing economy. Is it

> Capitalist or socialist? Commercial economy or gift economy? Market or hierarchy? Global or local economic impact? Regulatory arbitrage or self-regulatory expression? Centralized or decentralized value capture? Empowered entrepreneur or disenfranchised drone? Job destruction or work creation? Isolated or connected societies?
>
> *(p. 205)*

While scrutinizing what the sharing economy is, in the end, Sundarajan's (2016) answer is 'yes' to each of them, highlighting how the sharing economy escapes easy description and hence judgement. Nonetheless, he goes on to claim that the sharing economy will result in a democratization of economic opportunity that promises inclusive growth. For optimists, the concept of 'we-conomy' used by Stephany (2015) is a description that seems to capture the possibilities for an anti-hierarchical pattern of exchange in which sellers and buyers can transact without the dominance of large corporations.

EMMA GOLDMAN, 1869–1940

One of a small number of women in the history of traditional anarchist thought, Emma Goldman is one of its most important names. Having been born in the Russian Empire (modern-day Lithuania) to a Jewish family and then emigrating to the United States, Goldman became an active witness of all sorts of tectonic political changes taking place in Europe and North America. She was a prolific writer and activist speaking on a number of diverse issues, including capitalism, use of violence, sexuality, atheism, militarism and many others. Goldman parted ways with the suffragette movement, believing that women can be as easily corrupted as men in a voting process. However, she found many ways to incorporate gender politics into anarchism and generally asserted that patriarchy is another form of hierarchy like state or class to be done away with. Because of this, she is often called a founder of **anarcha-feminism** (see box in Chapter 4). Pertinent to the context of this book is the fact that Emma Goldman was an astute critic of capitalism, seeing it as a system dehumanizing people and depriving them of their liberty.

Gig work

'It's been called the Gig Economy, Freelance Nation, the Rise of the Creative Class, and the e-conomy, with the "e" standing for electronic, entrepreneurial, or perhaps eclectic,' says Horowitz (2011), while pointing out the major characteristics of work in the new economy. Although much attention has been given to gig work by the popular media, this labour side of the collaboration coin is relatively under-researched due to difficulties related to access to a fragmented population of workers and inherent complexities related to any definition. This empirical neglect is also highlighted by De Stefano (2016) concerning the legal rights of people engaged in gig work. It's easy enough to celebrate gig work in the abstract, but much of the work that it involves might be poorly paid and precarious.

There is also an ongoing debate whether the actual growth of the gig economy is a myth or a reality (De Stefano, 2016; Kuhn, 2016). Based on country statistics compiled by Stewart and Stanford (2017), it seems to be that the trend is exaggerated and concentrated in certain cities in the Global North. Of course, it might be that traditional labour force surveys are not useful to measure the rise of such an informal and diverse economy (Kuhn, 2016). It might also be that there is not one gig economy. For example, at the time of writing, Handy, providing home services, has a workforce of 5000 people, whereas Crowdsource has eight million members. These latter numbers alone make some parts of the gig economy a significant phenomenon (De Stefano, 2016). So we are not simply talking about small-scale non-hierarchical communities, but Big Gig players which seem very far away from anarchist ideas of everyday co-operation and **prefigurative** organization (see box in Chapter 2).

Indeed, much of this work is not that new anyway. 'Contingent' or 'flexible' labour are terms which have long been used by economists and sociologists to describe part-time work, temporary employment, subcontracting, outsourcing and home-based work (Barley and Kunda, 2006). Low-paid contingent labour usually comes with no security, pension or social benefits (Kalleberg, Reskin, and Hudson, 2000). The dual labour market theory suggests that 'secondary' jobs will always be for 'secondary' people – women, ethnic minorities, migrants and so on. However, the recent rise of the gig economy has also affected 'primary' jobs in which people take stable employment and career advancement for granted (Barley and Kunda, 2006).

Online platforms unbundle jobs into separate tasks and directly connect buyers and sellers (Farrell and Greig, 2016). The fundamental characteristics of gig work are not new, but the technology backing its growth is developing rapidly (Stewart and Stanford, 2017). Platforms are digital infrastructures that enable two or more groups to interact (Srnicek, 2017, p. 36). Farrell and Greig (2016, p. 5) define the gig economy, which they prefer to call the online platform economy, as economic activities involving an online intermediary that provides a platform by which independent workers or sellers can sell a distinct service or good to customers. There are many attempts to distinguish different types of gig work from each other. For example, Farrell and Greig (2016) made a distinction between labour platforms and capital platforms. According to these authors, labour platforms 'connect customers with freelance or contingent workers who perform discrete tasks or projects,' whereas capital platforms 'connect customers with individuals who rent assets or sell goods peer-to-peer.' Well-known examples of labour platforms may include TaskRabbit and Mechanical Turk. Platforms such as eBay or Airbnb are popular examples of capital platforms.

De Stefano (2016) provides a further distinction within labour platforms which he talks about as crowdwork systems and work-on-demand via app systems. Generally, tasks which can be priced, worked on and delivered online are subject to crowdwork systems through open websites. Here the platform provides a market-like environment matching workers with potential purchasers. Crowdwork systems connect a network of 'partners' – organizations and people collaborating on a global basis. Generally, tasks are extremely micro, menial and sometimes boring, but they require human intervention (e.g. tagging photos). In some other cases, larger and more meaningful work is crowdsourced (i.e. website development). Work-on-demand via app systems can provide solutions for buyers of labour who previously had to employ people in more traditional ways and with better guarantees. The platforms characterized as work-on-demand via app systems are also managed by companies which control the important aspects of the service being provided, such as sales, marketing and HR. There are inherent differences between crowdwork systems and work-on-demand via app systems in terms of payment and labour regulations. Payment is usually decentralized in crowdwork systems, centralized in work-on-demand via apps. Work-on-demand via app systems take more responsibility for core HR functions, such as selection, supervision and discipline than crowdwork systems (Stewart and Stanford, 2017). Crowdwork systems are more like a technologically enhanced version of capitalism as we know it, whereas work-on-demand via app systems could be imagined to be post-capitalist, at least in the sense that they appear to decentralize more of the decision making for both buyers and sellers.

Sundararajan (2016) claims that crowd-based capitalism will necessarily reshape state regulatory frameworks for work, social insurance, pensions and so on. The times and spaces of work will be very different in the future, but this is in part because much labour will then become precarious, short term and with no guarantees (De Stefano, 2016). For this reason, Stewart and Stanford (2017) argue that the regulatory problems should be overcome by creating rights for workers, not for employees. In that sense, policymakers should acknowledge that a driver is 'a driver' whether employed by a taxi company or through an Uber platform. This is a move towards the idea of workers as individual traders, not members of organizations who might be represented by trade unions involved in collective bargaining. For some scholars (Born and Witteloostuijn, 2013; Kitching and Smallbone, 2012; Kuhn, 2016), such freelancers have been defined as professionals providing expert services and depicted more as an entrepreneur rather than a worker. In that sense, people may view gig work as a useful way of fighting against income volatility (Farrell and Greig, 2016).

However, workers with entrepreneurial abilities, specialized skills, deep expertise or in-demand experience will be the winners of an economy which rewards those who can successfully pitch their skills (Mulcahy, 2016). Barley and Kunda (2006, p. 48) claim that making deals in the platform economy is more like 'haggling in a bazaar rather than shopping at the suburban mall . . . a bazaar without clear spatial and temporal boundaries.' Relatively secure employees become insecure entrepreneurs selling their skills, at the same time that they are being described as freeing themselves from the coercions and inefficiencies of bureaucracy.

Precarious work

Post-Fordist ideas about flexible or contingent labour became popularly discussed during the 1980s as a part of firms' overall outsourcing strategy. Since then, we have witnessed a tremendous growth of independent contractors and temporary workers. In the age of 'flexibility,' contingent labour was used for buffering purposes for seasonal ups and downs whilst facing fewer 'people issues' (Barley and Kunda, 2006) as well as cutting costs.

During the 1990s, understandings of the benefits of flexibility varied widely. Some cautioned that the expansion of contingent labour downgraded full-time employment and threatened the security of the workforce. Others believed that this expansion freed labour from outmoded industrialist loyalty-based working regimes and thus provided an opportunity for workers to regain the surplus value that they produced (Barley and Kunda, 2006). A growing number of people, according to Sundararajan (2016), started to feel worried about the future of work. After all, the key features of gig work are irregular work schedules, most or all of the capital used for completing the task is invested by the worker, there is no designated work-place, pay is based on a piece-rate payment system and the work generally requires some form of digital platform for mediation (Stewart and Stanford, 2017). In order to soften the negative aspects, optimistic euphemisms such as sharing economy, crowdsourcing or the collaborative economy are used to sell the idea of digitized irregular work (Sundararajan, 2016). So, perhaps the new economy isn't really that new or that attractive to workers?

> Today, careers consist of piecing together various types of work, juggling multiple clients, learning to be marketing and accounting experts, and creating offices in bedrooms/coffee shops/coworking spaces. Independent workers abound. We call them freelancers, contractors, sole proprietors, consultants, temps, and the self-employed.

This is how the Freelancers Union founder Sara Horowitz (2011) describes today's workforce. App based and platform technology now allows the outsourcing of what writers on 'post-Fordism' in the 1990s called 'functional' and 'numerical' flexibility (Kalleberg, 2011). It is now possible to contract out even CEO positions by using specialized staffing agencies. If labour supply exceeds labour demand, then platforms do not feel obliged to provide health insurance or pensions. The financial crisis of 2007–8 accelerated an erosion in workers' earnings and consequently increased their vulnerability to exploitative working conditions (Srnicek, 2017). This so-called 'demutualization of risk' means that in modern labour markets, employers can transfer costs and uncertainties from themselves to employees (De Stefano, 2016; King, 2014). Constant employment uncertainty means that gig workers live between feast and famine, and for many, the meaning of employment is redefined (Armstrong, 2017; Paulsen, 2014; Aubenas, 2011; Maier, 2004). Even those who teach you might be gig workers, precarious part-time academics with rent to pay (Hall, 2015; Standing, 2011). In any case, using temporary workers (or temps) for cost-cutting purposes might backfire in the long run. Simulations conducted by Fisher and Connely (2017) revealed that if temps are given the opportunity to become permanent workers, they work more effectively.

So if the collaborative economy is so one-sided in its power relations, then can it truly deserve comparison with anarchist ideas about the future of labour? It is certainly possible to describe gig work in terms of escaping hierarchical decision making, collectivizing provision of goods and services and the autonomy of the worker. The question is whether this is just window dressing for externalizing the costs of labour and capital, whilst big companies make even higher profits.

Conclusion

> Amazon Mechanical Turk and its affiliates ('**we**,' '**us**,' or '**our**') provide the Site to you subject to this Agreement.
>
> (https://worker.mturk.com/check_registration)

Who is this 'we, us, and our' in this section from the Amazon Mechanical Turk contract? One might expect that, in light of the inherent characteristics of collaborative consumption and work, it must be gig workers. In this contract, however, it is the company. The exaggerated promises for collaborative consumption and work highlighted by this apparent contradiction may be just some of the new features of a new form of capitalism. 'Are we heading toward an economy in which the on-demand many serve the privileged few?' asks Sundararajan (2016). Risk, uncertainty and employment insecurity have been endemic in market economies throughout the 20th century, but they were moderated by regulation by the state and collective bargaining by trade unions (King, 2014). Working individually in globally dispersed settings makes it hard for gig workers to be aware of their legal and regulatory rights, thus making collective action very difficult (Stewart and Stanford, 2017). Grassroots organizations such as Turkopticon, created by Amazon's Mechanical Turk taskers, or unionization attempts like the Freelancers Union mentioned earlier seem to be viable options for resistance. 'Turkopticon helps the people in the "crowd" of crowdsourcing watch out for each other – because nobody else seems to be' (https://turkopticon.ucsd.edu/). The Freelancers Union stands to strengthen the network and resources available for members, most of whom are working alone and facing various types of exclusion from basic employment and labour laws. The Freelancers Union is established as an insurance scheme and describes the tensions between individualism and collectivism through a philosophy they call the new mutualism. These characteristics are replicable – for example in the form of platform **co-operatives** (Scholz and Schneider, 2016, see box in Chapter 8) – and promise solidarity among a growing precariat. If we need new trade unions to counter the power of the new capitalists, these organizations of precarious, freelance, gig economy workers seem to be a solution. This means moving away from traditional left-wing mass unionization to locally organized forms of mutual solidarity. It might be that it is this collective resistance to the gig economy that might actually be the anarchist response, rather than the gig economy itself.

The answers to these questions go beyond the purely economic, if such a sphere of human life could ever be imagined. Anarchists have always understood that work is an integral part of what it means to live a rewarding and meaningful life, and hence a great deal of their writing and activism has focused on the organization of production and consumption. In most strands of anarchism, it is only social exchange that brings the responsibility, gratitude and trust that pure economic exchange cannot (Blau, 1964, p. 94; see also Chapter 17). Work should be an answer to the question, 'Who am I?', not merely a way of selling labour time in return for money. This means that an anarchist interpretation of a collaborative economy needs to address this need for **identity** (see box in Chapter 4), for a common culture, as well as for clear protections over the control and ownership of labour. As we have seen in other chapters of this book, on crowdsourcing or bitcoin, for example (see the other chapters in this section), technology does not determine social relations, so we should always be sceptical when someone suggests that society has changed. It is politics that determines social relations and that will shape the possibilities of an anarchist version of work and organization based on sharing labour and resources whilst avoiding hierarchy. The emergence of a genuinely mutual, co-operative version of the collaborative economy is possible, but it is not guaranteed.

Questions for further study

1   Imagine you are working for a ride-sharing company such as UBER or Lyft. Who do you think is your boss? What is the relationship between you and the customer, on the one hand, and you and the employer, on the other?
2   How would you define the sharing economy? How is it different from the forms of capitalism that came before it?
3   Based on what you know about anarchism from the various chapters in this book, what aspects of the sharing economy do you think fit well with anarchism? How could an anarchist version of the sharing economy be structured? What threats would there be to this kind of economy?
4   Flexible, contingent work has in the past promised freedom for those carrying out this work. Based on what you have read about the sharing economy and the problems it has created, do you agree with this?

References

Armstrong, S. (2017). *The New Poverty*. London; New York, NY: Verso.
Atsushi, M. (2014). *The Rise of Sharing: Fourth-Stage Consumer Society in Japan*. Tokyo: International House of Japan.
Aubenas, F. (2011). *The Night Cleaner*. Cambridge: Polity Press.
Barley, S. R., Bechky, B. A., and Milliken, F. J. (2017). "The Changing Nature of Work: Careers, Identities, and Work Lives in the 21st Century." *Academy of Management Discoveries*, 3(2), 111–115. http://doi.org/10.5465/amd.2017.0034
Barley, S. R., and Kunda, G. (2006). "Contracting: A New Form of Professional Practice." *Academy of Management Perspectives*, 20(1), 45–66.
Blau, P. M. (1964). *Exchange and Power in Social Life*. New York, NY: John Wiley & Sons.
Born, A., and Witteloostuijn, A. (2013). "Drivers of Freelance Career Success." *Journal of Organizational Behavior*, 34, 24–46.

Botsman, R., and Rogers, R. (2011). *What's Mine Is Yours: How Collaborative Consumption Is Changing the Way We Live*. London: Harper Collins Publishers.

Buczynski, B. (2013). *Sharing Is Good*. Gabriola Island, BC: New Society Publishers.

Cunliffe, A. L. (2014). *A Very Short, Fairly Interesting and Reasonably Cheap Book About Management* (2nd Edition). London: Sage Publications.

De Stefano, V. (2016). *The Rise of the 'Just-in-Time Workforce': On-Demand Work, Crowd Work and Labour Protection in the 'Gig-Economy'*. International Labour Office, Inclusive Labour Markets, Labour Relations and Working Conditions Branch. 2016 Conditions of Work and Employment Series: No. 71. Geneva: ILO.

DiMaggio, P. J., and Powell, W. W. (1991). "Introduction." In P. J. DiMaggio and W. W. Powell (Eds.), *The New Institutionalism in Organizational Analysis*. Chicago, IL: University of Chicago Press.

Ebert, R. J., and Griffin, R. W. (2017). *Business Essentials* (Global 11th Edition). Essex: Pearson.

Farrell, D., and Greig, F. (2016). "Paychecks, Paydays, and the Online Platform Economy: Big Data on Income Volatility." *JP Morgan Chase & Co. Institute*. Available at: www.jpmorganchase.com/corporate/institute/document/jpmc-institute-volatility-2-report.pdf (accessed 2 June 2017).

Fisher, S. L., and Connely, C. E. (2017). "Lower Cost or Just Lower Value? Modeling the Organizational Costs and Benefits of Contingent Work." *Academy of Management Discoveries*, 3(2), 165–186.

Gansky, L. (2010). *The Mesh: Why the Future of Business Is Sharing?* New York, NY: Portfolio Penguin.

Goodwin, T. (2015). "The Battle Is for the Customer Interface." Available at: https://techcrunch.com/2015/03/03/in-the-age-of-disintermediation-the-battle-is-all-for-the-customer-interface/ (accessed 12 November 2017).

Greenwood, R., Oliver, C., Suddaby, R., and Sahlin-Andersson, K. (2008). "Introduction." In R. Greenwood, C. Oliver, R. Suddaby, and K. Sahlin-Andersson (Eds.), *The Sage Handbook of Organizational Institutionalism*. London: Sage Publications.

Hall, L. (2015). "I Am an Adjunct Professor Who Teaches Five Classes: I Earn Less Than a Pet-Sitter." Available at: www.theguardian.com/commentisfree/2015/jun/22/adjunct-professor-earn-less-than-pet-sitter (accessed 23 October 2017).

Horowitz, S. (2011). "The Freelancer Surge Is the Industrial Revolution of Our Time." *Atlantic*, 1 September. Available at: www.theatlantic.com/business/archive/2011/09/the-freelance-surge-is-the-industrial-revolution-of-our-time/244229.

Kalleberg, A. L. (2011). *Good Jobs, Bad Jobs: The Rise of Polarized and Precarious Employment Systems in the United States, 1970s to 2000s*. New York, NY: Russell Sage Foundation.

Kalleberg, A. L., Reskin, B. F., and Hudson, K. (2000). "Bad Jobs in America: Standard and Nonstandard Employment Relations and Job Quality in the United States." *American Sociological Review*, 65, 256–278.

King, M. W. (2014). "Protecting and Representing Workers in the New Gig Economy: The Case of the Freelancers Union." In R. Milkman and E. Ott (Eds.), *New Labor in New York: Precarious Workers and the Future of the Labor Movement*, pp. 150–170. Ithaca, NY: Cornell University Press.

Kitching, J., and Smallbone, D. (2012). "Are Freelancers a Neglected Form of Small Business?" *Journal of Small Business and Enterprise Development*, 19, 74–91.

Kuhn, K. M. (2016). "The Rise of the 'Gig Economy' and Implications for Understanding Work and Workers." *Industrial and Organizational Psychology*, 9(1), 157–162.

Maier, C. (2004). *Hello Laziness: Why Hard Work Doesn't Pay*. London: Orion.

168 Ozan Ağlargöz and Feyza Ağlargöz

Mulcahy, D. (2016). *The Gig Economy: The Complete Guide to Getting Better Work, Taking More Time Off, and Financing the Life You Want.* New York, NY: AMACOM.
Paulsen, R. (2014). *Empty Labor: Idleness and Workplace Resistance.* Cambridge: Cambridge University Press.
Scholz, T., and Schneider, N. (eds.). (2016). *Ours to Hack and to Own: The Rise of Platform Cooperativism.* New York, NY: OR Books.
Srnicek, N. (2017). *Platform Capitalism.* Cambridge: Polity Press.
Standing, G. (2011). *The Precariat: The New Dangerous Class.* London; New York, NY: Bloomsbury.
Stephany, A. (2015). *The Business of Sharing: Making It in the New Sharing Economy.* London: Palgrave Macmillan.
Stewart, A., and Stanford, J. (2017). "Regulating Work in the Gig Economy: What Are the Options?" *Economic and Labour Relations Review,* 28(3), 420–437.
Sundararajan, A. (2016). *The Sharing Economy: The End of Employment and the Rise of Crowd-Based Capitalism.* Cambridge, MA: Massachusetts Institute of Technology Press.
White, S., and Koltrowitz, S. (2017). "From Wine to Watches, Sharing Sites Offer Slice of Luxury." Available at: www.reuters.com/article/us-luxury-internet/from-wine-to-watches-sharing-sites-offer-slice-of-luxury-idUSKBN1EE1QG?utm_campaign=tru eAnthem:+Trending+Content&utm_content=5a3a789a04d301271df625e1&utm_ medium=trueAnthem&utm_source=twitter (accessed 23 December 2017).

13

CROWDSOURCING AND DIGITAL PLATFORMS

Andreas Kamstrup and Emil Husted

Over the past 50 years, digitalization has had (and continues to have) an immense influence on how work is conducted and what we understand by the idea of 'work.' While some jobs have become redundant and obsolete, others have emerged and proliferated. For instance, the diffusion of the personal computer from the late 1970s and onwards has helped minimize the need for secretaries to write memos, but it has also helped increase the demand for IT support. From the mid-1990s, information and communication technologies (ICTs), such as e-mail systems, websites and instant messaging applications began to play an important role in the organization of work, allowing a lot of 'white-collar work' to be carried out independently of traditional space and time constraints (e.g. Castells, 1996; Huws, 2003; Scholz, 2013). This meant that such work could now be conducted with little more than an Internet connection: reports could be read without printing them, e-mails could be answered, databases and servers could be accessed and meetings could be held through conferencing technology. Since the turn of the millennium, technologies such as blogs, wikis and social media applications have added yet another dimension to the reorganization of work, with the 'crowdsourced' user taking centre stage as the primary content creator. It is in this context that the notion of 'the platform' was introduced, as many of these participatory design technologies are marketed as interactive platforms where users meet, create and consume digital content (e.g. van Dijck and Nieborg, 2009).

But do these new technologies provide for new power relations, or are they disguising the ways in which exploitation continues to take place? Is the web a place of corporate control pretending to be liberation? In this chapter, we explore how crowdsourcing has been articulated in mainstream business and management practice and examine through two case studies the anarchist potential of crowdsourcing, focusing on what it means for crowdsourcing to reflect anarchist principles.

This chapter will

- provide a brief overview of how online crowdsourcing platforms have been used by corporations,
- discuss the different ways anarchists have approached the question of technology and its role in society and in social change,
- identify the concept of 'affordances' as useful in analyzing technologies like crowdsourcing platforms from an anarchist perspective,
- present two case studies that show in different ways how crowdsourcing platforms can be assessed through anarchist principles, and
- ask whether crowdsourcing can be considered anarchist.

The digital age and crowdsourcing in business and management

In popular management literature, it is commonly argued that the consequences of these technological developments are overwhelmingly positive, since they increase creativity and innovation and free the worker from tedious and strenuous labour (e.g. Anderson, 2012; Kelly, 2011; Rheingold, 2012). For instance, the influential tech writer and consultant Clay Shirky (2009) argues that we live in an age that privileges new forms of organizing not bound by traditional hierarchies and formal structures. According to him, new digital technologies have made it possible to 'organize without organizations,' in the sense that collaboration today has become much more seamless than before. Similarly, Bruns (2008) argues that digital technologies have blurred the boundary between consumers and producers to the point where everyone becomes a 'produser' (both producer and user) of content. Finally, in their handbook of organizational behaviour, Huczynski and Buchanan (2013, p. 84) are even more explicit in highlighting the benefits of digitalization in relation to work and organization, as they argue that 'the exercise of knowledge, creativity, and problem-solving skills requires more freedom and flexibility than traditional bureaucracy allows, and technology makes this possible.' In contrast to this rather techno–optimist view of digitalization, a less mainstream tradition assumes a more critical stance in arguing that digital technologies do not necessarily allow for more creative collaboration or emancipated workers. Instead, it is argued that new digital technologies have re-introduced and accentuated economic inequality (Fuchs, 2014), leading to the emergence of a large underpaid 'gig' workforce (here, Uber-drivers are a common example). In fact, some even argue that digital technologies have helped form a new cyber-proletariat who produce – but do not own – the technological infrastructure of the digital economy (Dyer-Witheford, 2015).

TECHNO-OPTIMISM

Techno-optimism is the belief that the development of technology is ultimately a good thing that will prove beneficial to people. It is often contrasted with techno-pessimism, where technological development is seen as essentially a negative thing. Both of these views can be found in anarchism, both in the past and today. For Peter **Kropotkin** (see box in Chapter 3), for example, science and technology were essential parts of any activity that would help liberate people from domination. Other anarchists, such as the contemporary primitivist John Zerzan, instead see all but the most basic technology as fundamentally oppressive. We can see this debate played out in how many anarchists and other radicals approach the question of social media like Facebook. For some, platforms like Facebook allow us to communicate effectively, form relationships and even plan revolutionary activity in non-hierarchical ways. For others, Facebook is an entity that exists solely to collect personal information about us and to allow that information to be used to control us through targeted advertising or political campaigning. There is, of course, a position that sits between techno-optimism and techno-pessimism. Murray **Bookchin** (see box in Chapter 10), argues that while how much of technology has developed today is strongly linked to attempts at controlling us (and indeed controlling nature), this does not mean that technology cannot be designed in ways that serve our interests and even help create more sustainable ecological relationships.

A flagship phenomenon of work in the 'digital age' is crowdsourcing. The word was initially coined by Howe (2006) as a portmanteau of *crowd* and *outsourcing*, and it is commonly agreed that crowdsourcing involves a task being posed and communicated (i.e. outsourced) to a group of decentralized and digitally organized people (i.e. the crowd), who then start solving the problem (Brabham, 2013; Estellés–Arolas and González-Ladrón-de-Guevara, 2012). Despite this, the organizational dynamics of crowdsourcing are still not well understood (Kamstrup, 2017). One reason is that crowdsourcing does not represent a unified phenomenon but instead a multitude of platforms and practices. While some enactments of crowdsourcing are profit-driven and structured as competitions, others are more voluntary and support collaboration. However, common to most types of crowdsourcing is that they unfold on a designated digital platform.

One well-known example of crowdsourcing is *LEGO Ideas*, where the toy manufacturer invites its fan community to come up with new products in return for a small share of the revenue. Another example is *InnoCentive*, a platform that offers companies access to a crowd of highly trained natural scientists, who then assist the companies with complex tasks. Both of these platforms manifest a competitive dynamic, where only the best uploads receive monetary rewards. Amazon's *Mechanical Turk* is an entirely different form of crowdsourcing, sometimes referred to as 'human intelligence tasks' or 'micro-tasks' (Difallah et al., 2015). Here, crowd members receive a fixed – albeit small – compensation in return for solving trivial tasks, such as identifying motives in pictures or completing questionnaires. A third type of crowdsourcing is citizen science platforms, such as *Zooniverse* or *eBird*, where the crowd works to address scientific issues by analyzing and categorizing large amounts of data. While the first three examples include monetary compensation, either based on competition or fixed rates, citizen science is typically based on voluntary work.

At a first glance, the decentralized and self-governing nature of crowdsourcing could be seen as squarely aligned with anarchist ideals of organization, most famously described by Ward (1973) as voluntary, functional, temporary and small. For instance, Barnes et al. (2013, p. 27) argue that

> crowdsourcing enables individuals to access opportunities for employment regardless of location, and so can be argued to provide opportunities for participation in the economy. Importantly, crowdsourcing platforms can be viewed as empowering individuals by creating and providing a space in which they can self-select work, be creative and/or interact to solve problems as part of a wider community.

In this view, crowdsourcing constitutes a unique opportunity for empowered individuals to free themselves from constraining contractual obligations, while simultaneously realizing their creative and innovative potential. However, others argue that crowdsourcing constitutes a modern form of exploitation where the remuneration is low and/or insecure (Kleemann, Voß, and Rieder, 2008), and that it is difficult for crowd members to organize themselves independently (Felstiner, 2011). In this chapter, we will shed some light on the relationship between crowdsourcing and anarchism by exploring two very distinct platforms: *Innosite* (a platform that hosts architectural competitions) and *Tag Del* (a platform focused on public deliberation and voluntary work). We examine if and how crowdsourcing can be considered anarchist, but first we unfold how the concept of technology has been understood in anarchist thinking.

The question of technology in anarchism

For more than a century, anarchist thinkers have been divided in their views on technology as a means for achieving a freer and less-authoritarian society. While some have celebrated technology's ability to alleviate the burden of manual labour, others have argued that technological change only reinforces domination (Gordon, 2009). For instance, whereas Peter **Kropotkin** saw the invention of the washing machine as a welcome opportunity to 'liberate women from household drudgery' (Marshall, 1992, p. 328; see box in Chapter 3), Pierre-Joseph **Proudhon** (1847, Ch. 4, see box in Chapter 2) argued that such 'mechanical progress' would only 'deepen the abyss that separates the class that commands and enjoys from the class that obeys and suffers.' Along similar lines, Jacques Ellul (1964) argued that modern technology has outgrown human control and reduced humans to cogs in the machine of technical civilization. More recently, technological advances have been linked to climate change and environmental degradation, particularly within the stream of thought called 'anarcho-primitivism,' where the return to a hunter-gatherer society is seen as the most viable road to emancipation (e.g. Pearlman, 1983; Zerzan, 1994).

Importantly, anarchist resistance towards technology is not only an academic phenomenon. Political activists inspired by anarchist thinking have likewise been engaged in struggles against a wide variety of new technologies, such as nuclear technology, nanotechnology, surveillance technology, warfare technology, synthetic biology and artificial intelligence. However, as Gordon (2008) argues, one type of technology usually escapes the critical gaze of contemporary anarchists, namely information and communication technologies (ICTs). Since the so-called 'Battle of Seattle' alter-globalization protests in 1999, activists around the world have used e-mail lists and websites to coordinate their actions and to spread their messages. With the advent of applications such as Facebook and Twitter, the embrace of ICTs has reached unprecedented heights within activist circles, leading scholars like Manuel Castells (2012) to argue that they allow leaderless movements to mobilize support and coordinate activities much more effectively than they could prior to the rise of what he calls 'technologies of freedom' (Castells, 2009, p. 414). Recently, however, accounts that question ICTs' ability to sustain anarchist ideals have emerged (e.g. Swann and Husted, 2017), indicating that a more nuanced understanding of the relationship between anarchism and technology may be needed.

Bookchin and the concept of affordances

The American philosopher and historian Murray **Bookchin** (see box in Chapter 10), dedicated most of his writings to establishing environmentalism – or as he called it 'ecology' – as an important area of concern for anarchist thinking, thereby contributing to the advancement of so-called 'green anarchism' (Marshall, 1992, and Chapter 10). Inspired by the positive perception of technological progress found in the work of Peter Kropotkin (and parts of **Marxist** thinking, see box in Chapter 11), Bookchin firmly believed that 'appropriate' technology would play an integral part in the dissolution of hierarchy and the emergence of a society based on social and environmental sustainability (Bookchin, 1980). However, unlike Kropotkin's occasionally naïve faith in mechanical progress (Collister, 2014), Bookchin advocated an understanding of technology that not only considered the strictly material aspects of technologies but also the social and cultural context in which these are embedded. Bookchin's (1982) word for these composite ensembles of material, social and cultural forces is 'technics' (see also **Foucault**, 1982 and box in Chapter 4).

Taking his cue from Lewis Mumford's (1964) history of technological development, Bookchin establishes a distinction between *libertarian* and *authoritarian* technics. While the former category represents technics that facilitate diversity, spontaneity, mutualism and non-hierarchical relationships, the latter represents technics that foster hierarchies and domination (Bookchin, 1982, pp. 252–253). However, even though this distinction seems both tangible and easily operationalized, there is no hard and fast way of deciding whether certain technics belong to one or the other category. As he puts it, 'Technics does not exist in a vacuum, nor does it have an autonomous life of its own' (ibid., p. 223). Hence, no technics are inherently good or bad, libertarian or authoritarian; it all depends on their material features, practical usage and cultural context. Adding to this complexity is the fact that Bookchin never provided a method for assessing the character of different technics. To remedy this, we draw on the concept of 'affordances.'

The concept of affordances was initially coined by American psychologist James Gibson (1979) as a way of accounting for the way animals (including humans) perceive their natural habitat. Etymologically, the word is a nominalization of the verb 'to afford,' which means to offer or make something available to someone. Gibson's point is that animals perceive their immediate environment in terms of usage: a large rock may offer a resting spot to some animals and a hiding place to others. The rock has no meaning of its own. Instead, its meaning is a product of the animal's interaction with the features of the stone as well as the surrounding environment. Transporting these observations to the world of human beings, Gibson (1979, p. 139) suggests the act of writing a letter as an illustrative example. As an activity, letter writing requires a person who is both willing and capable of authoring a letter. But this is clearly not enough. It also requires a mailbox that is large enough to contain the letter and a postal system that ensures the letter reaches its destination. Hence, Gibson's affordance theory has three interrelated components: the objects (the letter and the mailbox), the actors (the author and the addressee) and the environment (the postal system). As he puts it,

> An affordance is neither an objective property nor a subjective property; or it is both if you like. An affordance cuts across the dichotomy of subjective-objective and helps understand its inadequacy. It is equally a fact of the environment and a fact of behaviour.
>
> *(Gibson, 1979, p. 129)*

More recently, Ian Hutchby (2001) has employed this idea in relation to contemporary ICTs, arguing that they afford certain types of interactions, depending on the social and cultural context in which they are used. For instance, the telephone was originally marketed as a way of broadcasting concert music to a wider audience but ended up as the primary medium for enabling two-way communication between private individuals. Similarly, the technical foundations of the Internet were invented during the Cold War to protect the communicative infrastructure of the American army from nuclear attack but ended up as a 'World Wide Web' connecting billions of people across the globe. The point of these stories is, of course, to show that the technical features of a given technology do not determine the way humans interact with them (see also Kamstrup and Jacobsen, 2018).

Importantly, however, this does not mean that technology is completely neutral until appropriated by human beings, as scholars like Keith Grint and Steve Woolgar (1997) seem to suggest. Clearly, the telephone and the Internet do not invite the same kind of interaction, because their technical features differ substantially (though the advent of instant messaging apps and the proliferation of smartphones have pushed the boundary to the point of convergence). As Hutchby (2001, p. 28) puts it, 'While it may be the case that the telephone was not originally marketed as a means of two-party interpersonal communication, the point is that it *affords* that form of interaction' (see also Winner, 1980). Even though the concept of affordances has been used to examine how the 'physicality' of objects shape action, it is important to note that it is equally powerful to study how computer software makes certain actions more likely than others (Husted and Plesner, 2017).

Next, we draw on the idea of affordances to study two Danish crowdsourcing platforms: *Innosite*, a platform that hosts architectural competitions, and *Tag Del*, a platform that facilitates public deliberation on societal challenges. Our purpose is to examine whether the platforms meet the criteria for libertarian and authoritarian 'technics,' as proposed by Bookchin (1982) or, in other words, to examine if and when crowdsourcing can be seen as anarchist.

The affordances of crowdsourcing

Recognizing the need for inventive thinking in the Danish building industry as well as the untapped potential of digital technology, the Danish Architecture Centre decided in late 2011 to launch a new online platform called *Innosite* that would 'enhance idea generation and the level of innovation in the built environment' (Innosite, 2011, n.p.). More specifically, the purpose of the platform was to outsource the creative part of architectural competitions to the general public, in the hope that this would generate more innovative ideas in a 'cheaper and faster' way than previously (Innosite, 2017, n.p.). As such, while the primary motivation for launching the platform was to harness the creative potential of the crowd by sidestepping the conventions of traditional architectural competitions, the Innosite project was firmly embedded in capitalist relations of production. By connecting 'those with a need' (i.e., building contractors) to 'those with the good ideas' (i.e. the crowd), Innosite not only allowed ordinary people to express their creative ideas, but it also provided companies with an opportunity to minimize the cost of ideation, otherwise performed by trained architects (Kamstrup and Jacobsen, 2018).

Two years after the birth of Innosite, another Danish crowdsourcing platform was launched by two young men who recognized the need for a more systematic approach to citizen involvement in general. The platform was called *Tag Del*, meaning 'take part,' and it aims to include ordinary citizens in the process of arriving at creative and tangible solutions to various societal challenges. In contrast to Innosite, Tag Del is a non-commercial platform where anyone can pose challenges and propose solutions. As one of the platform's founders explains, 'Challenges, propositions and comments are not allowed to contain commercial advertisements . . . No one has monopoly of ideas and solutions developed on the site' (Tag Del, 2013a, n.p.). Some challenges are submitted by municipalities and state agencies; others are submitted by NGOs and political parties. Some challenges concern social marginalization and vulnerability; others concern climate change and environmental decay.

The common denominator across these challenges is a shared appreciation of the public's role in resolving societal issues.

In the following three sections, we will go through each of the three components in Gibson's theory of affordances in relation to Innosite and Tag Del. First, we will consider the objects (the technical features of the platforms), then move on to the environment (the cultural context in which the platforms are embedded) and finally, turn our attention to the actors (the social interactions on the platforms). It should be noted, however, that the following analysis has been simplified. A proper affordance analysis would not treat the three components separately but integrate them into a more coherent analysis (for examples, see Fayard and Weeks, 2007; Kamstrup, 2017; Treem and Leonardi, 2013; Husted and Plesner, 2017).

Objects: the technical features

An Innosite contest begins when a 'competition brief' containing a challenge is uploaded and displayed to members. Importantly, this brief also presents the assessment criteria used to select a winner. The brief is composed by an organization which has a pressing challenge they need help solving. A contest is composed of an input stage and a selection stage. In the input stage, every registered (crowd) member can upload a proposal. The platform is designed so that it is as simple as possible to create a profile: it requires a profile name, a password and a profile picture. At any given time, only one challenge is active, and a challenge typically lasts eight weeks. When logged in, it is possible to upload a solution to the active challenge by using the upload button. When a proposal is uploaded, it is visible for all crowd members, and an evaluation option is automatically activated. Using this option, crowd members can rate each other's proposals. This rating can either be done by clicking a 'This idea inspired me' button or by giving one to five stars. These dimensions are similar to the assessment criteria given in the competition brief. Because of the design of the platform, this evaluation option is the primary way for crowd members to communicate with each other. In the second stage of the contest, the winner is chosen. Ideally, the best rated and evaluated proposals are presented for an appointed jury, who are brought together and tasked with finding the final winner from this preselection of proposals.

Both organizations and individuals can post challenges on the Tag Del platform. This is done by selecting a category for the challenge (education, transportation, environment and so on) and by writing a text that briefly outlines its scope and why it is important. It is also possible to add additional sources of information, such as pictures and videos, in order to provide users with the knowledge to respond constructively to the challenge. Finally, a realistic deadline must be provided for the challenge to encourage fast and focused responses. Once the challenge has been posted, users are able to respond. They do so by writing comments or by elaborating on other users' comments. Users are also able to support each other's comments by clicking a like-button similar to the one on Facebook. In the end, the responses are picked up by the 'challenge owners' and (ideally) brought to life. Unlike many other crowdsourcing platforms, there are no winners on Tag Del – or, rather, there are only winners, since all responses contribute more or less directly to solving the challenges. Accordingly, responses are by default displayed chronologically on the platform. One has to actively select 'popularity' as a filtering mechanism to sort responses according the number of likes received. There are no prizes to be won. People participate voluntarily in resolving other people's challenges, though the platform administrators frequently encourage challenge owners to praise all responses and to acknowledge the energy that users spend solving a challenge.

Environment: the cultural context

As mentioned, Innosite is operated by the Danish Architecture Centre, and the challenges uploaded on the platform are thus important to the Danish building industry. For instance, one contest called 'Sleep Tight' was co-formulated by three municipalities and concerned how to design and build cheap student accommodation in university cities. In another contest, called 'Dressed in Clay,' the crowd was asked how to use clay tiles and bricks in relation to both effective insulation and aesthetic design choices. More in the periphery, but still somewhat typical, is the contest 'Trash or Treasure,' in which the crowd was asked to come up with ideas to make waste management more interesting, easy and sustainable. In broader terms, the platform competitions can be compared to architectural competitions. The architectural competition is a century-old phenomenon that allows a client or contractor to ask architects for solutions to a given challenge (Lipstadt, 2003). Traditionally, an architectural competition is either open or invited, meaning that it is organized so that either anyone or only a select few can participate (Larson, 1994). In Denmark, there is a tradition for developing new competition formats, and Innosite can be seen as an attempt at increasing the openness of architectural competitions by extending the 'invitation' beyond traditional boundaries of participation. That said, the architectural competition is an established institution in the building industry, and architectural students are brought-up with 'competition' as a common mode of interaction.

The immediate environment of the Tag Del platform is not easily defined. Since there are no limits to the type of challenges found on the platform and no limits to the type of users engaged in solving these, it is difficult to situate Tag Del in a particular context. That said, the platform is clearly embedded in a narrative about the value of public participation in policymaking, which may be why some of its most active participants are municipalities and local branches of political parties. As noted in a promotional movie for Tag Del, 'collaboration is our biggest resource, which is why collaboration is the key to solving societal challenges' (Tag Del, 2013b). In terms of the challenges, the vast majority of these belong to the category called 'urban development.' For instance, one challenge concerned the pressing need to make Danish cities greener, while another involved a suggestion about giving new powers to certain districts of Copenhagen. Interestingly, this brings the Tag Del platform close to the Innosite platform in terms of cultural context. What sets the two apart is that the latter is situated in the competitive environment of architectural competitions, whereas the former is positioned in a context of collaboration and voluntarism. As we shall see, this an important point to keep in mind in trying to understand the social interactions that the two platforms afford.

Actors: the social interactions

Challenges posted on the Innosite platform typically receive somewhere between 50 and 100 responses, though some of the most popular ones have received close to 300 responses. The quality of the responses varies immensely. While some users only post a few lines of text, others upload large files containing technical drawings and blueprints. Needless to say, the winners almost always belong to the latter group, and at the time of writing, only once did a winner not upload elaborate drawings. The competitive nature of the platform renders interaction and collaboration between participants close to non-existent. For instance, even though the platform actively encourages users to interact with each other, this rarely happens, presumably because of the fear of promoting other proposals than one's own. Similarly, the possibility for users to write comments on each other's profiles has never been used. Instead of interacting and collaborating, users tend to look elsewhere for inspiration on how to respond to a challenge. The most frequently used source of inspiration is previous winners. This is possible because all former winning proposals are openly stored on the platform and can be accessed freely. Over time, this has resulted in newer proposals beginning to look like the older winning proposals, in the sense that they rely on similar architectural aesthetics and include many of the same elements.

Challenges posted on the Tag Del platform generally receive somewhere between a handful and several dozen responses. Though some users participate more regularly than others, challenges are typically picked up by a wide variety of users, who all bring different perspectives and competences to the discussion. The interactions on the platform take the form of brainstorm-like deliberations. One user responds to a challenge by proposing a solution, and others follow-up on that or suggest other solutions. There seems to be no preconceived quality criteria guiding the discussion and, thus, no limits to what counts as a valid proposal. As such, there are no visible evaluation processes going on, and it is extremely rare to see unofficial 'winners' or 'best proposals' announced by those posting the challenges. The tone on the platform is always friendly and accommodating towards new and alternative proposals. For instance, users often begin their responses by highlighting the challenge's significance and pertinence, and challenge owners will typically reply in an equally appreciative fashion. As one challenge owner concluded, having received 31 responses to his challenge about hitchhiking and the need to raise awareness about more communal modes of transportation,

> Dear everyone. I am overwhelmed by the amount of interest for this project. All your proposals have been dearly noted and are included in the attached

document. I have received so much positive response both here on Tag Del, but also on Facebook and elsewhere . . . Tag Del will continue to be our 'development portal,' where new ideas can be discussed and developed. You are also welcome to post a challenge yourself if you feel like taking initiative.

Is crowdsourcing anarchist?

Recalling Bookchin's conceptualization of libertarian technics, we can say that anarchist technologies should be characterized by four interrelated features: (1) *diversity*, (2) *spontaneity*, (3) ***mutualism*** and (4) ***horizontalism*** (see boxes in Chapters 17 and 9). In contrast, authoritarian technology is characterized by relationships of domination and hierarchy.

In terms of *diversity*, both Innosite and Tag Del were initially launched with the ambition of generating a multiplicity of diverse proposals for how to solve specific challenges. For instance, the purpose of Innosite was to 'enhance idea generation and the level of innovation' in the Danish building industry, and the same could be said for Tag Del in relation to public deliberation and voluntary work. However, only the latter platform seems capable of actually delivering on that ambition. While proposals on Tag Del are incredibly varied, not least because the interests and competences of those submitting proposals differ substantially, the proposals on Innosite are very similar. Presumably, the monetary prize associated with winning one of the competitions has encouraged users to look for inspiration from former winners, resulting in them imitating previously successful proposals in terms of architectural standards and aesthetics. The level of diversity – and innovation – on the Innosite platform is thus limited, which may be one of the reasons why the platform is now not used very much.

In terms of *spontaneity*, the Tag Del platform holds a significant advantage over the Innosite platform. While both platforms have relatively low entry barriers (it takes less than five clicks to become a member of the crowd, and the challenges posted on both platforms are often easily comprehensible), only the Tag Del platform affords spontaneous responses from its users. Once again, this has to do with the approach that users adopt in trying to win the Innosite challenges by uploading large PDF files containing blueprints and technical drawings as part of their proposals. This has rendered the process of responding to challenges a time-consuming activity that privileges only particular actors, such as trained architects and urban developers. In contrast, the deliberative and brainstorming nature of Tag Del affords much more spontaneous responses, since it requires little more than a few lines of text to participate in solving one of the challenges.

In terms of *mutualism*, the competitive structure of Innosite once again tilts the odds in Tag Del's favour. Originally, Innosite was conceived as a platform that would not only raise the level of innovation but also challenge the hyper-competitive spirit of architectural competitions by introducing digital infrastructure that allowed for collaboration and knowledge-sharing. However, the customs of secrecy in architectural competitions proved too difficult to break (Kreiner, 2007). Innosite users never use the technical features that support collaboration, presumably because they fear being victims of intellectual property theft. Even the seemingly harmless 'this idea inspired me' button is left almost completely untouched. On the Tag Del platform, the opposite seems to be the case. Users frequently elaborate on each other's responses and commend fellow crowd members for submitting interesting proposals. Of course, one can only speculate about what would happen if monetary prizes were introduced to Tag Del, but the case of Innosite suggests that this would significantly impact the level of mutualism on the platform.

Finally, in terms of *horizontalism*, we need to look at the evaluative structure of the two platforms. Whereas proposals on Tag Del are not subject to any kind of formal evaluation, the Innosite proposals are presented to a jury (consisting of experts in architecture and urban development and representatives from the organization that owns the challenge) who then pick a winner. The role of the jury is to interpret the official assessment criteria and to ensure that all winning proposals meet these. However, even though this mode of evaluation ensures that winning proposals are of a certain quality, it also renders the otherwise potentially horizontal process of crowdsourcing centralized and hierarchical. In fact, it is difficult to imagine a more hierarchical form of work organization than having an entire crowd labouring voluntarily in the service of a small jury who then, retrospectively, decide which of the 100 plus submitted proposals should be 'rewarded' with a paycheck. The Tag Del platform, in contrast, explicitly states that it only curates voluntary work: there are no prizes to be won, no paychecks to be collected and no profits to be made. This makes the evaluative structure informal, decentral and horizontal, resulting in a situation where all proposals are recognized as valuable but no proposals are ranked and rated according to fixed assessment criteria.

Measured by Bookchin's four characteristics of libertarian technics, the Tag Del platform is clearly much more aligned with anarchist ideals of technology, work and organization than the Innosite platform. Of course, this does not mean that there is nothing positive to say about Innosite. After all, the platform has helped challenge the monopoly of large architectural firms by inviting freelance architects and hobbyists to join competitions previously reserved for big companies. Innosite has also helped globalize architectural competition, thus allowing users across the globe to enter the race for monetary rewards. However, in relation to anarchist theory, Tag Del and Innosite are very different. While the former affords diverse and spontaneous responses from users, the latter affords resource-demanding responses that only well-trained and resourceful users are capable of delivering. Furthermore, while Tag Del affords mutualism in the shape of ongoing collaboration, Innosite affords internal competition and secrecy amongst users. And finally, whereas submitted proposals on Tag Del are exempt from any kind of formal ranking, proposals on Innosite are subject to a hierarchical and centralized mode of evaluation.

Conclusion

The voluntary and collaborative forms of crowdsourcing, like Tag Del, or citizen science projects, like Zooniverse and eBird, could be conceived as anarchist in their impulse and operation. Furthermore, fixed-rate platforms like Amazon's Mechanical Turk could perhaps also – with a significant wage increase and a diversification of tasks – be seen as representing some of the libertarian spirit that characterizes anarchist approaches to technology. At the very least, such platforms allow users to work in a self-governing fashion independently of traditional space and time constraints. But anarchist ideals of technology, work and organization are less evident in the hyper-competitive, reward-based and hierarchically evaluated crowdsourcing that is represented by platforms like Innosite, InnoCentive and LEGO Ideas. Here, corporate actors are allowed to save vast amounts of money by outsourcing tasks previously undertaken by in-house employees to an un(der)paid digital workforce. In cases like these, crowdsourcing merely becomes another way to exploit labour by using smart technology. The lesson, it seems, is that judgements about technics partly depends on the affordances of the technology, but we should never assume that technology is either good or bad in its effects. Anarchists are right to be sceptical sometimes and enthusiastic at others, because technology, whether ICT or anything else, is only ever given meaning by the people who make it and use it.

Questions for further study

1   How do you think mainstream business and management thinkers would talk about the digital age and crowdsourcing? Do you think they would be positive or negative about these developments?
2   How do anarchists think about technology? Are there different anarchist positions on the question of technology and its role in social change? What different positions do you think there might be?
3   What does it mean for a piece of technology, like a crowdsourcing platform, to be anarchist? What core principles does it need to reflect, and how does this differ from other, non-anarchist technologies?
4   This chapter has discussed two examples of crowdsourcing platforms. Find some other examples of crowdsourcing platforms, and use what you have learned in this chapter to explore whether they are anarchist or not.

References

Anderson, C. (2012). *Makers: The New Industrial Revolution.* New York, NY: Crown Business.
Barnes, S., Hoyos, M., Balduf, B., Behle, H., and Green, A. (2013). *Review of State of the Art and Mapping: Crowdemploy.* Warwick: Warwick Institute for Employment Research.
Bookchin, M. (1980). *Towards an Ecological Society.* Montreal: Black Rose Books.
Bookchin, M. (1982). *The Ecology of Freedom: The Emergence and Dissolution of Hierarchy.* Montreal: Black Rose Books.
Brabham, D. C. (2013). *Crowdsourcing.* New York, NY: John Wiley & Sons.
Bruns, A. (2008). "The Future Is User-Led: The Path Towards Widespread Produsage." *Fibreculture Journal,* 11(1), n.p.
Castells, M. (1996). *The Rise of the Network Society.* Malden, MA: Blackwell Publishers.
Castells, M. (2009). *Communication Power.* Oxford: Oxford University Press.

Castells, M. (2012). *Networks of Outrage and Hope: Social Movements in the Internet Age*. Cambridge: Polity Press.

Collister, S. (2014). "Abstract Hacktivism as a Model for Postanarchist Organizing." *Ephemera*, 14(4), 765–779.

Difallah, D. E., Catasta, M., Demartini, G., Ipeirotis, P. G., and Cudré-Mauroux, P. (2015). "The Dynamics of Micro-Task Crowdsourcing: The Case of Amazon Mturk." In *Proceedings of the 24th International Conference on World Wide Web*, pp. 238–247. Florence, Italy. International World Wide Web Conferences Steering Committee.

Dyer-Witheford, N. (2015). *Cyber-Proletariat: Global Labour in the Digital Vortex*. London: Pluto Press.

Ellul, J. (1964). *The Technological Society*. New York, NY: Alfred A. Knopf Inc.

Estellés-Arolas, E., and González-Ladrón-de-Guevara, F. (2012). "Towards an Integrated Crowdsourcing Definition." *Journal of Information Science*, 38(2), 189–200.

Fayard, A., and Weeks, J. (2007). "Photocopiers and Water-Coolers: The Affordances of Informal Interaction." *Organization Studies*, 28(5), 605–634.

Felstiner, A. (2011). "Working the Crowd: Employment and Labor Law in the Crowdsourcing Industry." *Berkeley Journal of Employment & Labor Law*, 32(1), Article 3.

Foucault, M. (1982/2002). "Space, Knowledge, and Power." In J. D. Faubion (Ed.), *Power: Essential Works of Foucault 1954–194*, Vol. 3, pp. 349–364. London: Penguin Books.

Fuchs, C. (2014). *Digital Labour and Karl Marx*. London: Routledge.

Gibson, J. (1979). *The Ecological Approach to Visual Perception*. Hillsdale, NJ: Lawrence Erlbaum Associates.

Gordon, U. (2008). *Anarchy Alive!* London: Pluto Press.

Gordon, U. (2009). "Anarchism and the Politics of Technology." *The Journal of Labor and Society*, 12(3), 489–503.

Grint, K., and Woolgar, S. (1997). *The Machine at Work: Technology, Work and Organization*. Cambridge: Polity Press.

Howe, J. (2006). "The Rise of Crowdsourcing." *Wired*, 4(6), n.p.

Huczynski, A., and Buchanan, D. (2013). *Organizational Behaviour*. Harlow: Pearson.

Husted, E., and Plesner, U. (2017). "Spaces of Open-Source Politics: Physical and Digital Conditions for Political Organization." *Organization*, 24(5), 648–670.

Hutchby, I. (2001). *Conversation and Technology – From the Telephone to the Internet*. Cambridge: Polity Press.

Huws, U. (2003). *The Making of a Cybertariat: Virtual Work in a Real World*. New York, NY: Monthly Press Review.

Innosite. (2011). "Ny åben innovationsplatform skal skabe øget innovation i byggeriet" [New Open Innovation Platform to Create Enhanced Innovation in the Building Industry]. Press Release. Available at: https://realdania.dk/nyheder/seneste-nyt/nyheder-uden-projekt-2011/innosite_211111.

Innosite. (2017). "Om Innosite" [About Innosite]. Official website available at: www.innosite.dk/info.

Kamstrup, A. (2017). *Crowdsourcing and the Architectural Competition*. Ph.D. dissertation, Copenhagen Business School, Frederiksberg.

Kamstrup, A., and Jacobsen, P. (2018). "Organising for Openness: What Happens When Crowdsourcing Meets the Architectural Competition?" *Nordic Journal of Architectural Research*, n.p.

Kelly, K. (2011). *What Technology Wants*. New York, NY: Penguin Books.

Kleemann, F., Voß, G., and Rieder, K. (2008). "Un(der)paid Innovators: The Commercial Utiliza-tion of Consumer Work Through Crowdsourcing." *Science, Technology & Innovation Studies*, 4(1), 5–26.

Kreiner, K. (2007). "Constructing the Client in Architectural Competitions." Paper presented at *The 23rd EGOS Colloquium 2007*.

Larson, M. S. (1994). "Architectural Competitions as Discursive Events." *Theory and Society*, 23(4), 469–504.

Lipstadt, H. (2003). "Can 'Art Professions' be Bourdieuean Fields of Cultural Production? The Case of the Architecture Competition." *Cultural Studies*, 17(3–4), 390–419.

Maeckelbergh, M. (2009). *The Will of the Many: How the Alterglobalization Movement Is Changing the Face of Democracy*. London: Pluto Press.

Marshall, P. (1992). *Demanding the Impossible: A History of Anarchism*. London: Harper Perennial.

Mumford, L. (1964). "Authoritarian and Democratic Technics." *Technology & Culture*, 5(1), 1–8.

Pearlman, F. (1983). *Against His-Story, Against Leviathan!* Detroit, MI: Black and Red.

Proudhon, P.-J. (1847). *System of Economical Contradictions: Or, the Philosophy of Poverty*. Boston, MA: Benjamin Tucker.

Rheingold, H. (2012). *Net Smart – How to Thrive Online*. Cambridge, MA: Massachusetts Institute of Technology Press.

Scholz, T. (2013). *Digital Labor: The Internet as Playground and Factory*. New York, NY: Routledge.

Shirky, C. (2009). *Here Comes Everybody: How Change Happens When People Come Together*. London: Penguin Books.

Swann, T., and Husted, E. (2017). "Undermining Anarchy: Facebook's Influence on Anarchist Principles of Organization in Occupy Wall Street." *The Information Society*, 33(4), 192–204.

Tag Del. (2013a). "Tagdel.dk – en ny platform for sociale løsninger" [Tagdel.dk – A New Platform for Social Solutions]. Article available at: http://trendsonline.dk/2013/03/14/tagdel-dk-en-ny-platform-for-sociale-losninger.

Tag Del. (2013b). "TAG DEL vores samfund" [TAG DEL Our Society]. Promotional movie available at: www.youtube.com/watch?v=Zj04soJXHIU&t=5s.

Treem, J. W., and Leonardi, P. (2013). "Social Media Use in Organizations: Exploring the Affordances of Visibility, Editability, Persistence, and Association." *Annals of the International Communication Association*, 36(1).

van Dijck, J., and Nieborg, D. (2009). "Wikinomics and Its Discontents." *New Media and Society*, 11(5), 855–874.

Ward, C. (1973). *Anarchy in Action*. London: Freedom Press.

Winner, L. (1980). "Do Artifacts Have Politics?" *Daedalus*, 109(1), 121–136.

Zerzan, J. (1994). *Future Primitive and Other Essays*. New York, NY: Autonomedia.

14

TRUST, FINANCE AND CRYPTOCURRENCIES

Enrico Beltramini

Introduction

In many business school textbooks, the exchange of value (for example, in the form of money) between people and organizations is understood to be a matter of trust and regulation (e.g. White, 1999; Hubbard and O'Brien, 2013). When it comes to a payment, for example, people have to trust a third party in order to complete the transaction, such as a bank or credit card company. These third party intermediaries are backed by a central monetary authority. The government-backed banking system tracks transactions and records statistics so that the government is aware of the movement of capital across its borders. The identity of the individual traders or purchasers is traceable, and their activity is monitored for patterns that might indicate illegal activity, such as money laundering. The traditional banking system, however, is both expensive and exclusionary in that it constitutes a socioeconomic barrier that keeps many in financial distress outside the transaction systems (Rethel and Sinclair, 2012). It also brings potential for error, excessive discretionary powers by the state and a high level of intrusion into users' privacy.

It is possible, however, to imagine an alternative system where exchanges are verified and transactions finalized but where neither the buyer nor the seller comes under the surveillance of the state or state-backed central banks. Such an alternative has the potential to provide for much faster, even real-time, transactions that minimize the cost of the process. An alternative financial transaction system like this could promise to be free from intermediaries and government surveillance, delivering a low-cost, secure and fast value exchange without compromising the privacy of its users. If your main introduction to systems of exchange has been through mainstream finance and accounting textbooks, then an alternative like this, while perhaps desirable, may seem unrealistic and fanciful. This system, however, has not only been imagined but actually built. It stands at the intersection of a distinct form of anarchism, cryptoanarchism, and a specific technology, blockchain, which distributes trust across an entire network of users. The potential for an entirely new decentralized financial system is clear.

This chapter will

- clarify the problem that cryptoanarchism aims to address,
- define cryptoanarchism as a distinct form of anarchism and examine the relationship between cryptoanarchism (the political theory) and cryptoanarchy (the social organization),
- explore the idea that bitcoin is a technology that embodies cryptoanarchic principles of organization, and
- introduce blockchain, a current technology that produces distributed trust and automated value transfer with application beyond banking.

The problem

Internet and related digital media can constitute spaces of independence from governments but also, at times, from corporations (Dahlberg, 2017, and the other chapters in this section). The dominant, utopian narrative suggests a vision of freedom in which technology in the hands of ordinary people is seen as enabling the formation of self-organized communities free from state and corporate power (Goertzel and Goertzel, 2015). The dystopian narrative instead expresses a vision of oppression in which technology in the hands of technocratic governments and profit-driven corporations is seen as allowing for the formation of centralized forms of prosecution, censorship and exploitation.

Throughout the 1980s, a generation of entrepreneurs, engineers, mathematicians and civil rights activists in the San Francisco Bay Area of the USA was torn between hope and fear. On the one hand, they were excited by the simultaneous emergence of two revolutionary forces: personal computers and the Internet. Their hope was that more and more PC owners would connect their machines to the fast-growing global computer network, creating an information revolution and a new digital society. On the other hand, they were worried by the simultaneous emergence of two equally dangerous possibilities: the end of private communication and the rise of digital profiling. Their fear was that more and more intrusive technology (today we would call this Big Data) would make possible mass surveillance and data-mining.

Consider private communication. In the material world, mail moves from citizen to citizen, delivering both authenticity and privacy. The recipient knows that the communication has been generated by the sender, and the content of the communication is known only to the recipient and the sender. Liberal democratic governments cannot usually open their citizens' mail without a warrant that has been issued by a judge. But in a digital world, email can be easily intercepted, and in turn, interception can evolve into mass surveillance. As a matter of fact, unpredictable social and economic crises can create the circumstances for governments to argue that a crisis requires extension of power, or a state of exception, in which the law is suspended (Agamben, 2005). In a material world, such mass surveillance would be visible and costly and could really only be enforced by a totalitarian regime. In a digital world, this mass surveillance is instead mostly invisible and fairly cheap and hence does not arouse a strong reaction. For many citizens, it seems perfectly compatible with democracy. The loss of privacy is usually reduced to a minor problem through the 'I have nothing to hide' argument. According to this argument, privacy is about hiding a wrong; if we are not doing anything wrong, we have nothing to hide. Privacy, however, is not about hiding a wrong but rather having control over our own communication and deciding with whom we want to share it. For example, we might have curtains over our windows so that people can't see into our home. This isn't because we are undertaking illegal or immoral activities but simply because we decide who can see us in our home and who cannot. The choice comes down to a passive acceptance of mass surveillance or to an active defence of our own privacy (Solove, 2011).

Let's move to the rise of digital profiling. In the material world, individuals can book hotels, transport, restaurant visits, movie rentals and theatre visits, as well as purchase food, pharmaceuticals, alcohol, books, news and religious and political material without fear of being monitored. Outside totalitarian societies, individuals are basically invisible to business and the state because of the costs and complexity of detailed surveillance. But in a digital world, movements, transactions and even web searches can be collected and used to create, piece by piece, a detailed picture of each individual in order to find out who they are and what they want. As early as 1985, David Chaum, who laid the groundwork for the idea of anonymous trade, warned of 'a dossier society, in which computers could be used to infer individuals' life-styles, habits, whereabouts and associations from data collected in ordinary consumer transactions' (Chaum, 1985, p. 1030). Private behaviours, tendencies and preferences become data and generate tremendous value for corporations.

In summary, a justifiable fear about untrustworthy governments and corporations drove a group of visionaries to anticipate that private information can be stored and misused – that is, used to sustain a state of exception in which we are all surveilled in order to better control us and to make money. These thinkers established a fundamental connection between digital communication and civil rights, based on a suspicion of the technologies used by governments and corporations to collect data that is generated from everything individuals, in their status of citizens and consumers, do online. Important decisions based on surveillance and digital profiling are made by governments and corporations, including decisions like people's citizenship status, their credit score and their employability. Accordingly, passive acceptance of corporate and governmental incursions into individual privacy and rights does not address the wider issue: what kind of society is it in which a few control and exploit the many? If governments and corporations are not trustworthy, then surely communication and trade on the web need to be completely reimagined in order that they can operate in a decentralized manner, without the possibility of surveillance by powerful authorities with intrusive technologies.

Cryptoanarchism

These concerns have led to the development of a technological form of anarchism in response to a perceived problem of loss of privacy, with blockchain as the technology that can deliver transactions while protecting privacy. The ideological source of cryptoanarchism is *The Crypto Anarchist Manifesto*, published in 1992 on the 'cypherpunks' forum by Timothy C. May, an early employee at the computer company Intel. In his view, 'anarchy' is no longer associated with social movements but instead with radical appropriations of technology. The vision of classic anarchists is that of changing and replacing social orders, while May instead thinks that the state will increasingly become an irrelevance. In a cryptoanarchy, the government is not destroyed but instead gradually severed from the life of the average citizen. The notion that freedom can be found in cyberspace is related to the rather anarchic character of the Internet. In the Internet as a whole, no hierarchy is possible, and no ruler can be firmly established because there are too many nodes in the network.

CRYPTOANARCHISM

Cryptoanarchism is a movement which uses information technology in order to send and receive information free from surveillance and control by powerful institutions (Levy, 2001; Rid, 2016). The group has also been termed 'cypherpunks,' as a derivation of 'cypher' and 'cyberpunk.' In tracing its history, we can understand it as the libertarian foundations of the movement that spawned bitcoin and blockchain. Notable pioneers of cryptoanarchism were Whitfield Diffie and Martin Hellman, the founders of public-key cryptography in the 1970s, and David Chaum, a researcher and entrepreneur in fields such as anonymous digital cash and pseudonymous trust and reputation systems in the 1980s and '90s. The cypherpunk movement originates with Eric Hughes, Timothy C. May and John Gilmore, the founders of a group that met in the San Francisco Bay Area in the early 1990s. The cypherpunks mailing list was formed at about the same time, and May published *The Crypto Anarchist Manifesto* in 1992. Julian Assange joined the mailing list in 1994, later the founder of the controversial *WikiLeaks* website in 2006, aiming to bring secret information to public notice. Finally, Satoshi Nakamoto (a pseudonym for a still-unidentified individual or individuals) created bitcoin in 2008. The unifying idea behind these projects is that strong cryptography will result in a decline in the power of the state and corporations through decentralizing economic transactions and social interactions.

The key notion in May's *Manifesto* is not 'political self-sovereignty' or 'social change'; it is 'encryption.' The fundamental quality of technology, as far as cryptoanarchists are concerned, is the ability to 'crypt,' to allow people to communicate online anonymously and to protect themselves from surveillance by government and any other centralized authorities. Encryption allows a virtual community of millions of users, operating outside control and interference, to exchange information with one another through two-way, fully anonymous systems. May declared that encrypted communication and anonymity online would 'alter completely the nature of government regulation, the ability to tax and control economic interactions, the ability to keep information secret.' The result would be nothing less than 'both a social and economic revolution' (May, 2001, p. 61). This is the vision of the *Manifesto*. There is only one way this vision will materialize, and that is by the creation of a decentralized system in which anonymity facilitates the trade of information.

Before we continue, let's first clarify some of the key terms in this chapter, including *cyberspace*, *cryptography* and *encryption*. By 'cyberspace,' we should understand the virtual space in which computer transactions occur, the online world of computer networks and the Internet. 'Cryptography' is the theory and practice of techniques for secure communication in the presence of third parties. 'Encryption' (or 'digital cryptography') is a method of storing and transmitting data in a particular form so that only those for whom it is intended can read and process it. Encryption is basically the process of making information hidden or secret, through the use of algorithms (or 'ciphers').

Perhaps most important, all of these terms need to be understood as being hosted within a 'distributed system,' a collection of autonomous computers linked by a network and equipped with distributed system software. Distributed systems are technologies that enable decentralized and autonomous forms of organization, such as bitcoin and blockchain. They also allow 'decentralized autonomous organizations' – companies and other economic organizations that are established and managed by means of distributed systems. A peer-to-peer network technology allows direct communication between anonymous peers instead of communication through a central node, where each node stores and forwards information to all other nodes.

With cryptocurrencies like bitcoin, the full extension of the cryptoanarchic project became evident. Anonymous trade is based on a decentralized form of trust. This source of trust is neither particular individuals nor central authorities and not even the programmers who developed the system. In fact, the core idea of decentralization is that the operation of a service is not blindly trusted to any single agent. Instead, responsibility for the service is shared across the network. Users can choose to remain anonymous, but transactions are public and visible to anyone with access to the system. Trust, a collective memory of all transactions, resides in the nodes that operate the transactions and in the distributed system that enables them. Even though the community may not have any reason to trust or depend on anonymous others, the rules that describe behaviour are designed to force participants to act fairly and consistently in order to participate at all, relying heavily on cryptographic techniques to allow participants to hold each other accountable.

Thus, cryptoanarchy has shown through bitcoin that anonymity is not a barrier to trade. On the contrary, anonymity not only protects from control through surveillance but also from retaliation and punishment. Anonymous users can exchange information or perform transactions without infringement of their private and singular freedoms. This cryptofinance is the practical realization of cryptoanarchism, an organizational form of finance transcending national boundaries and freeing individuals to consensually make whatever economic arrangements they wish to make.

From cryptoanarchy to bitcoin

It did not take long for cryptoanarchist thinkers to grasp the economic and financial implications of May's original intuition. A community of users, protected by pseudonyms, who exchange information on a distributed system can also trade economic value. The idea of a cryptoeconomy is already present, in a nutshell, in May's *Manifesto*. A physical transaction implies physical presence, or a public face. A digital transaction, however, occurs between faceless parties (parties without visible identities). For May, people can 'exchange information, conduct business, and negotiate electronic contracts without ever knowing the True Name, or legal identity, of the other' (May, 2001, p. 61). In other words, undisclosed parties make transactions through the mediation of anonymous retailers and cryptographic protocols with nearly total assurance against any traceability. But this comment only scratches the surface of what is at stake in cryptoanarchism.

Cryptoanarchists wish to demonstrate the irrelevance of government and other centralized powers, an aim that classical anarchists would doubtless agree with. To reach this goal, they attempt to show that government as a central provider of trust and control is not necessary in a digital society. Let me start with trust. We might well argue that trust, in terms of predictability and durability, has always been guaranteed by government or government-sponsored institutions, legal entities and other centralized authorities in banking and finance. But cryptoanarchism can guarantee trust through cryptographic software. Because the parties are undisclosed, the nature of trust and reputation is no longer dependent upon who the parties are but instead on their history, which can be accessed via peer review. As for control, again, consider the inherently anarchic and distributed character of the Internet. We might say that the absence of universal hierarchy and rules must lead to chaos, but within cyberspace, a digital community of anonymous users with a common purpose can actually build trust and a reputation-based economy. Agreed encrypted communication protocols secure online transactions and also protect anonymity. In his *History of Silicon Valley*, Piero Scaruffi, a trained mathematician-turned-programmer-turned-historian, correctly identifies the issue at stake in cryptoanarchism: what is the function of government in the digital era when computer algorithms maintain 'order' with no need for a police force? (Scaruffi, 2015, p. 345).

May's ideas were further developed by two computer engineers who never met in person but in 1998 published two unrelated conceptual pieces. Both authors focused attention on the financial and contractual side of transactions, although with different solutions. When he was still in college, Wei Dai posted a paper on the 'cypherpunks' forum noting that 'a community' requires 'a medium of exchange (money) and a way to enforce contracts.' He added that 'traditionally these services have been provided by the government or government sponsored institutions and only to legal entities.' A protocol is required that provides the same services 'to and by untraceable entities' (Dai, 1998). Wei Dai's theoretical solution is an anonymous distributed electronic cash system ('B-money') in which the cryptocurrency is governed collectively by the entire cryptocurrency system. The cryptocurrency works as a medium of exchange and uses cryptography to secure the transactions and to control the creation of additional units of the currency.

At the same time, Nick Szabo developed a system for 'bit gold,' which has been seen as a precursor to bitcoin. Like bitcoin and other cryptocurrencies that followed it, bit gold was an electronic currency system, basically a software that required users to complete a proof of work function with solutions being cryptographically assembled and published (Szabo, 1998). Szabo, an expert in law, also articulated the notion of 'smart contract' – that is to say, contracts that are empowered by cryptographic protocols and other digital security mechanisms and facilitate, verify or enforce their negotiation or performance (Szabo, 1996). Both b-money and bit-gold remained only theoretical projects: neither author ever concretely tried to put them into practice. Nevertheless, their visions were remarkably accurate and established a template that ties money and law together with digital cryptography and makes them into a tool to produce online anarchism. The importance of these contributions resides in their accuracy in forecasting the benefits and parameters of what became bitcoin, perhaps the most well-known online currency. It was the result of the work of an anonymous individual (or group of individuals) operating under the pseudonymous Satoshi Nakamoto (Nakamoto, 2008). The story of the search for the real identity of Nakamoto and their relationship with Wei and Szabo is fascinating but outside the scope of this chapter (Davis, 2011; L.S., 2015). Bitcoin is important in our story, but just as important is the infrastructure that makes this cryptocurrency work – blockchain.

From bitcoin to blockchain

Bitcoin is the starting point for at least three stories: crypto-currencies, or currencies that operate on an anonymous and distributed system and not controlled by a central government; peer-to-peer networks, autonomous and distributed systems that replace a centralized system; and finally, blockchain, a distributed mechanism creating trust within autonomous and decentralized organizations through an algorithm. Bitcoin's strongest proponents see encryption and distributed systems as a way to trade anonymously, freeing commerce from the grip of governments and protecting individuals' privacy from corporations. That vision isn't exactly a reality, because of the conservative ways in which these technologies have been understood. Across Silicon Valley and beyond, the idea of bitcoin as a consumer technology has been replaced by the notion that bitcoin is another piece of infrastructure, an Internet protocol used by experts. Similarly, the perception of blockchain has also changed from being a potential building block for a collective direct governance of currency to being a technology that serves as the underpinning for other, more conventional, financial services. It and similar distributed ledgers – in which all users store details of all transactions – can be used to oversee the movement of money to and from businesses and customers across the world. It can also be used to issue stock over the Internet via technology based on the bitcoin blockchain.

Yet the idea of a vast online ledger designed to oversee movement of money from one machine to another without the need for any central banking authority or government to validate the transactions can in fact serve as the basis for other much more radical applications and services. Thanks to the communal character of the distributed ledger, every transaction and its associated value are visible to anyone with access to the system, without passing through a third party, so long as they make a genuine investment in the network equations (solving computationally intensive equations that computer scientists call a 'proof-of-work'). Another characteristic of blockchain is the irreversibility of entries: once a transaction is recorded in the database and the accounts are updated, the records cannot be erased because they are linked to every transaction record that came prior (hence the term 'chain'). Finally, blockchain not only records transactions; it can also program transactions. The digital nature of the ledger allows users to set up algorithms and rules that automatically trigger transactions between nodes. With these characteristics of blockchain in mind, it is clear that blockchain can track the exchange of money, but it can also record anything else of value, including stocks, bonds and other financial securities.

Blockchain is a technology with disruptive potential well beyond banking. Industries such as car leasing and sale, Internet advertising and hedge funds seem to be enthusiastic about blockchain technologies (CB Insights, 2018). Some entrepreneurs are focussing on applying blockchain to health care: one possible application refers to securely sharing patient data from sources such as medical records, clinical trials, genomic testing and mobile devices (CB Insights, 2017). The idea is to provide a secure network for all sources of patient data, from electronic medical records to medical devices and pharmacies. In a nutshell, a distributed blockchain network could replace the central hospital/pharmacy. Another application is health claims and payment management. The current system of verification is time intensive and prone to inefficiencies. Blockchain can operate as a shared ledger system in which every new change is recorded, where patients control access and where patients, providers and even insurers can be allowed to securely view a patient's health time line in real-time, improving speed and transparency. Moreover, health care may benefit from a blockchain-based security system to record and secure every interaction involving citizens, who already carry unique identity credentials that link back to their health records. Plus, health care is a device-intensive industry and thus receptive to blockchain-based applications for supply chain networks. For example, a server synchronizes with blockchain protocols and has applications ranging from medical devices and pharmaceuticals to package tracking.

Today, blockchain is the object of grandiose speculation. It is envisioned as a means to reduce the complexity involved in business operations by enabling collaboration without central authorities and intermediaries (Guptha, 2017). Potential areas of application of blockchain technology are innumerable, encompassing insurance, the music industry and legal services, but the more radical vision is a blueprint for a new economy (Swan, 2015; Tapscott and Tapscott, 2016). In a nutshell, the idea is that blockchain technology supports not just a cryptocurrency but also billions of smart things in the physical world. This would be the Internet of (Every)Thing (IoT) – the name used for the connections between physical objects that through the Internet are able to send data to one another; for example, in your home, the thermostat or the fridge might be connected to the Internet and so sending data about their activities to an app on your phone, and you might be able to control them from that same app. This IoT needs a secured and trusted record of all exchanged messages as well as record keeping between smart devices. In an IoT world, any property (physical or digital) can potentially be registered in blockchain so that blockchain operates as the digital ledger of transactions that can record everything that has value to someone.

Blockchain is the subject of increasing attention and is having an influence on mathematics, computer science, engineering, law and economics. Business scholars Kavanagh and Miscione (2015) have investigated blockchain's organizational assumptions and implications, seeing it as a means of transforming transactions. The distributed trust network and anonymity are certainly two important characteristics of the blockchain mechanism, but the business community are primarily interested in the former (Barton, 2015). Indeed, prominent Silicon Valley venture capital investor Marc Andreessen, co-creator of the first commercial Web browser, Netscape, has listed the blockchain *distributed consensus model* as the most important invention since the Internet itself (Andreessen, 2016). The combination of distributed trust or distributed **consensus** (see box in Chapter 9) with Nick Szabo's idea of 'smart contracts' means that it becomes possible to embed the terms of a contract into a computerized transaction. This form of technology might even allow the enforcement of contracts to be decentralized, perhaps radically altering the way in which we can imagine the legal system and even the nature and negotiation of agreements. After all, if hierarchical authority is replaced by distributed consensus, then all sorts of social and economic arrangements can be reimagined.

Conclusion

The original idea behind bitcoin was the vision of a decentralized cryptocurrency which would empower a self-organized community of anonymous traders. In that context, blockchain is the distributed accounting platform that makes bitcoin possible. However, with bitcoin receding to become a behind-the-scenes technology, the role of blockchain becomes that of a general tool that keeps secure data in an encrypted ledger and controls access to it. Accordingly, banks and other financial operations can adopt blockchain technology to oversee the movement of stocks and potentially anything that carries value. This could mean that it gets adopted as a technology which re-engineers aspects of markets without challenging the inherently centralized character of the organization of those markets. Without the radicalism of decentralization, blockchain could just become a tool used by the powerful to store their data.

The original **techno-optimistic** idea behind blockchain was that it was a technology that no one person or entity would control (see box in Chapter 13). The power of the blockchain lies in its distributed nature and in its communal character according to which anyone is allowed to add data to the blockchain. However, the surge in the number of providers with their own centralized, proprietary blockchain technology (really just offering blockchain as a service) seems to defeat the original purpose of the technology. Moreover, the final result of this form of privatized blockchain is an arrangement in which value is still exchanged with using traditional intermediaries (bank accounts, credit cards and so on) or certain sorts of experts (in corporate finance, accounting and so on). To put it differently, the original cryptoanarchic vision of alternative organizations in which value is exchanged outside the control of government and banking institutions, and outside the scope of financial management, is in danger of being forgotten. As with the platform and crowdsourcing economy in the two previous chapters, business-as-usual and radical political interpretations of blockchain technology are at odds with each other. Nonetheless, the potential of distributed information technologies is very clear and their radicalism is appealing to cryptoanarchists. Realizing that potential will require that this technology is used to serve everyone, not just those who already have power within systems that measure and move financial value.

Questions for further study

1 How would you define 'cryptoanarchism'? In what ways is it similar or different to some of the other ways anarchism is defined in this book?

2 What do you understand by the terms *bitcoin* and *blockchain*? How do they present new approaches to economic exchange?

3 Do bitcoin and blockchain technologies reflect cryptoanarchist ideas? Can they be understood as examples of anarchist organization more generally? Why?

4 Is blockchain necessarily something revolutionary that will provide real social change? In what ways do you think a technology like blockchain could be incorporated into mainstream forms of economic exchange?

References

Agamben, G. (2005). *State of Exception* (K. Attell, Trans.). Chicago, IL: University of Chicago Press.

Andreessen, M. (2016). "On Twitter." 23 February. Available at: https://twitter.com/pmarca?lang=en.

Barton, P. (2015). *Bitcoin and the Politics of Distributed Trust*. Senior Thesis, Sociology and Anthropology, Swarthmore College.

CB Insights. (2017). "5 Blockchain Startups Working to Transform Healthcare." *Report on Bitcoin & Blockchain*.

CB Insights. (2018). "Banking Is Only the Beginning: 36 Big Industries Blockchain Could Transform." *Report on Bitcoin and Blockchain*, 1 February.

Chaum, D. (1985). "Security Without Identification: Transaction Systems to Make Big Brother Obsolete." *Communications of the ACM*, 28(10), 1030–1044. Available at: www. cs.ru.nl/~jhh/pub/secsem/chaum1985bigbrother.pdf (accessed 11 April 2017).

Dahlberg, L. (2017). "Cyberlibertarianism." *Oxford Research Encyclopedia of Communication*, Online Publication. Available at: http://communication.oxfordre.com/ view/10.1093/acrefore/9780190228613.001.0001/acrefore-9780190228613-e- 70?rskey=VYMVkL&result=1 (accessed 23 October 2017).

Dai, W. (1998). "B-Money." Available at: www.weidai.com/bmoney.txt (accessed 3 March 2017).

Davis, J. (2011). "The Crypto-Currency: Bitcoin and Its Mysterious Inventor." *The New Yorker*, 10 October. Available at: www.newyorker.com/magazine/2011/10/10/the-crypto-currency (accessed 5 May 2017).

Goertzel, B., and Goertzel, T. (eds.). (2015). *The End of the Beginning: Life, Society and Economy on the Brink of the Singularity*. Los Angeles, CA: Humanity+ Press.

Guptha, V. (2017). "The Promise of Blockchain Is a World Without Middleman." *Harvard Business Review*, 6 March. Available at: https://hbr.org/2017/03/the-promise-of-block-chain-is-a-world-without-middlemen (accessed 12 April 2017).

Hubbard, R. G., and O'Brien, A. P. (2013). *Money, Banking, and the Financial System* (2nd Edition). Boston, MA; London: Pearson.

Kavanagh, D., and Miscione, G. (2015). "Bitcoin and the Blockchain: A coup d'état in Digital Heterotopia?" In *Critical Management Studies Conference Proceedings*, University of Leicester.

Levy, S. (2001). *Crypto: How the Code Rebels Beat the Government Saving Privacy in the Digital Age*. New York, NY: Random House.

L.S. (2015). "Who Is Satoshi Nakamoto." *The Economist*, 2 November. Available at: www. economist.com/blogs/economist-explains/2015/11/economist-explains-1 (accessed 23 April 2017).

May, T. C. (2001). "Crypto Anarchist Manifesto." In P. Ludlow (Ed.), *Crypto Anarchy, Cyberstates, and Pirate Utopias*, pp. 61–64. Cambridge, MA; London: Massachusetts Institute of Technology Press.

Nakamoto, S. (2008). "Bitcoin: A Peer-to-Peer Electronic Cash System." Available at: http:// bitcoin.org/bitcoin.pdf (accessed 18 April 2017).

Rethel, L., and Sinclair, T. J. (2012). *The Problem With Banks*. London: Zed Books.

Rid, T. (2016). *Rise of the Machines: A Cybernetics History*. Brunswick, Victoria: Scribe Publications.

Scaruffi, P. (2015 (2011)). *History of Silicon Valley*. CreateSpace Independent Publishing Platform.

Solove, D. J. (2011). *Nothing to Hide: The False Tradeoff Between Privacy and Security*. New Haven, CT; London: Yale University Press.

Swan, M. (2015). *Blockchain: Blueprint for a New Economy*. Sebastopol: O'Reilly Media Inc.

Szabo, N. (1996). "Smart Contracts: Building Blocks for Digital Markets." *Extropy*, 16. Available at: www.alamut.com/subj/economics/nick_szabo/smartContracts.html (accessed 23 April 2017).

Szabo, N. (1998). "B-Gold." Available at: http://unenumerated.blogspot.com/2005/12/bit-gold.html (accessed 25 March 2017).

Tapscott, D., and Tapscott, A. (2016). *Blockchain Revolution: How the Technology Behind Bitcoin Is Changing Money, Business, and the World*. New York, NY: Random House.

White, L. H. (1999). *The Theory of Monetary Institutions*. Malden, MA; Oxford, UK: Blackwell Publishers Inc.

PART VI

Markets and exchange

15

MARKETING, ADVERTISING AND PERSUASION

Amanda Earley

In order to sell products and services, we need to 'market' them. That is to say, it is assumed that methods of persuasion and influence must be used to 'sell' everything, from cars and perfumes to books like this one. Promotion, communication and marketing are all subjects covered in business and management studies. Marketing, in particular, has branched out to become a separate discipline with its own key textbooks. You can even pursue a separate degree in marketing and/or communication at any level, from a BA to an MBA. However, there is nothing in these textbooks or these degrees that would begin to explain marketing from an anarchist point of view, and that would question some of the core common sense of marketing. This chapter will introduce you to an anarchist perspective on marketing.

The chapter will introduce a particular approach to anarchism. Then, it presents a brief introduction to the concept of marketing. After these basics are covered, two cases of 'possible anarchist marketing' are considered: the aesthetic 'anarcho-capitalism' of the advertising executive Charles Saatchi and the case of the Occupy Wall Street protest in 2011. Regarding the former, I invite you to question whether anarcho-capitalism can really be anarchism at all, if capitalism inherently entails rule by the financially powerful. Meanwhile, using the Occupy case, I will show that the notion that marketing can be used by 'real anarchists' is also questionable. I will argue that marketing is an inherently capitalist and hierarchical communication tactic which cannot be effectively deployed by anarchists in the world as it is. This chapter hence asks you to consider whether we should view marketing and anarchism as antithetical, as necessarily opposed to one another.

This chapter will

- introduce marketing, discussing its history as a commercial and academic field;
- provide a definition of anarchism from an anthropological perspective that focuses on ethics and rejecting authority;
- discuss two examples of marketing activities that have been characterized as anarchist; and
- ask whether it is possible to have an anarchist form of marketing.

A brief history of marketing

Marketing refers to all of the activities required to bring goods, services and even 'ideas' to market (Kotler and Levy, 1969). While advertising is the most immediately recognizable marketing technology to non-experts, marketing can also include public relations, retailing, distribution/logistics and strategy (Fill, 2013). As far as when marketing emerged, it is arguably as old as commerce. One of the earliest money economies emerged in Ancient Greece, and that society's thinkers had much to say about the nature of marketing practice. As documented in the work of William Kelley (1956), the philosopher Plato disagreed with 'price discrimination,' or charging two prices for the same product – a standard marketing practice today, as anyone who has ever booked a plane ticket through a website that uses dynamic pricing knows. Aristotle, another Greek philosopher, believed that while the economics of the home were virtuous, the economics of commerce were savage and a risk to peaceable society.

That said, marketing as we know it is a more recent phenomenon. It can be described as a product of industrial capitalism and required great concentrations of wealth and resources, which were only possible via imperial control of international relations, the pinnacle of which was colonialism (the actual control and administration of foreign territories in the interests of the imperial centre). While this seems like a guaranteed money-making scheme, there was soon a crisis – a crisis of over-production – as supply greatly outstripped existing demand (Amin, 1997; Bukharin, 1917).

Marketing emerged to fill this gap, encouraging mass consumption throughout Europe and the United States via new forms of retail, such as shopping arcades, and new forms of communication, such as the use of catalogues (Ellis et al., 2010). The colonies, too, were turned into markets for goods, often with catastrophic effects. Having already suffered the plunder of their resources on terms backed up by military force, they were soon subject to 'dumping' – a practice by which overproduced goods are dropped in other countries so as to protect prices within the producing country. These uncontrolled floods of cheap goods destroyed local industries in those countries, as local craftspeople could not compete (Amin, 1997). Over time, techniques of marketing have advanced with new communications technologies (from newspaper adverts to social media ones), and imperialist international trade has been rebranded as 'international marketing.'

Marketing first became a formalized academic discipline of study in the United States. Early marketing departments were often dominated by practitioners from industries such as milk transportation (Bartels, 1951; Maynard, 1941). However, scholarship in these areas was deemed insufficiently academic, leading to the Ford and Carnegie Foundations (Pierson, 1959; Gordon and Howell, 1959) insisting that it had to become more technical and scholarly to maintain a legitimate place within university systems (Ellis et al., 2010; Gemelli, 1997). Reacting to this, a group of American marketing academics wrote a series of (often dissenting) opinion pieces, attempting to present a more rigorous notion of what the field was. Two main camps are defined by the work of Philip Kotler and Shelby Hunt. Kotler and his collaborators suggested that marketing was not just the territory of capitalist businesses. They argued that churches, universities and even socialist governments should – even *must* – use 'social marketing' to promote their causes and achieve desired change (Kotler and Levy, 1969). Hunt disagreed, arguing that marketing should be almost exclusively the domain of for-profit organizations (1976).

In the decades since, a form of compromise has emerged, effectively that marketing claims a centrality to business practices and is therefore primarily oriented toward capitalist organizations but acknowledging social marketing as a smaller and under-resourced practice and academic discipline (Ellis et al., 2010). This has meant that marketing has increasingly been seen as integral for a wide range of non-profit, charity and government actors (Lee and Kotler, 2011). As such, marketing can once again be best defined as a variety of distribution and communication technologies which are employed by a wide range of social actors in order to create behavioural change in others.

What is anarchism?

In this chapter, I understand anarchism to be a philosophical position in which the autonomy of the individual is inviolable, and as such, there is no legitimate defence of hierarchy or authority (Graeber, 2004). While some other chapters of this book refer to certain major works of anarchist philosophy as the 'starting point' of various streams of anarchism, this chapter diverges on this point. Instead, I adopt David Graeber's anthropological perspective, which finds anarchism to be one of the oldest and most pervasive belief systems. It is perhaps even a 'natural' form of human organization, which only disappears when authorities emerge and repress primitive forms of cooperation in order to suit their own interests (Graeber, 2013, and Chapter 17).

It is important to note that this definition of anarchism gives a central role to ethics (codes of good behaviour) and responsibility (duty to others). Indeed, the vast majority of anarchists believe that cooperation and **mutual** support are essential for our survival and quality of life (see box in Chapter 17). They believe that responsibility lies within *each* individual. However, this does not make ethics 'voluntary' or an 'individual choice.' Anthropological evidence from contexts without formal systems of government or authority shows that agreement about acceptable standards for living together emerge in all cultures. Members of traditional communities rarely diverge too far from these agreed rules, as they know they rely on others for their well-being and know that their well-being will be negatively affected by poor conduct (Graeber, 2013).

From this evidence, it can be argued that poor ethics in contemporary society actually arises from our *departure* from anarchist forms of cooperation – and not from some sort of naturally uncivilized behaviour which has to be repressed by the state. While Marxism and anarchism are often seen as warring philosophical factions (Graeber, 2004), a Marxist concept may be of use to explain why. This concept is called 'primitive accumulation.' In Marx's work (1867), and that of many later scholars, the term is used to describe the initial transition from communal societies to hierarchical ones. **Marx** argued that primitive accumulation, the beginnings of the concentration of wealth in a few hands, was always grounded in theft and often in physical violence, and there is anthropological evidence to support this (Harvey, 2005, see box in Chapter 11).

Like Marxists, many anarchists would contend that formal, hierarchical society is grounded in violent dispossession, in the enclosing of what was originally held in common. This means that they would argue that contemporary society has not eliminated violence or abuse, but that 'ordered' societies have facilitated some of the greatest atrocities of human history (e.g. every major war, the subjugation of women, slavery, the holocaust and so on). The sophisticated systems of discipline (like prisons, the army, the police) which have emerged from hierarchical society arguably do little to prevent these wider forms of violence.

In the case of crimes which mimic primitive accumulation, where property is removed from communal control and taken by those in positions of power, condemnations are rare and often easily dismissed. This may sound like an outrageous claim, but note that prosecutions of bankers in the 'global financial crisis' have been minimal and light touch to this day (Scannell and Milne, 2017; Eisinger, 2014), despite it being one of the worst financial crises of recent years. Meanwhile, criminalizing those who are already dispossessed, often through their social class or ethnicity, is routine. Imprisonment and carrying a criminal record then produce further stigma and economic deprivation, making theft and violence for survival all the more necessary (Bauman, 2004).

We can use concepts like 'ideology' to describe sets of beliefs that benefit the ruling classes and which are promoted as common sense, such as that we need hierarchical structures which provide people to govern us. A stable structure of ideology is called a 'hegemony,' a word which describes a situation within which ideology is the prime method of governing people instead of violence. This means that elaborate structures of socialization are actively deployed to naturalize an unequal state of affairs while, if the anthropological arguments are accepted, it is anything but natural. These structures include schools, television, film, journalism, government communications and (of course) marketing and advertising.

HEGEMONY

In the most general sense, hegemony denotes some form of domination of one nation-state over others – political or economic control, for instance.

> However, in the context of this chapter, it refers to a notion of cultural hegemony as developed by the Italian Marxist Antonio Gramsci (1891–1937). The idea behind it is that a ruling class – capitalists – can manipulate people's perceptions and cultural norms to the point that one desired worldview becomes dominant, almost seemingly natural. The outcome of this is such that power gets consent for its rule without any recourse to violence. Given what you learn about marketing and its ensuing practices in this chapter, you can notice that it represents one of the most potent hegemonic, and hence also political, tools of the present-day domination of some people over others.

If you are a newcomer to anarchism, it may seem like this is far too much to 'undo.' You might think that imagining a world without all these institutions is just idealistic. But does that mean that we should never challenge common-sense ideas or try to see behind the business school stories about the benefits of capitalism? It seems to me that there is an important ethical imperative to reveal ideology, and to promote truth, once you see it. In 1964, the Italian novelist and intellectual Italo Calvino travelled to Cuba and met with the revolutionary leader Che Guevara:

> Calvino: 'The European working class isn't interested in this talk about sacrifice. Or in the association of socialism with sacrifice and voluntary work. They are interested in cars and TV and higher wages. They support the Party because it leads the fight for higher wages. And they have a right to want this.'
> Guevara: 'I'm very happy for the European working class with their higher wages. But don't forget who is paying for those wages. We are – millions of exploited workers and peasants in Latin America, Africa and Asia.'
>
> *(quoted in Cope, 2015)*

Telling the truth about the world that you see is an important first step in exposing power and its abuses.

Anarchism and economy

Some of the main questions within anarchist thought concern how an economy should be organized and how we should get to that state of affairs. In answering this question, we should start by actually defining economy – something many textbooks fail to do. Put simply, economy refers to systems of resource production and distribution, and all societies have some form of economy (see Chapter 11, and Swedberg, 2003; Carruthers and Babb, 2000).

Many anarchist positions could be described as some form of anarcho-communism which advocates for a non-hierarchical society with some sort of communal and/or **co-operative** way of organizing production and distribution

(Gelderloos, 2015, see box in Chapter 8). However, there are other anarchists who argue that some sort of forced redistribution is not justified because it interferes with people's freedoms, and that uneven distribution of wealth is not necessarily wrong (Rothbard, 1978). Indeed, many 'anarcho-capitalists' believe that differences in earnings and accumulation are understandable and justifiable and that systems of authority obscure these legitimate differences in earnings based on merit and hard work. Here, earnings may refer to those of an individual, a firm or a country (Molyneux, 2017; Oliver, 2013). Though rarely describing itself as anarcho-capitalist, a libertarian, free market capitalism would also be a sort of anarcho-capitalist philosophy. The popularity of a traditional liberalism that stresses individual freedoms has decreased over the past few decades, and it has become apparent that 'neoliberalism' (a liberalism in which certain firms and nations use government structures and military and financial institutions to further their interests) is the actual order of the day. Many commentators would argue that neoliberalism is actually much more profitable for elites than true free market liberalism (Harvey, 2007).

It seems to me that anarcho-capitalism − because of its reliance on liberalism − cannot really be a true anarchism. Indeed, the fact that anarcho-capitalism does not advocate for radical redistribution may inherently preserve hierarchy, in that hierarchies are largely defined in terms of income and wealth, resulting in a society which is always already stratified by power (Panitch and Konings, 2008).

Building on this foundation, we now arrive at our key question: what is the intersection of marketing and anarchism? The sections that follow draw upon the two models of anarchist economics (the anarcho-capitalist and anarcho-communist) to identify two of the (rare) points at which marketing and anarchism could possibly intersect. The first considers the anarcho-capitalism of maverick marketer Charles Saatchi and as such draws upon the traditional (capitalist) model of marketing. The second considers how the anarcho-communist movement Occupy Wall Street used a version of social marketing to amplify its message.

The case of Charles Saatchi

Charles Saatchi is a renowned baron of the advertising industry. He has been known for 'throwing out the rules' and taking on ad campaigns that others would not, often advocating controversial changes to social behaviours. An example of one of his best-known campaigns is an image of a pregnant man, with the caption 'Would you be more careful if it was you that got pregnant?' This advert, from 1970, challenged received views on social issues such as birth control (Hatton and Walker, 2005). A more recent example can be seen in the partnership of his flagship agency and the organization Amnesty International, which campaigns for the release of political prisoners, and in which the agency deployed the memory of the martyred US anarchist heroes Sacco and Vanzetti (Saatchi and Saatchi, 2016) to make a fairly generic appeal about 'the global fight against injustice.'

Saatchi is also a renowned player in the arena of art collecting. His strategy throughout the 1990s was to buy most of the work produced in London art schools, hedging his bets that some would become incredibly valuable. In time, he ultimately managed to inflate the value of his collection and to inspire bidding wars within the field of art collection more generally (Thompson, 2008; Hatton and Walker, 2005). Key to Saatchi's art collecting style is shock – gaining attention by assaulting viewers with controversial and at times offensive images. While this is a trend that can be seen throughout his collecting and his exhibitions, many consider the 1997 *Sensation* exhibition to be the clearest statement of his intent. This was a show in which Damien Hirst's shark preserved in formaldehyde was presented as art – a gesture that was widely criticized inside and outside the art world at the time. Like his advertising, this is an area where he is willing to experiment with ultra-radical political positions. Numerous artworks in his collection reference anarchism specifically, including a *Sacco and Vanzetti* painting by Dominick Lombardi, *Anarchy in the UK* by Carrie Reichardt, *Anarchy* by Conrad Crispin Jones, *Anarchy* by Rick Lumsden and Michael Vincent Manalo's *In Order to Bring Peace and Also Anarchy*. Several exhibitions at Saatchi's gallery have also taken on the theme, including the 2017–18 *Art Riot* show which focused on the work of the collective Pussy Riot and some of their other Russian contemporaries, such as Blue Noses. Saatchi's exhibitions are always public and presented as a display of shock art, but they are also often understood by critics as a form of self-promotion conducted to elevate the value of his own collection (Thompson, 2008; Hatton and Walker, 2005). It is also notable that Saatchi is not above having expensive private exhibitions within his art spaces as well. In the autumn of 2017, he hosted a show called *Inside Pussy Riot*, an 'immersive theatre experience,' which accompanied the *Art Riot* show and cost £29.15 for entry.

That show can be used here as an example of the contradictions inherent within Saatchi's strategy. To begin, visitors were given no warnings as to what it means to 'go into' Pussy Riot and were advised not to 'spoil' the experience by reading reviews. Having had the experience, I can tell you that what happens is that you are temporarily imprisoned. The experience begins with a protest wherein you have to wear a balaclava, which soon ends with you 'arrested' and (very lightly) thrown to the ground. In a booking room, you see one of your compatriots get stripped down to a bra and underpants. You go through a sham court process and are sentenced to manual labour. You have to do meaningless activities like count pennies under tremendous time pressure, and then a guard comes by and destroys your count. Toward the end, you are locked in a pitch-black room, unsure of what will happen next.

This case study raises two issues in relation to marketing. The first are the class issues. This was an experience not only for people adequately 'cultured' (class-socialized) to go to the Saatchi Gallery but also for London residents and tourists who can pay to be imprisoned for fun. In other words, a playful element of radical and dissident politics is reproduced for those who almost definitely benefit handsomely from capitalism and without any explicit sense of challenging it (see also Chapter 16). The theatre group responsible, Les Enfants Terribles, went for a completely staged approach to the prison camp experience. You learn immediately that the strip-searched individual is part of the theatre troupe. The court is literally portrayed in the style of a carnival. The guards' tone is so over-the-top that it's not scary so much as laughable. In such an immersive experience, there was perhaps a real opportunity to shock attendees into consciousness of some harsh political realities, but ultimately the approach taken is of entertainment to be consumed by those who can afford to pay for it.

Ultimately, the anarchism of multi-millionaire business mavericks such as Saatchi is no anarchism at all. It is not aimed at the abolition of authority, whether state or market, instead presenting a version of anarchist aesthetics as shock, as an experience for art tourists. Moreover, it does not push for redistribution or communal economics and as such does not fight the hierarchical organization of society. Perhaps worst of all, Saatchi has actively furthered the uneven distribution of value and wealth by creating a small class of super-wealthy artists while the majority of cultural producers have highly precarious livelihoods (see Thompson, 2008). So, while Saatchi at least nominally combines marketing and anarchism, we see that there is no legitimate intersection between a committed anarchist theory and practice and his use of anarchistic aesthetics.

The case of Occupy Wall Street

A very different site for exploring the relationship between marketing and anarchism can be found in the case of Occupy Wall Street, the anarcho-communist mass movement which emerged in New York's Financial District in the autumn of 2011, spreading across the Global North in subsequent weeks. The movement was well-known to have made extensive use of advanced communications strategies and was particularly noted for its use of social media marketing, even being lauded as one of the best branding exercises of the year (Dumenco, 2011).

In understanding what the Occupy activists did, it is helpful to have an understanding about the nature and meaning of media practices. Following Fuchs (2013), let's take a 'neutral' approach to media, seeing any particular media practice or technology as neither inherently positive nor negative. Advertising, for example, could be quite progressive or quite conservative – it depends on what it was trying to achieve and how. Importantly, this neutral perspective reminds us of the continuities between old and new media, which are more common than we often think. Webpages which have few videos (like Facebook), for example, tend to be read quite like old-fashioned newspapers. Individuals jump around from one article to another. Adverts on Facebook must also follow similar principles as newspaper adverts to 'work.' Rules for contemporary newspaper adverts are that they should generally have short, catchy text and evocative images (Leiss et al., 2005). These ideas stem from observations of media effects – the fact that certain media tend to produce particular patterns of reading and interpretation.

While some of the scholarship on Occupy takes a 'cyber-utopian' tone, suggesting that the widespread use of social media produces new flatter and more democratic forms of organization and communication, there are other important perspectives on the issue (see Fuchs, 2014; Costanza-Chock, 2012). There was actually a wide variety of media practices at Occupy Wall Street, involving the full range of traditional media, such as handbills, newspapers, badges and placards. Social media, like Facebook and Twitter, were simply additional avenues for spreading the same messages. While there are some media-specific effects (such as the need for brevity on Twitter), many common principles of communications still applied. For example, the repeated use of the 'Occupy' name, slogans such as 'We are the 99%' and imagery were pretty much what one would expect from traditional branding. Ultimately, the question of whether Occupy actually engaged in 'marketing' seems unavoidable, as there were a number of Occupy groups and activities directly aimed at disseminating their ideas more widely. Moreover, in my experience, many in the movement worked in marketing or were aware that they were engaging in marketing as part of their work in the movement. Indeed, it was widely reported that Occupy Wall Street had formal public relations representation (e.g. DiGiacomo, Griffith, and Caparell, 2011).

Examining the biggest archives on Occupy Wall Street, housed at the Tamiment Archive in New York University's Bobst Library, helps to further understand the movement's marketing practices. Occupy communications – particularly those produced by very central and very formal subgroups of the movement – frequently used visual conventions associated with marketing communications, such as branded imagery, taglines and memorable phrases and logos (Leiss et al., 2005). In one instance, Occupy Wall Street even produced a traditional TV advertisement and tried to buy air time on the Fox News channel (Grossman and Sauvage, 2011; Tankersley, 2011). Yet if we consider the effectiveness of Occupy Wall Street as a marketing organization, we can conclude that the creative skills in the group were quite high but that the resources of the movement were inadequate to achieve their goals through marketing means. This included not only financial resources but also resources like social legitimacy, which meant that using 'marketing' as an activist group seemed to be a practice with relatively little reach.

Still, 'social marketing' scholars and practitioners espouse the inherent value of taking on impossible tasks. Take this quote from Lee and Kotler (2011, p. 15), leaders of the social marketing field, as a case in point:

> In social marketing, the competition is most often the current or preferred behavior of our target audience and the perceived benefits associated with that behavior, including the status quo. This also includes any organizations selling or promoting competing behaviors (e.g. the tobacco industry) . . . For a variety of reasons, we think social marketing is more difficult than commercial marketing. Consider the financial resources the competition has to make smoking look cool, yard cleanup using a gas blower easy, and weed-free lawns the norm.

This quotation comes from a key text on social marketing practice, as a defence of why social marketing is worthwhile but at the same time that it acknowledges the difficulty of that practice. One might ask why anyone would engage in a marketing battle with small resources, against organizations *that actually profit* from advocating the opposite? This is one of the challenges social marketing of the type Occupy Wall Street tried to engage in will always face.

One possible answer to this question can be found in the early academic social marketing literature. The inventors of the social marketing concept were intrigued by the social movements of the 1960s but felt constrained by their place within marketing departments in business schools (reviewed in Andreasen, 2003; see also Andreasen, 1997 for his personal account). Rather than question whether marketing is the place for activism at all, they instead decided to insert marketing into social causes. This decision can be read as not only a product of their place in business schools but also the influence of the repression of people identified as 'communists' in 1950s America. In their writing, they clearly state that they felt the need to identify a system which could allow for progressive social change but without 'top-down' state intervention. They believed that 'letting markets decide' was less likely to be seen as challenging to the established order. It would allow progressive voices to be heard but without introducing government regulation to force such voices to the front (for example, by guaranteeing television air-time to specific political positions).

'Letting the market decide,' however, does not necessarily solve the problem of social marketing. There are massive power asymmetries between those who can buy media coverage and those who consume the media (Fuchs, 2013). As such, consumer decisions are not 'free decisions' but are persistently shaped through persuasive forms of advertising, by those who seek to benefit from certain decisions (Mosco, 2009). With this in mind, it seems that marketing may *not* be a neutral tactic, not a practice that can simply be adopted by people who wish to oppose capitalism and hierarchy. In the world as it is, where access to media requires massive sums of money, marketing, whether social or not, is necessarily a capitalist practice. In addition, where access requires the legitimacy of existing political institutions (for example, in the UK where much of the media landscape is regulated by the government), it is not free from the influence of the state. One of the crucial challenges facing movements like Occupy, then, is how to get a message out, to engage in something like social marketing, while dealing with access to media that is guarded by wealth and authority.

Conclusion

This chapter has presented an introduction to anarchism for marketing, an introduction to marketing for anarchism and two cases which highlight some of the rare intersections between the two. Yet in these cases it is anarchism that becomes diluted and weakened. The 'anarchism' of Saatchi and his colleagues is little more than a marketing ploy. It is a capitalist tactic to the core, not aimed at the eventual dissolution of hierarchy and the production of more democratic and free social relations but instead a kind of shock aesthetic. The case of Occupy Wall Street, in contrast, shows what happens when a genuinely anarchist organization attempts to 'market' itself. While the motivations of such an attempt are perfectly credible, if marketing is a practice which requires the resources and technologies of capitalism, then it may be very poorly suited to the task of changing the opinions of the 99%, to paraphrase one of Occupy's slogans.

After taking all of this in, you may question why a chapter on marketing and anarchism was written at all, if they are indeed in such inherent opposition. Let me suggest a few responses. First of all, it provides some clarity about anarcho-capitalism in relation to other forms of anarchism and particularly in relation to its use in marketing. It seems to me that anarcho-capitalism is not anarchism at all, because it does not aim at producing an anarchist social order (see also Chapter 16). Secondly, for those interested in political activism, it suggests that marketing is unlikely to produce radical social change. It even raises questions about the potential successes of traditional social marketing causes, especially in cases where non-profit actors are competing directly with for-profit actors. Finally, for all readers, it opens the question of what marketing is and does, so that they can address and perhaps contest it in their organizing and everyday lives. Building on contemporary developments in ethics (Badiou, 1998), you now arguably face an 'ethical dilemma': you can no longer claim impartiality or ignorance but must decide yourself what to do next. In a society in which our choices are so profoundly shaped by the marketing of capitalism, it is difficult to ever be in a neutral position.

Questions for further study

1   Based on what you have read here, do you think that anarchists can also be capitalists? What are the contradictions in trying to be both at the same time?
2   Think of examples of 'social' marketing. What are the problems with trying to persuade people to support certain social causes or change their behaviour so as to be more environmentally friendly?
3   If anarchists care about freedom, should they be using techniques of persuasion to encourage people to think and act in different ways? Are there arguments that anarchists should never use any form of marketing?
4   If anarchists do reject all forms of marketing, what other forms of communication can they use to inform people about their ideas? How would these be different from marketing?

References

Amin, S. (1997). *Capitalism in the Age of Globalization*. London: Zed Books.
Andreasen, A. (1997). "From Ghetto Marketing to Social Marketing; Bringing Social Relevance to Marketing." *Journal of Public Policy & Marketing*, 16(1), 129–131.
Andreasen, A. (2003). "The Life Trajectory of Social Marketing." *Marketing Theory*, 3(3), 293–303.
Badiou, A. (1998/2001). *Ethics: An Essay on the Origin of Evil* (P. Hallward, Trans.). London: Verso.
Bartels, R. (1951). "Influences on the Development of Marketing Thought, 1900–1923." *Journal of Marketing*, 16 (July), 1–17.

Bauman, Z. (2004). *Work, Consumerism, and the New Poor*. Maidenhead: Open University Press.

Bukharin, N. (1917). *Imperialism and World Economy*. Createspace Independent Publishing Platform.

Carruthers, B. G., and Babb, S. L. (2000). *Economy/Society: Markets, Meanings, and Social Structure*. Thousand Oaks, CA: Pine Forge Press; Sage Publications.

Cope, Z. (2015). *Divided World, Divided Class: Global Political Economy and the Stratification of Labour Under Capitalism*. Montreal: Kersplebedeb.

Costanza-Chock, S. (2012). "Mic Check! Media Cultures and the Occupy Movement." *Social Movement Studies*, 11(3–4), 375–385.

DiGiacomo, F., Griffith, C., and Caparell, A. (2011). "Occupy Wall Street Protestors Picked up by Public Relations Firm Workshouse Pro-Bono." *New York Daily News*, 3 October. Online edition. Available at: www.nydailynews.com/entertainment/gossip/occupy-wall-street-protesters-picked-public-relations-firm-workhouse-pro-bono-article-1.959968.

Dumenco, S. (2011). "Occupy Wall Street, the Brand." *Ad Age*, 19 October. Online edition. Available at: http://adage.com/article/trending-topics/occupy-wall-street-brand/230516/.

Eisinger, J. (2014). "Why Only One Top Banker Went to Jail for the Financial Crisis." *New York Times*, 30 April. Online edition. Available at: www.nytimes.com/2014/05/04/magazine/only-one-top-banker-jail-financial-crisis.html.

Ellis, N., Fitchett, J., Higgins, M., Jack, G., Lim, M., Saren, M., and Tadajewski, M. (2010). *Marketing: A Critical Textbook*. London: Sage Publications.

Fill, C. (2013). *Marketing Communications* (6th Edition). Harlow: Pearson.

Fuchs, C. (2013). *Social Media: A Critical Introduction*. London: Sage Publications.

Fuchs, C. (2014). *OccupyMedia! The Occupy Movement and Social Media in Crisis Capitalism*. Hants: Zero Books.

Gelderloos, P. (2015). *Anarchy Works: Examples of Anarchist Ideas in Practice*. Bristol: Active Distribution.

Gemelli, G. (1997). *From Imitation to Competitive-Cooperation: Ford Foundation and Management Education in Western Europe*. Florence, Italy: European University Institute.

Gordon, R. A., and Howell, J. E. (1959). *Higher Education for Business*. New York, NY: Columbia University Press.

Graeber, D. (2004). *Fragments of an Anarchist Anthropology*. Chicago, IL: Prickly Paradigm Press.

Graeber, D. (2013). *The Democracy Project*. London: Penguin Books.

Grossman, G., and Sauvage, D. (2011). "Occupy Wall Street Commercial." Available at: www.youtube.com/watch?v=5O_Ao9w1u7c.

Harvey, D. (2005). *The New Imperialism*. Oxford: Oxford University Press.

Harvey, D. (2007). *A Brief History of Neoliberalism*. Oxford: Oxford University Press.

Hatton, R., and Walker, J. (2005). *Supercollector: A Critique of Charles Saatchi*. London: Institute of Artology.

Hunt, S. (1976). "The Nature and Scope of Marketing." *Journal of Marketing*, 40(3), 17–28.

Kelley, W. T. (1956). "The Development of Early Thought in Marketing and Promotion." *Journal of Marketing*, 21 (July), 62–67.

Kotler, P., and Levy, S. J. (1969). "Broadening the Concept of Marketing." *Journal of Marketing*, 33 (January), 1–15.

Lee, N., and Kotler, P. (2011). *Social Marketing: Influencing Behaviors for Good*. Los Angeles, CA: Sage Publications.

Leiss, W., Kline, S., Jhally, S., and Botterill, J. (2005). *Social Communication in Advertising: Consumption in the Mediated Marketplace* (3rd Edition). Milton Park, Oxon: Routledge.

Marx, K. (1867). *Capital* (Ben Fowkes, Trans.) (Vol. 1). New York, NY: Penguin Books.

Maynard, H. H. (1941). "Marketing Courses Prior to 1910." *Journal of Marketing*, 5 (April), 382–384.

Molyneux, S. (2017). *Practical Anarchy: The Freedom of the Future*. Createspace Independent Publishing Platform.

Mosco, V. (2009). *The Political Economy of Communication*. London: Sage Publications.

Oliver, J. M. (2013). *The New Libertarianism: Anarcho-Capitalism*. Createspace Independent Publishing Platform.

Panitch, L., and Konings, M. (2008). "Demystifying Imperial Finance." In L. Panitch and M. Konings (Eds.), *American Empire and the Political Economy of Global Finance*. Houndsmills: Palgrave.

Pierson, F. C. (1959). *The Education of American Businessmen*. New York, NY: McGraw-Hill Book Company.

Rothbard, M. N. (1978). *For a New Liberty: The Libertarian Manifesto*. Auburn, AL: Ludwig von Mises Institute.

Saatchi and Saatchi. (2016). "Saatchi & Saatchi Partners With Amnesty International on Human Rights Appeal #HeresToYou." Available at: http://saatchi.com/pl-PL/news/saatchi-saatchi-partners-with-amnesty-international-on-human-rights-appeal-herestoyou/.

Scannell, K., and Milne, R. (2017). "Who Was Convicted Because of the Global Financial Crisis?" *Financial Times*, 9 August. Online edition. Available at: www.ft.com/content/de173cc6-7c79-11e7-ab01-a13271d1ee9c.

Swedberg, R. (2003). *Principles of Economic Sociology*. Princeton, NJ: Princeton University Press.

Tankersley, J. (2011). "Occupy Wall Street's Marketing Crisis: What Would an OWS Brand Look Like?" *The Atlantic*, 23 October. Online edition. Available at: www.theatlantic.com/business/archive/2011/10/occupy-wall-streets-marketing-crisis-what-would-an-ows-brand-look-like/247175/.

Thompson, D. (2008). *The $12 Million Stuffed Shark: The Curious Economics of Contemporary Art*. London: Aurum Press.

16

INNOVATION AND ENTREPRENEURSHIP

Alf Rehn

That companies need to 'innovate or die' has become one of the leading clichés of our time. It is an article of faith in contemporary society that we live in an age of such tumultuous change that a company can survive only by utilizing its creative powers to continuously create newer and better products or services. This is also why so many CEOs, professors and even politicians continuously repeat claims about the critical importance of innovation – for companies as well as for countries. However, it is not always easy to say exactly what innovation is, as it comes in many forms. The same can be said for creativity, which we might innately understand and at least at times recognize but which is still not completely understood as a human faculty. What we do know is that creativity can be wild and crazy and definitively doesn't play by the rules. In a similar manner, innovation is often talked about as a revolutionary force, one that can 'disrupt' industries and nations. It shouldn't come as a surprise, then, that creativity and innovation are at times referred to as anarchistic or that those who realize innovative ideas are described as something similar to anarchists.

To make sense of such comparisons, we need to understand what anarchism is or at least what we think it is. To some, it looks like pure chaos, the absence of order and civilization. To others, it looks like no more of 'the man' and a chance to be free. To some, it might even look like a land of opportunity, one where the rules are suspended and no-one rules, where one might test out things that were previously forbidden. And what does an anarchist look like? If you would have asked people some 50 years ago, they would probably have pointed to the cartoon depiction of early anarchists, all clad in black, sporting bushy beards and carrying cartoon bombs. This popular depiction is a nod to Mikhail **Bakunin**, one of the key founders of socialist anarchism (see box in Chapter 7), as well as to the notion of anarchists as violent revolutionaries. If you ask today, quite a few would point to direct action groups such as Antifa (Anti-Fascist Action) or Black Bloc protestors – black clothes, scarves, ski masks and the like, marching, chanting and occasionally throwing rocks.

Today, there is a third image of the anarchist, one which connects to the notion of anarchy as opportunity. This is the young person in khakis and a polo shirt, laptop at the ready, wanting to pay in bitcoin. The Ayn Rand-reading, libertarian, anti-authoritarian anarcho-capitalist rarely marches and is unlikely to have a deep understanding of Bakunin yet still stands as a peculiar twist in the tale of anarchism. This particular breed of anarchist enjoys breaking at least some rules, desires (a specific kind of) freedom and further, whilst scorned by many, stands as a symbol of the way in which anarchism has been co-opted, possibly perverted and definitively recast within the broad field of innovation, entrepreneurship and free-market capitalism (see also Chapter 15).

This chapter will discuss anarchy with and without anarchism, particularly with reference to business thinking and education. Whereas many of the disciplines taught at a conventional business school are opposed to anarchism on a fundamental and philosophical level, not all of them are. A few – such as innovation and entrepreneurship – exhibit a more complex relationship to anarchism, even if it would be problematic to assume that they are, therefore, 'anarchism-friendly.' What I will do is discuss the way in which these two specific disciplines within management studies – innovation and entrepreneurship – deal with something we might call *the fetish of anarchy* and also consider how this might be counteracted. It will deal with a simplistic idea of what it means to be anarchistic and the way in which behaving without regard for or in opposition to hierarchy or institutional rules becomes central to the ideals of innovation and entrepreneurship.

This chapter will

- explain the basics of creativity, innovation and entrepreneurship;
- show that how we tend to think about them is aligned with ideas about anarchy and anarchism;
- discuss how this doesn't necessary amount to more than a flirtation with freedom and is still in line with 'proper' management thinking; and
- stimulate a discussion about anarchic thinking and the possibilities of freedom in innovation and entrepreneurship.

Creativity, innovation and all that

Creativity is something we often refer to, but at the same time, it isn't always easy to define. We might, to begin, say that creativity is the faculty through which human beings can create new ideas. In part, this is thanks to human beings having a capacity for imagination (i.e. to think of things or about things in a way that isn't bound by what we know about the world). For instance, if you read this book, it is very likely that you know of ketchup as a condiment. If you think about ketchup, you will in all likelihood think of red tomato ketchup, quite possibly even of a specific brand like Heinz. If a person would completely lack imagination, this is where it would end. Ketchup is red and made of tomatoes, and that's it. For a person with imagination, this needn't be so. You might have heard of other types, like walnut ketchup, mushroom ketchup and banana ketchup, and can think of several other forms – maybe a zucchini ketchup or a kale one? And why stop there? Why not make ketchup different colours? Maybe a black ketchup or one with stripes like toothpaste? (The funny thing is, Heinz actually explored this and launched the EZ Squirt brand of ketchup for kids – with colours like Blastin' Green, Funky Purple, Stellar Blue, Passion Pink, Awesome Orange and Totally Teal.)

This, the capacity to think of forms of ketchup you've never seen before, could be called imagination or creativity. The exact boundary between the two is difficult to pinpoint, but we usually talk of imagination when we refer to the capacity to think wholly without boundaries (imagine a ketchup with actual blinking stars in it and which magically cures hangovers) and creativity when we use these skills to solve problems, create new art or think up a new product. What Heinz did with the EZ Squirt ketchup was thus to first take the imaginative leap to coloured ketchups and then creatively developed Funky Purple.

Here, we can also start talking about innovation. It takes imagination to create an innovation, but a thought can be imaginative without being realizable. I can, for instance, imagine a kind of beer that not only doesn't give me a hangover but also makes me better looking and burns away the fat around my waist. I'd pay for such beer, but sadly I have no idea how to go from my idea to actually making it happen. It's a creative thought but not a realizable one. Sometimes, though, imagination can take the leap to reality. When the first iPod was released, it had "1000 songs in your pocket" as a tagline. Now, to us old enough to remember the time before such products, that seemed almost as magic slimming beer, but Apple had managed to make it happen. Innovation, then, is *the successful realization of a creative idea that is accepted in a use-context and/or system of exchange.*

This can refer to the market economy we all know, the one where products and services are bought and sold, but it can also refer to something far wider. A social innovation, for instance, needs to be accepted in the system of exchanges that organizes the activities it wishes to innovate – which can be based on gifting and generosity rather than market exchange. As an example, we might think of the principle of free health care. For a very long time, the notion that the state would guarantee health care for all (or at least most) seemed like a completely impossible idea – and many in the US still think it is. The idea did take root in several countries, however, leading to institutions such as the National Health Service in the UK. The system of exchange here obviously wasn't one of consumers and companies but rather the *political* and *institutional* context, where the idea needed to be supported by enough of the voting public to be possible to implement and get enough traction among the involved institutions to be feasible.

The progress from imaginative idea, by way of creative adaptation, to full-blown innovation, is thus neither self-evident nor easy to model and/or define. We can point to successes and failures at each point along the way but not always give a perfect explanation for why some ideas develop and work and others do not. Nor do we always know why innovations succeed or fail, as so many things can either support or impede them. What we *do* know is that in order to succeed, organizations as well as people need to be able to break with the way in which things have normally been done in their field and explore ways of thinking and acting that may well be against the assumed rules and norms of the field in question. It is here we can find the connection to various conceptions of anarchy, anarchism and anarchist thought.

Social and technological innovation

Imagination, as a faculty, could well be described as an anarchistic energy. It cares not for what is allowed, what is best practice or what is possible and is our mind at its most free. It follows that creativity is in this way also linked to freedom, such as in freedom of thought. If we lacked imagination and creativity, we would still be living in societies dominated by chieftains, the most powerful person in the tribe or the community declaring him- or herself ruler, and that's that. It was our imagination that allowed us to think beyond chieftains and kings, which gave us democracy (a rather nice little social innovation, even in its less perfect modes), and it is imagination that enables us to imagine a world without governments and similar formal institutions. Creativity, whilst possible to use in a plethora of ways, thus also opens up ways of thinking and acting that break with existing structures, including but not limited to laws (both a burglar and a smuggler can be very creative (see Clay and Phillips, 2016)), institutions (think of the way in which modern art developed by challenging existing art institutions (see Chipp, 1968)), and governments (for instance by creating a currency that is in no way connected to a central bank (see Narayanan et al., 2016)).

Many innovations follow from this. A **co-operative**, for instance, was and is a social innovation that broke with existing forms of ownership and control of work (see Chapter 8, and the box in Chapter 8). **Open source software** was both a product and a process innovation that broke with the prevailing notion that software needs to be a commodity and needs to be governed and created by a corporation (see box in Chapter 1). Anarchism itself was an innovative idea about governance and politics. This of course does not mean that all innovations follow the same path, as most innovations (at least at the moment) exist squarely as commodities in the sphere of market capitalism. This hasn't, however, stopped people from drawing upon the underlying anarchist ethos and, through this, using anarchist ideas in the general field of innovation.

If we for instance look at the way in which we often talk about innovators in the public discourse, these are often described with words that are meant to evoke some of this anarchic energy – maverick, revolutionary, rebel. Innovation itself can be described as radical, disruptive or transformative. This does not mean that innovation or innovators always are, rather that when we talk about them, we often reach for such terms. Facebook, poster-child of startup entrepreneurship, used to have a mantra of "Move fast and break things," by which it wanted to emphasize just how little one cared about the rules, and this has spread into culture at large. Companies such as Uber flaunted how they didn't care about the governmental regulations set up to control the taxi industry and were both hailed and rewarded for this, whereas one of the hottest technologies in the world (at the moment I write this) is crypto-currencies and the blockchains that power them – the latter being a form of keeping tabs on who has what that works not through one centralized form of government but by a distributed ledger where it is the community rather than an official that is in charge (sound familiar?). Some cryptoanarchists have taken all this to mean that true revolutionary power lies not in politics and political ideas but rather in technology and the intrepid entrepreneurs who harness it (see Chapter 14).

The anarchy of entrepreneurship

If creativity is about new thinking and innovation about new creations, then entrepreneurship might be said to deal with new ventures. Now, if you think that those differences sound rather vague and like there's a lot of overlap between the categories, you're absolutely right. You can have entrepreneurship without much of either creativity or innovation – opening up yet another takeaway or hairdresser is entrepreneurial but not necessarily innovative – but we still often implicitly connect creativity, innovation and entrepreneurship.

An entrepreneur, then, is someone who starts a business or an organization, although the word has in modern entrepreneurship research been used to describe everything from artists to revolutionaries (Baker and Welter, 2018). In public discourse, the term is mostly used about people who start new businesses, particularly those who start novel and risky ones. A hairdresser working for him- or herself is technically just as much an entrepreneur as the programmer who founded Rosa, the dating app for anarchists (which sadly doesn't exist, yet), but is still more likely to be referred to as 'small business,' as separate from entrepreneurship. Some think that the latter term should be reserved primarily for individuals who try to achieve something more than surviving and getting an income and who instead take risks in order to grow the company by doing something new. Today, this kind of entrepreneurship is sometimes referred to as 'startup entrepreneurship.'

What an entrepreneur does in an economic system, particularly in a market economy, has been described with the concept 'creative destruction' (Schumpeter, 1942, yet even cooler in the original German as used by Sombart, 1913: '*schöpferische Zerstörung*'). This has its roots in the thinking of Karl **Marx** (see box in Chapter 11), who was interested in the ways in which capitalism both generates new ideas and new companies but at the same time continuously destroys capital and commodity values. This line of thinking was taken up by Joseph Schumpeter, whose famous line from *Capitalism, Socialism and Democracy* was that capitalism requires 'the perennial gale of creative destruction,' and in his thinking, the person who enacted this was the entrepreneur. These people saw a new way to create value, from either new products, new technology, new markets or new ways of working, and whilst this is of course creative, it also carries with it a destructive aspect. For instance, the emergence of digital photography was of course a boon for a number of companies, including companies that make mobile phones. Yet this innovation and the entrepreneurs who built companies around it also destroyed value – think for instance of the companies who produced traditional cameras and film and the many one-hour photo shops that had to close.

Schumpeter thus saw that innovation and entrepreneurship was a dynamic but also somewhat chaotic energy, one that drove the economy onwards. He was, much like Marx, pessimistic regarding how sustainable this was in the long run, but many other economists and others took the concept from him and established that this dynamism needn't have any boundaries, that it could generate continuous development and growth. The entrepreneur, then, stands at the centre of the economy as a kind of engine, continuously bringing new innovations and new developments, whilst also driving slower, less dynamic companies and organizations out of business. The concept can of course be used in other contexts as well. We might for instance consider the emergence of modern art a kind of entrepreneurship (see Chapter 15), and the same dynamic can be found in basically every creative endeavour.

Politics, too, can be viewed through the same lens. The emergence of 'social anarchism,' as a criticism of 'state communism,' and Bakunin's subsequent feud with Marx could be described as both innovation in action and creative destruction (among other things, it led to the demise of the communist First International). Here, Bakunin was by far the more radical, a thinker who would not compromise when it came to having no government and no state. Marx wanted nothing to do with the free-for-all that Bakunin suggested. Bakunin was the true disruptive force here, arguing for real innovation (and thus destruction). Where Marx argued for transitionary models of centralized organization (such as the dictatorship of the proletariat), Bakunin saw every attempt to negotiate with the powers that be as failing the revolutionary project. In the end, whilst both had their champions within the First International, Bakunin was expelled for protesting against Marx's proposal that the aim should be a state led by the proletariat – something utterly unthinkable for the anarchists. What this led to was a split between socialist and anarchist factions and arguably a sharpening of both positions. In other words, we might say that both socialism and anarchism as we know them emerged out of a destructive dynamic that in the end pushed both movements forward – even if the First International didn't survive. (It split, confusingly, into two separate First Internationals, who held their own, competing congresses.) By positioning himself differently to Marx, Bakunin could rally a new dynamic, and it is interesting to note that where the first congress of the anarchist First International in St. Imier was considered a great success, the sixth congress of the Marxist wing was by most seen as a failure and was disbanded three years later. Whilst he would have hated the very notion, it is almost as if Bakunin emerges here as an entrepreneur, in the Schumpeterian sense. Bakunin did, after all, argue that 'the passion for destruction is a creative passion, too!' (Bakunin, 1842).

The entrepreneur as anarchist and the anarchist as entrepreneur

The notion of the entrepreneur as an agent of creative destruction has, as already intimated, led to a tendency to see entrepreneurs as wild, freewheeling pirates. Books on entrepreneurship for a popular audience can have titles such as *Rules for Revolutionaries: The Capitalist Manifesto for Creating and Marketing New Products and Services, Business Model Generation: A Handbook for Visionaries, Game Changers and Challengers*, or *The Upstarts: How Uber, Airbnb, and the Killer Companies of the New Silicon Valley Are Changing the World*. Startup conferences liberally use terms such as *disruption* (from 'disruptive innovation,' a term coined by Clayton Christensen), *transformation* and *radical change*, and these same phrases then turn up when entrepreneurs describe themselves. Today, you can even go to an online store such as startupvitamins.com and buy a T-shirt with the slogan 'Be Amazing. Be Revolutionary.' and complement this with an 'Innovate or Die' cap and an 'Always Challenge the Old Ways' coffee mug.

All this might seem silly and/or harmless, but it also communicates something about the way in which the field sees itself. Because an entrepreneur, at least by the Schumpeterian definition, challenges existing systems, there does exist an implied link to 'revolution,' even if it might be a tenuous one. Similarly, as entrepreneurs by definition work for themselves, there is a narrative of freedom. Such ideas, particularly when they are presented as heroic accounts of being your own master and overthrowing old industries and even come with merchandise, can be very attractive. We should also in this context remember that the anarchist tradition has always been more open to a certain kind of entrepreneurial activity and small industry than the more statist socialists were. Where communist countries often forbade entrepreneurship outright, **Kropotkin** (1912, p. 111, see box in Chapter 3) writes in his *Fields, Factories and Workshops*:

> But wherever the direct intervention of taste and inventiveness are required, wherever new patterns of goods requiring a continual renewal of machinery and tools must continually be introduced in order to feed the demand, as is the case with all fancy textiles, even though they be fabricated to supply the millions; wherever a great variety of goods and the uninterrupted invention of new ones goes on, as is the case in the toy trade, in instrument making, watch making, bicycle making and so on; and finally, wherever the artistic feeling of the individual worker makes the best part of his goods, as is the case in hundreds of branches of small articles of luxury, there is a wide field for petty trades, rural workshops, domestic industries, and the like.

With this in mind, it might seem almost logical that in the more radical parts of the entrepreneurship scene, one can find an emergent anarchist tradition, if a very specialized such. Rather than representing the kind of thinking around community and **mutual** aid (see box in Chapter 17) that emerged out of the anarchism of

Kropotkin and Bakunin, this is something more akin to the individualist or egoist anarchism espoused by Max Stirner, which emphasized individual freedom. It's radical form, surprisingly popular among a certain kind of startup entrepreneurs, called 'anarcho-capitalism,' is aggressively anti-state and basically argues for a totally free market, with no state controls or laws (see e.g. Rothbard, 1978, and Chapter 15). Another form of anarchist thought that often inspires the same people is 'crypto-anarchism' (see Chapter 14), where the freedom to keep one's communications encrypted and private is emphasized. With technological developments in crypto-currencies, this has made anonymous counter-economies possible, something that is looked upon with favour by anarcho-capitalists. Here, it can be difficult to know where the line between anarchism and libertarianism should be drawn, as both emphasize freedom and reject the state as a power structure. The difference often comes down to positions held on private property rights. Where anarchists such as **Proudhon** (see box in Chapter 2) have seen private property and the control thereof as antithetical to true freedom and argued for shared or communal owner-ship of at least the means of production, libertarians and anarcho-capitalists hold that the right to own property is a form of freedom and shouldn't be curtailed. So whilst both camps wish to see the abolishment of the state, the latter group has proposed that law and order be upheld by privately funded corporations, paid for by private property owners, whereas the former group would see this as an affront to anarchist ideals of community and a shared pursuit of happiness.

MAX STIRNER, 1806–1856

Stirner was a German philosopher who was a major influence on the develop-ment of nihilism, existentialism and individualist anarchism. He proposed a radical anti-authoritarian and individualist critique both of modern Western society and its proposed cures of humanism, socialism, communism and anar-chism. All religions and ideologies, he argued, rest on empty concepts that serve merely to conceal the self-interest at their heart. Recognizing the inher-ent self-interest in institutions such as the state, church or school destroys their claims for legitimate authority and power. Stirner suggests that once these false claims have been exposed and the individual's drive for self-realization, or egoism, recognized as the only valid aim for a human being, then freedom can be obtained. Stirner advocates a 'union of egotists,' a freely entered into asso-ciation with others to enable all to more effectively realize their self-interest. Though often thought of as an individual anarchist as a result, Stirner rejected anarchism as a collective movement and revolution and any social movement aimed at reforming existing institutions. The power to create oneself comes from complete autonomy and the rejection of all pre-existing meaning struc-tures. Stirner's ideas contrast with the more collectivist spirit of communism.

> The notion that self-interest lies at the foundation of all social structures and values may be a useful corrective to the rose-tinted view that so often underestimates the problems of accommodating the deep-rooted self-interest of human beings within collective projects.

The difficulty here might be posed as a question: whose anarchy is it anyway? Many in the anarchist movement do not consider anarcho-capitalists real anarchists, as the movement has been so strongly anti-capitalist. Similarly, **cryptoanarchism**, with its focus on technology and anonymous markets, isn't always easy to connect to more classical anarchist thought or the traditional forms of anarchist activism (see box in Chapter 14). Both can, depending on your perspective, seem like anarchism in name only. That said, anarcho-capitalist entrepreneurs do exist, and their individualist form of anarchism isn't without precedent. Further, the manner in which entrepreneurship captures innovation and the energies connected to it does have important lessons for anarchism as well. Few if any anarchists would question the importance of human imagination, creativity and ingenuity, and the creation of alternative forms of social organization is today often powered by technological innovation (see the chapters in the previous section), making it important to understand the complex relationships between the fields.

Anarchism and its frenemies

A frenemy is someone who doesn't actually like you but pretends to do so, often for reasons to do with social networks. For instance, we might pretend to be friendly with a very powerful person in our community, even though we actually hate that person. It seems to me that the fields of innovation and entrepreneurship, both as fields of study and fields of practice, are something like frenemies to anarchism.

Creativity, as a field, might have the most unproblematic relationship to anarchism, regardless of tradition. Since anarchism is positioned as an ideology of freedom and since creativity requires and draws upon the same, it isn't surprising that key anarchist thinkers emphasized the importance of creativity (and imagination), which encourages idea generation without concern for how institutions or the state would view them. Creativity breaks with common sense and draws liberally from the anarchic dynamism of imagination.

The relationship between innovation and anarchism is far more fraught. Looking to innovation as a field of study, it is clear that it does celebrate the importance of breaking with old systems and teaches that destruction is the price we pay for progress. The field has tended to celebrate 'disruptive innovation,' a form of innovation where a competitor utilizes underserved markets and developments in technology in order to destabilize even the biggest and oldest actors in an industry (think, for example, about how Airbnb challenged the hotel industry). This might seem well in line with a philosophy of freedom but is in fact very far from an anarchist ethos. For whilst one celebrates tales of plucky underdogs who challenge industry stalwarts, this interest has only very rarely extended to challenging the system within which most innovations have been created – the capitalist market. Some recent developments in the field have flirted with such issues – there is a greater interest regarding social innovations, for instance – but overall the interest innovation studies has in freedom is very much a tempered one.

We can see something similar in the field of innovation practice. Yes, there are books out there such as *The Misfit Economy: Lessons in Creativity From Pirates, Hackers, Gangsters, and Other Informal Entrepreneurs* (Clay and Phillips, 2016) and people commonly talk of breaking rules, but it is also very clear that few if any active commentators in the field advocate anything remotely like an anarchist worldview. It is by necessity wedded to the central myth of 'creative destruction.' The innovator is a breaker of rules and frameworks, but only in a limited way, owing to a need to stay aligned with the institutional logic of capitalism. Innovation consultants might talk about 'thinking outside the box,' but they are dependent on major corporations as clients, which means that there are many boxes that remain completely unchallenged.

Entrepreneurship studies, for its part, has shown some interest towards more radical forms of activism, but this has always been a marginal occupation. For every study done on workers collectives, there are at least a hundred done on 'typical' entrepreneurial companies. The field does talk continuously about topics such as risk-taking and opportunity recognition, but both are always presented in a way where it becomes obvious that the risks are economic rather than existential and the opportunities that the field wants to help people recognize are very much market opportunities rather than attempts to rethink the market economy and the role of the state. The field emphasizes how entrepreneurship is a way to enact human freedom but rarely strays away from the assumption that this freedom needs to take place within a capitalist system. And here lies the rub. Anarchist thought has the potential, if taken seriously, to present a very different, more open perspective on entrepreneurship, in effect making the possibilities for entrepreneurship as social change considerably broader. This should be a good thing, as more perspectives and more possibilities to study enrich thought. This, however, has proven to be a bridge too far for most, and it in effect self-regulates itself to be smaller, and more limited, keeping anarchist thought a frenemy at best.

In entrepreneurship practice, as I've noted, there is a flirtation with anarchist ideas and a tendency to present oneself as something of an anarchist. The latter, however, is often more of an affectation than anything else, a way to mark oneself as a breed apart. So, whilst self-identifying as a 'maverick' or a 'punk entrepreneur' may seem like an engagement with anarchism, it can be a very superficial one. Considerably more interesting is the tendency to adopt some ideas regarding radical freedom, or even thinking in and with communities, within contemporary entrepreneurship discourse. Whilst many anarchists do not consider anarcho-capitalism or other radical forms of individualist anarchism as proper anarchism, these are still engagements with these ideas. Similarly, some entrepreneurship pundits have talked about the sharing economy (the part of the economy where one can trade/share goods or services – such as a place to sleep [Airbnb] or a car ride [Uber]) as real-izing some of the ideas of community and mutual aid that early anarchists espoused (Sundararajan, 2017). The latter argument does require some mental acrobatics to hold but also goes some way to show that whilst the field is still wedded to the capitalist economy, some of the ideas of freedom that anarchist thought has brought have found at least an imperfect resonance here, in frenemy territory.

Conclusion

What we might then say, overall, is that neither the field of innovation nor that of entrepreneurship actually wishes for anarchy, but both still have a fetish for it. The radical freedom present in anarchy, and theorized in anarchist thought, is something that the fields have a specific affinity for but which at the same time neither field can fully embrace. In the case of entrepreneurship, this has been handled by the emergence of anarcho-capitalism and crypto-anarchism, forms of anarchist thought that are more palatable. In the case of innovation, this has been handled within discussions on creativity or by turning attention to disruption, instead of engaging with the full spectrum of social innovation. In both cases, anarchic ideas have been turned into objects held at a distance, something one might occasionally make a move towards, such as when an innovation professor expresses giddy joy regarding the opportunities inherent in blockchain technology, but which one never com-mits to.

In the field of practice, this fetishization becomes even more pronounced, with corporate actors trying to rebrand themselves as 'revolutionaries,' yet never fully exploring the possibilities therein, and with concepts of radical freedom literally becoming slogans. Anarchy and freedom become concepts in a PowerPoint pres-entation but are avoided in practice and politics. In this way, an unreflected and culturally mandated notion of 'anarchy' becomes central to the aesthetic image of innovation management, something to preach, not practice. It sounds good and gives off just the right counter-cultural vibe, but in the end, it is a colonized and neutered form.

This is a shame, for fields like innovation and entrepreneurship always state that they work with and are interested in new thinking. From the anarchic energy of imagination, through the innovation potential of an entirely new way of social organization, to the 'wide field for petty trades, rural workshops, domestic industries, and the like' that Kropotkin speaks of, anarchism and anarchist thought could enrich these fields and social life more generally, if they moved beyond mere fetishism.

Questions for further study

1   Can you name some entrepreneurs who have been described as 'mavericks' or 'rule-breakers'? Why do you think they have been described in this way? Are these descriptions accurate?

2   What do we mean when we say that an innovation is 'revolutionary'? What kind of effect are we describing, and how far-reaching is this effect?

3   Conservatism, a belief in the importance of tradition and maintaining existing institutions and relationships, is normally thought to be the opposite to radical change or innovation. Can there be such a thing as conservative creativity?

4   Discuss whether anarcho-capitalism is a form of anarchism. Why? Why not?

5   What might it mean for innovation to truly embrace anarchism? How would this kind of innovation differ from the kind you might read about in mainstream management textbooks?

References

Baker, T., and Welter, F. (eds.). (2018). *The Companion to Entrepreneurship*. London: Routledge.

Bakunin, M. (1842). "The reaction in Germany." Available at: https://theanarchistlibrary.org/library/mikhail-bakunin-the-reaction-in-germany

Chipp, H. B. (1968). *Theories of Modern Art: A Source Book by Artists and Critics*. Berkeley, CA: University of California Press.

Clay, A., and Phillips, K. M. (2016). *The Misfit Economy: Lessons in Creativity From Pirates, Hackers, Gangsters and Other Informal Entrepreneurs*. New York, NY: Simon and Schuster.

Kropotkin, P. (1912). *Fields, Factories and Workshops: Or Industry Combined With Agriculture and Brain Work With Manual Work*. Nashville, TN: Thomas Nelson & Sons.

Narayanan, A., Bonneau, J., Felten, E., Miller, A., and Goldfeder, S. (2016). *Bitcoin and Cryptocurrency Technologies: A Comprehensive Introduction*. Princeton, NJ: Princeton University Press.

Rothbard, M. N. (1978). *For a New Liberty: The Libertarian Manifesto*. Auburn, AL: Ludwig von Mises Institute.

Schumpeter, J. (1942/1994). *Capitalism, Socialism and Democracy*. London: Routledge.

Sombart, W. (1913). *Krieg und Kapitalismus*. München: Duncker & Humblot.

Sundararajan, A. (2017). *The Sharing Economy: The End of Employment and the Rise of Crowd-Based Capitalism*. Cambridge, MA: Massachusetts Institute of Technology Press.

17

EXCHANGE BEYOND THE MARKET

Richard J. White and Colin C. Williams

Everything that standard management and business textbooks talk about – production, buying, selling, workplace, motivation, structuring your business – takes place strictly in the context of the market. Businesses are established, people are hired, services and goods are sold and then the money is counted. This is a very simplified sequence of activities, but that is largely what would be covered in most management courses. However, even in the most money-driven settings, there are many activities that take place and are not reducible to money. Think of when people work overtime just because of a sense of duty or care, give advice without asking anything in return or break the rules in order to help a customer. What is common to all these examples is that they might generate value, but they are not motivated by the generation of value (see Chapter 10). In fact, caring for others, voluntary work and gift giving happen all around us and are at the centre of every-day life. It should not surprise us then that they happen in for-profit organizations too, as ordinary people ignore money and act, either individually or in groups, in ways that support each other. In this chapter, we will discuss how a lot of everyday economic life is practically anarchist, or rather, that we very often live like anarchists, even if we are encouraged not to.

This chapter will

- introduce and discuss the idea of *Homo economicus* and the forms of organization and exchange it entails,
- suggest that this view of human beings and human society is not natural but constructed to reinforce certain economic arrangements,
- point towards anarchist values of fairness, cooperation and mutual aid that better reflect how people organize their daily lives, and

- highlight examples of these anarchist values in practice in everyday life, with a focus on our home lives, our commutes and our lives at university.

A trap of *Homo economicus*

Pick up most management textbooks published in the last 40 years, and you will find *Homo economicus*. A specific type of *Homo sapiens* (human being; from the Latin *homo* (human) and *sapiens* [wise]), *Homo economicus* is the embodiment of a supposedly rational version of human nature, describing the dominant motivations, perceptions and values of the human condition. For example, in their natural setting, *Homo economicus* acts apolitically and competitively, driven by the overriding need to 'maximize [their] own well-being' (Nyborg, 2000, p. 306). In their relation to others, and to society, they act out of self-interest in pursuit of tangible goals and care about other people 'only insofar as they affect [their] final consumption of wealth' (Gintis, 2000, p. 312). In business schools, students are often encouraged to apply this common-sense reading of the nature of human beings in order to understand the appropriate organizational principles that emerge from it.

However, what if we were to personalize this question of human nature and think about our own sense of values, motivations, perceptions and experiences that inform how we treat others in a given situation, with those of the *Homo economicus*? Many of us would probably distance ourselves from such a construct, finding the 'common-sense' rhetoric about human nature which informs our management textbooks impossible to identify *ourselves* with.[1] This then raises the question: what *is* human nature? The core aim of this chapter is to try to show how problematic this question is and offer instead an argument to say that whatever human nature may or may not be, *Homo sapiens* are fundamentally *social* animals. Demonstrated through our relationships with others and reinforced by the motivations that underpin these relations (sociability, mutual aid, cooperation and so on), we argue that these actions are highly consistent with anarchism and can be found in anarchist forms of organization (see also Chapter 3). The chapter asks that you adopt what Scott (2012, p. XII) would describe as an 'anarchist squint' with which to see and understand yourself and the world around you. In doing so, as well as challenging our own understanding of what anarchism is and what anarchists do, it 'will also become apparent that anarchist principles are active in the aspirations and political action of people who have never heard of anarchism or anarchist philosophy.'

Thinking and acting like an anarchist at this time of huge crises has practical consequences. There are many persuasive reasons to believe that we currently live in 'an age that is desperately in need of . . . alternatives to the stasis of hierarchical social relations [which can be found through] mutual aid, voluntary association, direct action, horizontality, and self-management' (Springer, 2016, p. 1). If this is the case, then recognizing how we often act and think like anarchists through the everyday examples focussed on in this chapter, might encourage us to consciously *see* the world more fully 'as an anarchist.' Furthermore, the challenge as to how to apply this new anarchist imaginary in our everyday world, in ways which encourage us to engage and organize *differently with others*, perhaps even in ways that will help inspire a 'spirit of revolt' (Souza, White, and Springer, 2016, p. 16) is something to reflect on long after this chapter – and this book – has been read.

The rest of our chapter is divided into three parts. The question of what it might mean to act or think 'like an anarchist' will be the focus of the next section. Then to illustrate the discussion at hand and help you to relate to it, the main body focusses attention towards anarchist forms of motivation and organization with reference to (1) your home/place of residence, (2) your community and (3) the university campus. The final section of the chapter will encourage you to act more purposefully in ways to make both ourselves – and others more generally – aware of the centrality of anarchist practice in everyday life and society and the opportunity that this brings.

Thinking and acting like an anarchist

David Graeber argues that 'Anarchists are simply people who are capable of behaving in a reasonable fashion without having to be forced to. It is really a very simple notion' (2000, n.p.). Rejecting the common sense that caricatures anarchism in a wholly negative light and demonizes anarchists as perpetrators of reckless violence who desire the destruction of 'civilized' values, it may be of surprise (and relief) to note that two key concepts lie at the heart of anarchism and anarchist practice: freedom and autonomy.

In many ways, the relationship between the two is deeply entwined. Crucially, anarchism anchors the location of freedom and autonomy within the individual, from which it then radiates outwards across society. In other words, neither freedom nor autonomy are 'things' that can be externally granted to individuals by 'starting from the State and working downwards' (Christopher et al., 1995, p. 83). Thinking about freedom quickly brings into focus questions of power and inevitably the **intersectional** nature of oppression, exploitation, subjugation, violence and the multiple sources (and sites) where these occur (see box in Chapter 5). In this way, the idea of (individual) autonomy becomes a central point of concern. Paul Goodman (2011, p. 32), for example, suggests that

> To me, the chief principle of anarchism is not freedom but autonomy. Since to initiate, and do it my way, and be an artist with concrete matter, is the kind of experience I like, I am restive about being given orders by external authorities, who don't concretely know the problem of the available means. Mostly, behaviour is more graceful, forceful, and discriminating without the intervention of top-down authorities, whether State, collective, democracy, corporate bureaucracy, prison wardens, deans, pre-arranged curricula, or central planning.

Anarchism in this context is defined in opposition, or in contrast to, other forms of organizing. To use Colin Ward's framing (1982, p. 14) anarchism 'is a description of a mode of human experience of everyday life, which operates side-by-side with, and in spite of, the dominant authoritarian trends of our society.' Drawing attention toward anarchism in the context of everyday life is important in emphasizing the social embeddedness of the individual. For the most part, anarchists make no overt statements about human nature. Instead, they will emphasize how and why people engage with others in the way they do, and this goes a long way to understanding who and what we are. As geographer Simon Springer (2016, p. 132) concluded, 'after spending the last few years reading anarchist philosophy, I now realize I was born an anarchist. In fact we all were.'

Avoiding claims about 'the human condition' (whether people are born good or evil, for example), many anarchists would be confident in arguing the case that humans are *social* animals. People have a fundamental desire and need to engage with others. As Cornelius Castoriadis (1922–1997) – a political philosopher and a highly influential figure across academic and activist communities – argued, 'People can exist only within society and through society' (2010, p. 45). In this way, Ward (1982) suggests, we might understand anarchists to be 'people who make a social and political philosophy out of the natural and spontaneous tendency of humans to associate together for their mutual benefit.' Here, the emphasis on engaging on grounds of 'mutual' benefit is a critical one. The famous anarchist philosopher Peter Kropotkin (1901/1998, p. 180) emphasized that a tendency toward mutual aid is 'deeply interwoven with all the past evolution of the human race.' It is a direct rebuttal to the idea that human beings are motivated first and foremost by self-interest or self-gain, are asocial beings, are competitive rather than cooperative and so on. Understanding human nature as being inherently social and co-operative is central to how many assertions about how society – an anarchist society – should be organized.

MUTUAL AID

Mutual aid is one of the cornerstone concepts of anarchist political philosophy and its associated practices. It was fully developed by Peter **Kropotkin** (see box in Chapter 3) in his book *Mutual Aid: A Factor of Evolution*, which explored mutually beneficial cooperation and reciprocity. He emphasized the principles of mutual aid against social Darwinists, who insisted that competition was the main factor of survival of the fittest individual species. While recognizing the presence of competitive struggle in the animal kingdom, he insisted that cooperative behaviour was downplayed yet was crucial for collective survival of species in harsh environments. After all, if cooperation facilitates individual survival, then it is encouraged by natural selection. This finds confirmation with the views of contemporary biology and as such is not just a well-meaning political idea. Principles of mutual-aid are at the heart of such organizations as trade unions, **cooperatives** (see box in Chapter 8) and social movements and also, as this chapter demonstrates, are pervasive in our everyday lives.

An explicit focus of attention for anarchists is to explore anarchism in everyday life though the relationships, forms of organization and modes of exchange which seem to work best for most people in practical terms. By situating a radical politics in everyday life, anarchists resist and reject any tendency for ready-made, narrow blueprints or appeals to a utopia that individuals and society should dogmatically adhere to.

> We anarchists do not want to emancipate the people; we want the people to emancipate themselves. We do not believe in the good that comes from above and imposed by force; we want the new way of life to emerge from the body of the people and correspond to the state of their development and advance as they advance. It matters to us therefore that all interests and opinions should find their expression in a conscious organisation and should influence communal life in proportions to their importance.
>
> *(Malatesta, 1965, p. 90)*

This means rejecting the idea that blueprints or absolute schemes should be used to inform and determine a political programme of change in society. Indeed, for Rudolf Rocker (1938), to seek to do so was not just evil, but 'The *greatest* evil of any form of power is just that it always tries to force other rich diversity of social life into definite forms and adjust it to particular norms.'

So political 'revolution,' from an anarchist perspective, is imagined as an ongoing, self-determined process, which is embodied in Castoriadis's understanding of autonomist society:

> I first used the concept of autonomy, extended to society, in the sense of 'collective management.' I have now been left to give it a more radical content that is no longer collective management (self-management), but the *ongoing, explicit self-institution* of society, meaning a state in which the community knows that its institutions are its own creation and has been able to regard them as such, to re-examine them and transform them. If you accept that idea, it defines a unified revolutionary project.
>
> *(2010, p. 41)*

At a time of prolonged economic, political and environmental crisis, such as the current period we live in, embracing the complex diversity of contemporary society at 'the human scale' is necessary in order to avoid the problems with grand schemes and plans. This allows us to start making the everyday changes today that will help shape our future.

It is important to recognize the examples of cooperation, mutual aid and alternative modes of consumption and production that are embedded in the here and the now. 'The anarchist envisages a different kind of federal society, one in which the responsibility begins in the vital nuclei of social life, the workplace and the neighbourhoods where people live' (Woodcock, 1986, p. 25). Valuing those precious and often overlooked spaces and times, we can recognize justice, solidarity, freedom and autonomy in our own lives as a first step. The second is to focus on how to harness and enrich these spaces and also radiate them ever further outwards and upwards within society, both now and in the future. To these ends, the chapter invites you to think about three places:

- Your home
- Your community
- Your university campus

Everyday anarchism: home and community

To encourage *your* anarchist imaginary to come to the fore, think carefully about the building blocks of social life and, indeed, about your own life and experiences. Think about the seemingly ordinary, routine and perhaps small points of everyday engagement with other people that you have experienced so far today and perhaps will look forward to over the rest of the day. These will, without doubt, provide some meaningful examples of anarchy in action. For example, if you are living in shared accommodation, then this might include making your housemate(s) a cup of tea, taking the bins out, leaving the kitchen tidy (so as not to risk friendships and the milk going sour), agreeing to drop off a housemate's book at the library on his or her behalf, offering to take lecture notes, bringing back food or medicines if a housemate is sick or buying tickets for a nightclub or sporting event. Assuming you are not charging a premium rate for these services and/or you have not been coerced into doing so but have done so voluntarily, then you are acting like an anarchist. On the way to campus, maybe you have given someone directions, offered to give your seat up on the bus for somebody else, treated the bus driver as a human being with respect and been courteous to the 'freedoms' of fellow commuters on the bus (e.g. music levels kept low and personal, not engaging in loud conversations on your mobile phone or not putting your feet on the seats). Perhaps you held a door open for someone or even gave money or food to a homeless person. Adhering to these social rules and expectations is indicative of our expectations of what any 'good,' 'decent' human being tends to do.

The focus on these ordinary practices and informal coping strategies and how these are organized in ways to complete a range of material tasks or provide emotional support have underpinned much research focussed on highlighting the pervasive nature of 'alternative' economies in so-called formal capitalist societies (White and Williams, 2016). Within this literature, there is an explicit focus on 'community self-help,' which covers a diverse spectrum of activities that are not formally provided by the market or the state. One type of community self-help is referred to as self-help or self-provisioning. This largely concerns unpaid work (anything from child care to cooking and cleaning, as well as forms of household maintenance such as decorating and gardening) undertaken for and by household members. The second type is mutual aid, which means unpaid work that is undertaken by extended family or community networks.

Research conducted through time use surveys and household work practice surveys in the UK, and Western 'capitalist' economies more generally, has explored the extent of participation in community self-help as well as barriers to it (White and Williams, 2016). The results have found non-capitalist, informal modes of work and organization to be both pervasive and desirable. From an explicitly anarchist reading of these practices of community self-help, in terms of how people organize and how the products of labour are distributed, it reminds us of the slogan suggested by the French anarchist geographer Élisée Reclus: 'From each according to ability, to each according to the principle of solidarity' (Ward, 2010, p. 222). When engaging with family and non-family relations, altruism, reciprocity, mutual aid, volunteerism and **horizontalism** (see box in Chapter 9) are the assumed ways that people relate to each other. In the management textbook, it might seem as if *Homo economicus* is everywhere. But research into what people actually do suggests that anarchist practices of exchange and distribution are powerful in informing our own sense of **identity** (see box in Chapter 4) and our complex relationships to others.

Anarchism at the university

Having thought about our home and our commute to work, the third place we want to look at is the university campus itself. We might begin by looking at the intellectual content of your business or management course. Think about the theoretical or methodological assumptions embedded within the research that is drawn on and the relevance and application of the knowledge you are meant to acquire. What end does it serve? In many parts of the world, higher education is being increasingly defined by marketization and commodification, wherein 'goods and services are increasingly produced and delivered by capitalist forms of monetized exchange for the purpose of profit' (Williams, 2005, p. 14). Ultimately, these processes have transformed the university's overt role and purpose away from being a 'public' to a 'for profit' entity, a change that many university employees disagree with (Heath and Burdon, 2017).

Unsurprisingly, there is a longstanding critique of the nature of learning and pedagogy by anarchists (e.g. Goodman, 2011; Parker et al., 2014), and many would agree with Springer (2016, p. 20) when they suggest that

> While education has often been touted as a path to freedom and enlightenment, all too often it operates as a mechanism that stupefies through the promotion of ignorance, prejudice, and submission to authority.
>
> *Springer (2016, p. 20)*

How might we draw attention to the everyday presence of anarchism on campus? One obvious example would be to recognize the many inter-connected forms of interaction and modes of organization that we engage in directly that make the university possible. For example, think of how you and your fellow students queued up when waiting for the last lecture or seminar you had. Did you do so in an orderly way? Was there quarrelling or fighting or jostling? How might this mode of organizing play out when reflecting on broader experiences of waiting in line? When the lecturer arrived, how did you then decide where to sit? Our guess is that was mostly undertaken in a self-organized and voluntary manner. Perhaps, in a small class in a big lecture theatre, the lecturer may have asked you to 'move closer to the front,' but usually no explicit guidance or instruction is necessary.

Reflect on the learning experience during that last lecture/seminar. Did the lecturer play a dominant role from start to finish? Or, alternatively, was a conscious attempt made to encourage and facilitate more engaged, informal, shared and safe spaces between and within the class to discuss and debate the issues at hand? Did everybody speak and listen 'appropriately' – respectfully listening when 'the speaker' was talking or not speaking for 'too long' and speaking in respectful tones (not shouting or ranting) when given the opportunity? If, on an unfortunate occasion, somebody transgressed and violated these rules, how was that addressed? Did the lecturer encourage the person to self-reflect? Or appeal to authority, reprimand him or her, send him or her out and threaten to report him or her?

Assuming the discussion was engaging, maybe even inspiring, perhaps you (or a peer) might have stayed behind and asked the lecturer some questions or followed up a discussion after the class? We mention this because as employees of the university, your lecturers will have various contact time allocated for teaching, which can be distributed across all related activities: lectures, seminars, tutorials, dissertation supervision, fieldwork and so on. Beyond the hour lecture then, if working to the rule of their formal contract, they would be within their rights to not volunteer an extra five or ten minutes or even more to entertain these questions (or equivalent issues). It is instructive to see how these unpaid minutes add up. When looking across the education sector as a whole, for example, the Trade Union Congress, the body representing the various trade unions in the UK, drew on unpublished Office for National Statistics data from the Labour Force Survey (July–September 2016) and the Annual Survey of Hours and Earnings (2016). Their analysis found that people working in education are among those most likely to be putting in unpaid overtime and clocking up 12.1 free hours a week. The trade union for many members of university staff in the UK said the figures highlighted how staff working in schools, colleges and universities continue to go above and beyond the call of duty and put in the extra unpaid mile. The analysis revealed that over half of people working in education (51.8%) do extra unpaid work (UCU, 2017).

This is a difference that makes all the difference. Modes of organization and exchange in which support is given regardless of financial remuneration is still the lifeblood that animates and gives life to the university. This is despite the authoritarian top-down style of governing that is increasingly, forcibly, administered to these spaces. For another example, think about the acknowledgements written in the academic books you read. As Nocella and Juergensmeyer (2017, p. XIX) note,

> Acknowledgements are so critical and a radical humbling of oneself because it publicly notes that no one is an island and that everyone is interdependent and needing support because we are living creatures and part of an ecosystem, where everyone is interwoven and interdependent of one another.

Unfortunately, much of the collaborative element, particularly where remarkable intellectual and technological achievements have been made, has often been obscured by its attribution to the success of individuals rather than groups or networks. This should not be surprising in one respect because, as Cumbers (2012, p. 70) observes, 'The failure to treat knowledge production and economic action as socially embedded and interactive processes also applies to most of mainstream economics with its focus upon atomized individuals and market exchange.' To take one example, we might suggest Schaffer's (2015) analysis of the multi-billionaire Elon Musk. She argues that

> Musk's success would not have been possible without, among other things, government funding for basic research and subsidies for electric cars and solar panels. Above all, he has benefited from a long series of innovations in batteries, solar cells, and space travel.... The problem with such portrayals is not merely that they are inaccurate and unfair to the many contributors to new technologies. By warping the popular understanding of how technologies develop, great-man myths threaten to undermine the structure that is actually necessary for future innovations.

A generation ago, academics were also warning of the dangers of the proliferation of property rights over knowledge. Focusing attention on the privatization of bio-medical research, Heller and Eisenberg (1998, p. 698) argued that the result 'may lead paradoxically to fewer useful products for improving human health,' resulting in what they termed as an 'anticommons,' the privatization of public goods. With this in mind, think how different history may well have turned out if the British computer scientist Tim Berners-Lee decided to patent 'his' invention of HyperText Transfer Protocol, which led to the World Wide Web. Imagine if this had been a private network with no social media or public resources like *Wikipedia* or all the many news and information sites you often use to do your research (see **open source** box in the introduction).

COMMONS

Land over which members of the community could exercise customary rights, such as the right of grazing or collecting. In England, the rights of commons were eroded by the enclosures that began in the 12th century and was largely completed by the end of the 19th. In modern use, the commons has acquired a broader meaning to include not only land but also other natural resources (water, biodiversity) and cultural resources (traditional knowledge, information and creative works) which were openly available to all. There have been many attempts to protect the commons from modern forms of enclosure, in particular corporate encroachment through privatization and marketization. Reclaiming the commons has become one of the rallying calls of the anti-capitalist movement. The **Open Source** Software movement (see box in Chapter 1) is also an attempt to keep software within the public domain through copyleft licensing that ensures that anyone can use or modify a programme, but no one can appropriate it through copyright or patent laws. In addition, there have been campaigns to reclaim privatized water as a common resource, to defend the right of small farmers to use common land against the threat of eviction and privatization or to reclaim public spaces for public use by taking direct action against developments.

It seems to us that a rich and diverse range of common resources and ideas helps to generate better ideas (see Hess and Ostrom, 2007), just as a range of forms of self-help and mutual aid supports us in our everyday lives. Our final section focuses on the possibilities of anarchism to help recognize and grow this world. As Paul Goodman suggests,

> In any present society, though much and even an increasing amount is coercive, nevertheless, much is also free. . . . In creative work, in passion and sentiment, in spontaneous recreation, there are healthy spheres of nature and freedom: it is the spirit of these that we most often extrapolate to all acts of utopian free society, to making a living, to civil life and law.
>
> *(2011, p. 35)*

The real challenge is never only 'out-there' in the future, but always personal and now, involving us and what we do and the ways in which we can extend this in order to create 'new living institutions, new groupings, new social relationships . . . for [our] own futures' (Malatesta, 1965).

The future: extending anarchism in the everyday

We have argued that encouraging a deeper understanding of anarchism also means a greater awareness of the ways in which everyday forms of anarchist organization can be seen in our own lives. This sort of anarchism involves you, the reader, as a central protagonist, not a detached and neutral observer on the sidelines. Moreover, this reading of anarchism is not asking you to *imagine* what an anarchist society

234 Richard J. White and Colin C. Williams

might look like but to recognize that what gives our society meaning is largely rooted in a primitive form of anarchist sensibility. So how can this encourage us to think about the desirability of anarchism and the ways of extending anarchist practices to challenge domination and bring forward a more socially just, collective and emancipated world?

Anarchist practices encourage us to recognize our own agency and think creatively about the power that we have and how we can use it. What can we do, *in addition to what we do already*, to encourage social, economic and environmental justice to flourish? In other words, how can we (in company with others) think and act in ways that extend 'spheres of free action until they make up most of social life' (Goodman, 2011, p. 34)? One point to strongly emphasize here is the need for absolute consistency between 'means' and 'ends.' Anarchists who desire a non-violent, non-coercive future must, at fear of contradiction, engage in non-violent, non-coercive forms of direct action as a means to achieve this (see Baldelli, 1972).

The three sites we covered in the chapter demonstrate the practical ways in which non-market forms of engagement and organization are embedded in our everyday lives, so let us conclude by exploring one of these in a little more detail. Within the university, there are a great many inspiring and purposeful forms of direct action which are largely consistent with anarchism (Clare, G. White, and R. J. White, 2017). Individually, and working with others, areas to think about here include resisting and challenging the increasingly commodified 'for profit' nature of university spaces and organizing positively in ways that can reclaim higher education institutions and open up new alternatives for transformative action to take root (see Nocella and Juergensmeyer, 2017; Springer, 2016; Thompson, 2017). We can also critically explore everyday spaces and situations (what goes on in the lecture theatre or library, for example) to focus attention on the ways in which these spaces are connected to broader configurations of hierarchical oppression and exclusion that exist across and beyond the campus (e.g. capitalism, sexism, racism and classism). This would mean acting in ways that can maintain and foster cooperation, democratic involvement and solidarity between faculty, staff and students. This would certainly be highly desirable if it built new, meaningful bridges with minority and vulnerable student groups who routinely experience persecution and exclusion and in cases where the freedom of speech is threatened.

Moving confidently away from the self-interested, competitive norms and asocial motivations that are believed to inform human nature, captured in *Homo economicus*, what this chapter has hoped to encourage is a greater understanding of how we are in fact motivated by 'anarchist' principles of fairness, cooperation and mutual aid. Recognizing ourselves as social animals, we can also appreciate how these values underpin the way in which others engage with us. They are, after all, the core foundations of meaningful relations, be they with colleagues, friends, neighbours or those we love. Far from being a utopian ideal, anarchist forms of organizing are already deeply familiar to us. They are already happening in our everyday lives, with people who are known and familiar to us, as well as with those we share buses and seminars with. Ultimately, anarchist ideas offer up futures that are radical and vital antidotes to top-down governance and coercive forms of organization. As Maletesta (1891) believed, if you can

> convince the public that government is not only unnecessary but extremely harmful, then the word anarchy, just because it means absence of government, will come to mean for everybody: natural order, unity of human needs, and the interests of all, complete freedom within complete solidarity.

Looking at the world and ourselves through an 'anarchist squint' will prove to be empowering, not least through firmly rejecting the spectre of *Homo economicus*, which continues to haunt mainstream management organization textbooks. In this way, embracing a practical understanding of anarchism perhaps also enriches our continual quest for meaning, and might speak to those existential questions that we carry with us about the nature of life and our relations with others. On a more applied level, without appealing to authority, anarchist practice offers original, radical and new ways of analyzing problems, identifying the most appropriate solutions and working out what types of organization might be needed. There is nothing to stop us thinking and acting in ways that help create emancipatory anarchist modes of organizing, because we are demonstrably not (only) creatures of the market. And we can do this from where we stand, in the here and in the now.

Questions for further study

1   Think of the three areas of anarchist practice discussed in this chapter (home, the commute and the university). From your own experience, can you think of examples that confirm what the chapter has said about everyday fairness, cooperation and mutual aid?
2   Can you think of any processes or forces that encourage other values such as those of market-based selfishness? How do these pose a threat to everyday forms of cooperation?
3   The cases discussed here are focused on small-scale examples of anarchist values in organization and exchange. What might larger, more wide-reaching examples of these same values look like? How could they be used to extend the practices discussed in the chapter to the scale of a corporation or of society as a whole?
4   Anarchism has been defined here as having to do with some common ideas of fairness, cooperation and mutual aid. Do you think adhering to these ideas makes someone an anarchist? Is there anything more that is needed for a person, group or form of organization and exchange to be called 'anarchist'?

Note

1   The paper, 'Are You an Anarchist? The Answer May Surprise You!' (2000), by the anthropologist and anarchist activist David Graeber has been influential in how this chapter

has been structured and organized. There – and here – readers are invited to pay close and careful attention to how they would respond to a number of 'everyday' scenarios or questions and why they would choose to act or organize themselves in this way.

References

Baldelli, G. (1972). *Social Anarchism*. Harmondsworth: Penguin Books.

Castoriadis, C. (2010). *A Society Adrift, Interviews & Debates 1974–1997* (E. Escobar, M. Gondicas, and P. Vernay, Eds.). New York, NY: Fordham University Press.

Christopher, B., Robinson, J., Sansom, P., and Turner, P. (1970 (1995)). "The Relevance of Anarchism." In D. Rooum and Freedom Press (Eds.), *What Is Anarchism? An Introduction*. Available at: https://libcom.org/files/donald-rooum-and-freedom-press-ed-what-is-anarchism-an-introduction.pdf (accessed 14 May 2018).

Clare, N., White, G., and White, R. J. (2017). "Striking out! Challenging Academic Repression in the Neoliberal University Through Alternative Forms of Resistance: Some Lessons from the UK." In A. Nocella and E. Juergensmeyer (Eds.), *Taking Back Our Universities: Strategies to Fight Against Academic Repression and the Corporatization of Higher Education*, pp. 15–31. New York, NY: Peter Lang.

Cumbers, A. (2012). *Reclaiming Public Ownership: Making Space for Economic Democracy*. London: Zed Books.

Gintis, H. (2000). "Beyond Homo Economicus: Evidence from Experimental Economics." *Ecological Economics*, 35(3), 311–322.

Goodman, P. (2011). "Freedom and Autonomy." In S. Goodman (ed.), *The Paul Goodman Reader*. Oakland, CA: PM Press.

Graeber, D. (2000). "Are You an Anarchist? The Answer May Surprise You." *The Anarchist Library*. Available at: https://theanarchistlibrary.org/library/david-graeber-are-you-an-anarchist-the-answer-may-surprise-you (accessed August 2019).

Heath, M., and Burdon, P. (2017). "Academic Resistance: Landscape of Hope and Despair." In A. Nocella and E. Juergensmeyer (Eds.), *Taking Back Our Universities: Strategies to Fight Against Academic Repression and the Corporatization of Higher Education*, pp. 33–45. New York, NY: Peter Lang.

Heller, M. A., and Eisenberg, R. S. (1998). "Can Patents Deter Innovation? The Anticommons in Biomedical Research." *Science*, 1 (May), 698–701.

Hess, C., and Ostrom, E. (eds.). (2007). *Understanding Knowledge as a Commons: From Theory to Practice*. Cambridge, MA: Massachusetts Institute of Technology Press.

Kropotkin, P. (1901/2018). *Mutual Aid: A Factor of Evolution*. Plano, TX: SMK Books.

Malatesta, E. (1891). "L'Anarchia." Available at: https://theanarchistlibrary.org/library/errico-malatesta-anarchy.

Malatesta, E. (1965). *His Life and Ideas* (V. Richards, Ed.). London: Freedom Press.

Nocella, A., and Juergensmeyer, E. (eds.). (2017). *Taking Back Our Universities: Strategies to Fight Against Academic Repression and the Corporatization of Higher Education*. New York, NY: Peter Lang.

Nyborg, K. (2000). "Homo Economicus and Homo Politicus: Interpretation and Aggregation of Environmental Values." *Journal of Economic Behavior & Organization*, 42(3), 305–322.

Parker, M., Cheney, G., Fournier, V., and Land, C. (2014). "The Question of Organization: A Manifesto for Alternatives." *Ephemera*, 14(4), 623–638.

Rocker, R. (1938). "Anarchy: Aims and Purposes." Available at: www.panarchy.org/rocker/anarchy.html (accessed August 2019).

Schaffer, A. (2015). "Tech's Enduring Great-Man Myth in MIT Technology Review." Available at: www.technologyreview.com/s/539861/techs-enduring-great-man-myth/?utm_campaign=add_this&utm_source=facebook&utm_medium=post (accessed 14 May 2018).

Scott, W. (2012). *Two Cheers for Anarchism*. Princeton, NJ: Princeton University Press.

Souza, S. M. L. de, White, R. J., and Springer, S. (2016). "Introduction: Subverting the Meaning of Theory." In S. Springer, R. J. White, and S. M. L. de Souza (Eds.), *Introduction Transgressing Frontiers Through the Radicalization of Pedagogy: Anarchism, Geography and the Spirit of Revolt*, pp. 1–26. Lanham, MD: Rowman and Littlefield.

Springer, S. (2016). *The Anarchist Roots of Geography: Towards Spatial Emancipation*. Minneapolis, MN: University of Minnesota Press.

Thompson, R. (2017). "Reclaiming Campus as an Event Site: A Comparative Discussion of Student Resistance Tactics." In A. Nocella and E. Juergensmeyer (Eds.), *Taking Back Our Universities: Strategies to Fight Against Academic Repression and the Corporatization of Higher Education*. New York, NY: Peter Lang.

UCU. (2017). "Education Workers Putting in Long Hours of Unpaid Overtime." Available at: www.ucu.org.uk/article/8693/Education-workers-putting-in-long-hours-of-unpaid-overtime (accessed August 2019).

Ward, C. (1982). *Anarchy in Action*. London: Freedom Press.

Ward, D. (2010). "Alchemy in Clarens: Kropotkin and Reclus, 1877–1881." In N. J. Jun and S. Wahl (Eds.), *New Perspectives on Anarchism*. Plymouth: Lexington Books.

White, R. J., and Williams, C. C. (2016). "Valuing and Harnessing Alternative Work Practice in a Neoliberal Society." In S. Springer, K. Birch, and J. MacLeavy (Eds.), *The Handbook of Neoliberalism*. London: Routledge.

Williams, C. C. (2005). *A Commodified World*. London: Zed Books.

Woodcock, G. (1986). "Anarchism: A Historical Introduction." In G. Woodcock (Ed.), *The Anarchist Reader*. Glasgow: William Collins Sons.

18

CONCLUSION

What to do with this book

Martin Parker, Thomas Swann and
Konstantin Stoborod

Textbooks are sometimes quite useful because they tell us what we need to know in order to understand, and perhaps pass exams, in a particular area of knowledge. Their learning points, lists, questions and **boxes** are designed to help readers digest complex ideas. In that sense, textbooks are authoritative. They provide us with a kind of truth. The origin of the word textbook is from the idea of something being woven together, like a textile, but its earliest use in English meant a book printed with wide spaces between the lines in order that scholars or students could insert their own notes or translations. This older sense of textbook suggests a different texture of weaving, that of a mixing of the understandings of the author and the reader. That is really what we would like you to do with this book – to read between the lines and make the ideas useful for you and the things that you want to do. But how can we move from words to world?

Quite a few of the chapters in this book have claimed that anarchism isn't really a theory at all but a practice. That is to say that it is all very well talking and writing about equality and freedom, or prefiguration and democratic decision making, but it is another thing to be involved in it. The classic anarchist writers often offer beautiful language and inspiring visions of the future, but there is a big gap between talk and action, thinking and doing. So what could you do with the ideas in this book? How could you make them yours?

We could respond to this question in two broadly different ways. One would be a pessimistic dismissal of anarchism, or any radical suggestions for changing the world, because it is simply too hard. Instead, we accept that the way that things are done now is the best way, not because we are at all happy with it, but because it is too difficult to change. That's just the way that things are, so stop being a whining snowflake and get on with it. The weight of the present is too heavy for us to shift, and we are resigned to the way that things are because of inertia. After all, what can any one of us do? Protesting against global capitalism is like complaining about gravity. It is what it is. So in the case of business and management, it will be business as usual, because that is what most businesses want and what most policy makers assume and what most textbooks say.

That's all very well, in which case reading this book was really just another exercise in doing what your teacher told you to do. It might have been recommended as supplementary reading, in which case you read it, or some of it, and then moved on. You can write an essay, graduate and carry on as if nothing has happened. The problem with that response is that it effectively denies that any change could ever happen, and we know from history that isn't the case. There are moments when radical social innovations do take place, whether these are revolutions, responses to new forms of technology or huge changes in people's assumptions. For example, a century ago, women and black people were not expected or allowed to go to university at all. Now, probably half the students using this book on their undergraduate degrees are women, and many will be people of colour. Or think about the social changes which produced free health care in many European states or that abolished slavery or that gave all adults the vote or that legalized gay marriage and so on. At the time, these were radical breaks with tradition, and many conservative forces fought against them. They were struggles to change the world, and they worked, and the fact that they worked allows us to say that social change does happen – from slavery to democracy, from poverty to affluence, from racism to diversity, and so on.

So why do we find it so hard to imagine that we could change economic life? It seems that this is partly because we are continually told that the laws of the market, combined with supposed truths about human nature, mean that the inevitable and best outcome is managerial capitalism. Both of these assertions rely on the idea that human beings are essentially self-interested, motivated to gain as much 'utility' for themselves as they can. This, it is said, explains why they are in competition with one another, *Homo economicus* always trying to gain an advantage and build the biggest pile of cash. It's a view of people which is pretty bleak and that, if widely assumed to be true, might even encourage the very behaviour which it describes (Ghoshal, 2005).

But is it true? Are we only motivated by economic gain? Imagine that you are at home, and one of your parents is cooking for you. Would you expect to pay for your dinner? Calculating the cost of the ingredients and a fair rate for the hour or two of labour? Or if you lend some money to a friend who is a bit short this week, do you expect that person to pay interest? If you have ever given to charity or engaged in some sort of voluntary work, did you do it because you hoped to benefit economically? These examples – and many others – demonstrate that there are huge areas of our lives in which we do not appear to be motivated by money, or even by some sort of expectation of return, and this is why the anarchist David Graeber believes that our everyday behaviour is actually rather anarchist in a very ordinary way (2000). The way we talk about our everyday lives continually makes reference to ideas that seem to have very little to do with the rational calculating machine assumed by the 'law' of the markets and 'human nature.' Love, friendship, sacrifice, community, justice, empathy, duty and belonging all imply some other sort of motives, different accounts of what human beings are and how they might exchange services, goods and favours with each other.

In their now rather famous 'iceberg' metaphor, post-capitalist theorists Gibson-Graham suggest that the formal waged economy is only one element in understanding wider networks of exchange (2006). They use voluntary work, gift giving, barter, co-operatives, activities around the temple or church, under-the-table work, the family, self-provisioning and many other examples to suggest that the capitalist economy should actually be understood as only one form of exchange among many others. It is only the tip of a very large iceberg, and most forms of 'economic' life don't follow its rules. Indeed, it might well be that the idea of *Homo economicus* really only applies in quite specific and narrow circumstances. As novelists, poets and artists of all descriptions have shown us, people are complicated and contradictory creatures, capable of overwhelming stupidity and endless small acts of love and kindness. The sphere of behaviour classified as 'the economic' is, in pre-industrial societies, embedded in all the other aspects of human lives – family, politics, farming, religion and so on. It is only in modern societies that we might identify something called the economy which is somehow 'disembedded' from how human beings live together (Polyani, 1944/2001). And even then, this sort of description only seems to hold for some people, in the spaces and times of their working lives. We are very rarely economic robots, driven only by calculations of personal interest.

So if 'human nature' is not simply economic selfishness, and there are lots of examples of behaviour that doesn't appear to follow the 'laws' of the market, then why could we not also imagine a different sort of economic system? Markets are made by human beings after all, so they are the result of all sorts of human choices. Consider 'Fairtrade' for example, a form of kite mark for labour standards which means that consumers pay more money for certain products – coffee, tea, sugar and so on – because they want to ensure that the producers get a fair price for their work. If we were simply maximizing our utility, then the global Fairtrade market would not be worth the nearly eight billion Euros it was estimated at in 2016 (Fairtrade International, 2017). Why would consumers pay more for something they could get cheaper? It makes no sense, if we are only ever *Homo economicus*.

These sort of 'irrational' behaviours suggest that it could be easier to reinvent economic life than might be assumed, and this opens up the possibility of a second response to the question of what you might do with the ideas in this book. Just like other aspects of human activity, politics and ethics are central considerations in this book. Perhaps changing the world isn't impossible after all, because human beings make the economy, not robots. This book, rather than being irrelevant, then opens up the possibility of thinking about work and organizations differently, as matters subject to ethical and political judgement, not the operation of natural laws. This is an argument which has even greater weight now, at a moment when the viability of our species on the planet is in question if we continue with the forms of production and consumption that characterize our present age. One of the slogans of the activist group Extinction Rebellion is 'There is no Planet B.' The natural limits of global capitalism make it vital that we develop a different economy which produces low-carbon, high-inclusion and high-democracy work. Changing the world is possible – and absolutely necessary.

And this is precisely why anarchism is of such relevance at the present moment. As we hope to have convinced you in the rest of this book, the tired image of anarchists as being people who couldn't organize a tea party in a cake shop is very far from the truth. Ever since its beginnings, anarchism has been centrally concerned with how to organize – whether considering the rules that we live by, the way we make decisions, the different forms of small-scale and large-scale association, our relationships with nature and so on. As Matthew Wilson puts it, anarchism tries to experiment with 'rules without rulers' (2014). It is, quite simply, the most radical way of thinking about how human beings could arrange their affairs to maximize personal freedom and collective flourishing. That is why anyone interested in management should take anarchism seriously and not dismiss it as idealistic, impractical or just historical (Swann and Stoborod, 2014).

Indeed, it is quite easy to think about anarchism as being the only really radical form of organization theory, one in which each of the variables that constitutes a particular form of organization is placed in question and forms of organizational design are not assumed. In this book, we have chapters which have taken ideas from personal development, organizational structure, human resource management, decision making, organizational culture, marketing, leadership, innovation, finance, accounting, business ethics, technology and so on but turned them on their head. Any given conventional business organization reflects particular decisions made about each of these variables, like building blocks being used to make a model of something. In most cases, the blocks are used to make something that looks a great deal like everyone else's model because the answers are already assumed. Anarchist ideas allow us to imagine that we could assemble a different kind of organization, one in which decision making was shared, hierarchy was minimized, accounting was used as information for everyone, culture was a shared collective experience and so on. This is a way of thinking about organizing as multiple, varied and specific in its response to particular circumstances and challenges. Anarchism leaves organizing open, rather than assuming that there is one best way to manage in all circumstances.

Because organization is then left open – not subject to 'laws' of efficiency or profit – questions of ethics and politics can be given full consideration. The sorts of values which motivate anarchists are those that are hard for anyone to disagree with as ideals – personal freedom, the encouragement of the same freedoms for others, collective and democratic decision making and responsibility to others and the planet. It is, in a sense, only a 'radical' movement because these values are so absent in our current economy and political system. Perhaps the most dangerous argument in mainstream textbooks, the one that is most insidious because it is rarely stated explicitly, is that these ideals can never become common practices in business and management. Indeed, the sort of attitude which is often encouraged, in gameshows like *The Apprentice* and self-help guides to having a successful career, is that ruthlessness, self-promotion and calculation will get you the rewards you desire. Business, we are continually told, is red in tooth and claw and has no time for losers, so be a winner.

If you really believe this, then this book is not for you. Put it down now and go off and make your millions. But if you do want to 'make the world a better place' – a statement which lots of people will agree with – then what should you do next?

Of course, in the spirit of anarchism, that is up to you, but here are some ideas. First, as with all the anarchists we have mentioned in the book, always question what you have been told. Are human beings really selfish? Do businesses always need to grow? Is the new economy fairer and more democratic than the old economy? Are people motivated mostly by money? Do we have to have leaders in order to make organizations function? Schools of business and management, perhaps like the ones that you are being taught within, have some rather predictable responses to these questions and tend to reward students who repeat what the teachers have said (Illich, 1971; Parker, 2018, see box in Chapter 10). But if your teachers have asked you to 'critically evaluate' something in an essay or exam, why not use that suggested freedom to think about the problems with mainstream ideas? What would an anarchist say about your responsibility to make up your own mind and say what you believe?

Second, when you are thinking about your assignments or dissertation, it is always tempting to use one of the big and famous organizations that are widely believed to be examples of business success. Apple, Virgin, Google, Walmart, Amazon and many others have millions of words written about them, and it is easy enough to find a 'case study' which will keep your teachers happy. But why not do some research into a worker co-operative, a credit union or social movement? Or a different sort of organization altogether – a library, a circus, a band of pirates or Hell's Angels gang. If you want to, pick a local shop or café which is worker owned and controlled or which tries to source its products and services locally or that refuses to use plastic packaging. Though they are not as visible as one of the big companies, they might be very happy to talk to you about their ideas, about why they are trying to do business in the way that they are, perhaps making a living while not trying to do any harm or giving some of their profits to a social cause that they believe in. And, for some of these organizations, they might already be influenced by anarchist ideas, whether they know it or not.

Finally, the economy is yours, is ours, so why not try to influence it in what you do next? As many of the chapters in the book have clearly stated, anarchism is not just a set of ideas but a practice, a way of thinking about how a life should be lived. In order to understand a particular sport, you could read its rules, a numbered list of dos and don'ts on paper, but the sport only comes to life when played. It's the same with anarchism. The theory is meant to inform a practice, to encourage you to reflect on the life that you live and the difference between that and the life you want to live. 'Taking back the economy,' as Gibson-Graham et al. have suggested (2013) is taking back what is already ours. The problem is that we don't think it's ours and tend to think that we must play by the 'rules' which are already established and are then repeated within business schools, the churches of capitalism. But there is no reason to assume that you have to graduate and just become an employee or set up and own your own business which makes you lots of money. Why not help to set up a business that is owned by the people who work for it and that makes decisions collectively? Why not make sure that whatever you do as a job results in zero or negative carbon emissions or think about ways of consuming which minimize waste and maximize the amount of time you spend with people you care about?

These are not 'academic' questions, in the sense that word is often used to mean irrelevant, largely disconnected from practical matters. You may have encountered anarchism for the first time in this academic text, but we are keen that it doesn't stay there, trapped between the covers of a book. You can ignore the problems that face us all, that face everyone on this planet. You could close this page now, having read the textbook and taken whatever notes you need. As an anarchist would always say, it is your choice. So never mind the essay or revising for the exam, what will you do?

References

Fairtrade International. (2017). "Building Fairtrade Markets: Annual Report 2016–17." Available at: https://annualreport16-17.fairtrade.net/en/building-fairtrade-markets/.

Ghoshal, S. (2005). "Bad Management Theories Are Destroying Good Management Practices." *Academy of Management Learning and Education*, 4(1), 75–91.

Gibson-Graham, J. K. (2006). *A Postcapitalist Politics*. Minneapolis, MN: University of Minnesota Press.

Gibson-Graham, J. K., Cameron, J., and Healy, S. (2013). *Take Back the Economy: An Ethical Guide for Transforming Our Communities*. Minneapolis, MN: University of Minnesota Press.

Graeber, D. (2000). "Are You an Anarchist? The Answer May Surprise You." *The Anarchist Library*. Available at: https://theanarchistlibrary.org/library/david-graeber-are-you-an-anarchist-the-answer-may-surprise-you (accessed August 2019).

Illich, I. (1971). *Deschooling Society*. New York, NY: Harper and Row.

Parker, M. (2018). *Shut Down the Business School*. London: Pluto Press.

Polyani, K. (1944/2001). *The Great Transformation*. Boston, MA: Beacon Press.

Swann, T., and Stoborod, T. (2014). "Did You Hear the One About the Anarchist Manager?" *Ephemera*, 14(4), 591–609. Available at: www.ephemerajournal.org.

Wilson, M. (2014). *Rules Without Rulers*. Winchester: Zed Books.

INDEX

Note: Page numbers in *italics* indicate figures; page numbers in **bold** indicate tables.

accounting 153; anarchist economy and 149–151; challenges of 151–153; financial and management 141–142; history of 143–144; need for 145–147; problem with markets 147–149; purpose of 147; value in theory 129–130
advertising case of Charles Saatchi 204–206
affirmative action 47
affordances, concept of 173–175
Airbnb 157, 159, 162, 220, 222
Albert, Michael 150
Alexander II 28
Alibaba 159
Amazon 27, 144, 165, 181, 242
Amin, Idi 115
Amnesty International 204
anarcha-feminism 43, 64, 161
anarchic selves-growth 65–66
anarchism 13; alternatives in practice 91–92; Bookchin and concept of affordances 173–175; classical 28; connections to global networks 18; cooperative action 19; crowdsourcing and 179–180; crypto- 187–189, 220; culture and 99–101; decision making in 89–90; definition 27, 201–202; economy and 149–151, 203–204; epochs of anarchist thinking **27**; everyday 229–230, 233–235; frenemies and 220–222; green, 173; ideas and organization 19–21; importance of equality 107; intersectional 129; organizational culture and 109; origins

of ideas in late 19th century 15–18; postanarchism 28, 30, 50, 62–63, 90; practical 29; prefiguration in 16–17; question of technology in 172–175; sharing ideas with management 22–23; at university 230–233
Anarchism (Woodcock) 27
anarchist(s): alternatives in leadership 116–119; interest in networks 4–5; managers 14–15; response to business ethics 77–78; self-management 61–64; theory of value 133–138; thinking and acting like 226–229
anarcho-syndicalism 65, 90, 106
anarchy: of entrepreneurship 216–217; *Anarchy in Action* (Ward) **27**, 28
Anarchy Works (Gelderloos) 94
Andreessen, Marc 192
Antifa (Anti-Fascist Action) 212
Apple 149, 214, 242
Apprentice, The (game show) 241
Aristotle 200
Assignment Tactics 33
Auftragstaktik 33
authoritarian 173
authority: disenchantment of world *114*; enunciative 113, *114*; institutional 113, *114*; of leadership 115; leadership and 120–121; origins of leadership and 112–115; of position 115
autodidacticism 100
Azteni, Maurizio 116

Badiou, Alain 74
Bakunin, Mikhail 21, 28, 90, 91, 112, 113, 142, 160, 212
balanced jobs 150
Baldwin, James 49
Banks, Iain M. 66
Barnard, Chester 115
Bauman, Zygmunt 74, 77
Beautiful Team, The 101–102
Belle Equipe 102, 103
Benjamin, Walter 24
Berners-Lee, Tim 232
Bey, Hakim 62–63
Beyond Race and Gender (Thomas) 47
Big Data 185
bitcoin 187, 188; cryptoanarchy and 189–190; blockchain and 190–192
bit gold 190
Black, Bob **27**, 28, 31, 63
Black Bloc protestors 212–213
Black Power 51
blockchain 187, 188; bitcoin and 190–192; distributed consensus model 192; technology of 191–192
Blue Noses 205
Bookchin, Murray 91, 133, 135, 136, 138, 171, 173, 179
brand value 32
Brazil, companies taken over by workers in 117–118
business, digital age and crowdsourcing in 170–172
business ethics 69, 70–76, 79; anarchist response to 77–78; approaches to *70*; conservative *70*, 71–72; critical *70*, 72–75; industry of 77; morality and 69; practical *70*, 75–76
Butler, Judith 30

Calvino, Italo 203
Capitalism, Socialism and Democracy (Schumpeter) 216
capitalist self-management 59–61
caring labour 44
Carnergie Foundation 201
Carr, Albert 72, 75
Castells, Manuel 173
Castoriadis, Cornelius 227, 228
Chaum, David 186, 187

Chicago Police Department 64
Chile, self-management in community centre in 118–119
China, Danyang-Kunshan Grand Bridge 6
Chomsky, Noam 74
classical anarchism 28
climate change 6, 132, 145, 148, 154, 172, 175
CNT (Confédération Nationale du Travail) 98, 101
Coco Cola 75
Cold War 174
collaboration 29, 157–158; in consumption and work 158–160; gig work 161–163; precarious work 163–165; sharing economy 160–161
collective property 134
commons 4, 134, 232–233
common sense, management 23–24
communication, private 185–186
Conquest of Bread, co-operative 101
Conquest of Bread (Kropotkin) 102
consensus 51, 104, 192; central features of process **94**; decision making 92–94, 119–120
conservative business ethics *70*, 71–72
consumption, collaborative 158–160
control, in organizations 86–89
conviviality 137
cooperation, principle of 89
cooperative action 19
co-operatives 100, 117, 165, 227; The Beautiful Team 101–102; companies taken over by workers in Brazil 117–118; Conquest of Bread 101; Omega boiler manufacturer 117–118, 120; organization 203–204; self-management in community centre in Chile 118–119; social innovation 215; Suma Foods 7–8
creative destruction, concept 216
creativity, innovation and 213–215, 220
Crenshaw, Kimberlé 58
critical business ethics *70*, 72–75
Critique of the Gotha Program (Marx) 141
crowd 171
Crowdsource 162
crowdsourcing 157; affordances of 175–179; anarchism and 179–180; in business and management 170–172; cultural context of environment 177–178; social interactions of actors 178–179; technical features of objects 176–177
crowdwork systems 162–163
cryptoanarchism 187–189, 220; from cryptoanarchy to bitcoin 189–190

Crypto Anarchist Manifesto, The (May) 187, 188, 189
cryptocurrencies: from bitcoin to blockchain 190–192; cryptoanarchism 187–189; from cryptoanarchy to bitcoin 189–190
cryptography 188
Culen, Julia 36
culture: anarchism and 99–101; at work 102–105; *see also* organizational culture
Culture, The 66
cyberpunk 187
cyberspace 188
cypherpunks 187

Dai, Wei 190
Danish Architecture Centre 175, 177
Danyang-Kunshan Grand Bridge in China 6
Darwin, Charles 28
de Beauvoir, Simone 42
decision making 85; anarchist 89–90; consensus 92–94, 119–120; power and 85–86
De Cleyre, Voltairine 129
Delivering Happiness (Hsieh) 34
Derrida, Jacques 30, 78
Diffie, Whitfield 187
digital age: business and management 170–172; digital cryptography 188; digital profiling 186–187
direct control 59
diversity 179
diversity management 42–44, 53–54; business case for 47–48; enthusiasm for 48; refusing group identity labels 51–52
division of labour 16, 17
do it yourself (DIY) 17
Du Pont Group 143
Duvivier, Julien 102

East India Company 143
EasyCar 159
EasyJet 159
eBay 162
eBird 171, 180
economics 125; everyday anarchism 229–230, 239–240; everyday life 224
economy: anarchism and 203–204; anarchist 149–151; gig work 161–163; need for accounting 145–147; precarious work 163–165; problem with markets 147–149; sharing 160–161; taking back 242–243; value in 241–242
education, anarchism at the university 230–233

effort of remembering 24
Ego and Its Own, The (Stirner) 30
Ellul, Jacques 172
El Productor (magazine) 14
encryption 188
entrepreneurship: anarchism and its frenemies 220–222; anarchist as entrepreneur 218–220; anarchy of 216–217; books on 218; entrepreneur as anarchist 218–220
enunciative authority 113, *114*
environmentalism 173
equal opportunities management 47
European Union 5
Extinction Rebellion 5, 95, 240

Facebook 159, 171, 173, 176, 206, 207
Fairtrade Foundation 7
Fairtrade market 240
Fayol, Henri 21, 115
feminists: Marxists 53; segregated labour 44–45
Fields, Factories and Workshops (Kropotkin) 218
financial crisis (2007–2009) 149, 164
First International 217
Fleming, Peter 60
Ford Foundation 201
Ford Pinto 76, 130–131, 132, 139
Fortune (magazine) 35
Foucault, Michel 30, 49, 61, 87, 90, 173
Fox News channel 207
Franks, Benjamin 78
freedom 57; self-management 59–61
Freelance Nation 161
Freelancers Union 164, 165
Friedman, Andy 59
Friedman, Milton 71–72, 78

Gelderloos, Peter 94–95
General Motors 33, 159
Gibson, James 174
Gig Economy 161
gig work 161–163
Gilmore, John 187
Gioia, Dennis 76
global financial crisis 149, 164, 202
Global Justice Now 144
Global Policy Forum 144
GNA software 4
Goldman, Emma 43, 62, 64, 161
Goodman, Paul **27**, 28, 29, 226, 233
Goodwin, Tom 159
Google 149, 242
Gordon, Uri 88
Graeber, David 201, 226, 235n1, 239

Gramsci, Antonio 87, 203
Gray, Lily 131
Great Depression 159
green anarchism 173
Grimshaw, Richard 131
Grint, Keith 174
Guevara, Che 203

Hahnel, Robin 145, 147, 150
Haudenosaunee Confederation 119
hegemonic 87
hegemony 202–203
Hellman, Martin 187
Hell's Angels gang 242
Herman, Edward 74
hierarchy 26
Hirst, Damien 205
History of Silicon Valley (Scaruffi) 189
Hitler, Adolf 115
Holacracy 35–36
Holloway, John 63
Homo economicus 224, 230, 239–240;
    human nature 225, 234–235; trap
    of 225–226
Homo sapiens 225
horizontal, self-management 57
horizontalism 179, 180, 230
horizontality 116
Horowitz, Sara 164
Hsieh, Tony 34
Hughes, Eric 187
human life, value of 130–132
human nature 9, 225, 227, 234, 239, 240
Hunt, Shelby 201
Hutchby, Ian 174
Hyper Text Transfer Protocol 232

Iacocca, Lee 131
identity 31, 50, 63, 103, 166, 230; national
    18; self-management 58; of worker 111
identity work, concept of 60
ideology 202
IKEA 157
Illich, Ivan 9, 127, 136, 137, 138
imagination 215
inclusion management 46–48; business case
    for diversity 47–48; equal opportunities
    47; rejecting work 52–53
industrial capitalism 9; rise of 13
Industrial Revolution 1, 21, 22, 24, 128,
    143, 145
Industrial Workers of the World 64
information and communication
    technologies (ICTs) 169, 173
InnoCentive 171, 181
Innosite 172, 175, 176, 178, 179, 180, 181

innovation: creativity and 213–215; social
    and technological 215–216
institutional authority 113, *114*
International Co-operative Alliance 100
Internet 145, 149, 169, 174; anarchic
    character of 187–189; bitcoin and 191;
    blockchain and 192; independence from
    government 185
Internet of Everything (IoT) 192
intersection 45
intersectional anarchism 129
intersectionality 58, 63
intersectional nature 226

Jackall, Robert 75–76
Jones, Conrad Crispin 205

Kelley, William 200
Khankhoje, Pandurang 15, 16, 18
Kotler, Philip 201
Kropotkin, Peter **27**, 28, 28–29, 34, 61, 102,
    145, 147, 160, 171, 172, 173, 218, 227

La Aurora (magazine) 14
LaborMe app 159
Labour Force Survey 231
labour markets: difference and inequality
    of 44–46; rejecting work 52–53;
    reproductive labour 44; segregated jobs
    45–46; segregated labour 44–45
La Questione sociale (periodical) 14
La Tribune Libre (periodical) 15
leadership 111–112; anarchist alternatives
    to 116–119; authority and 120–121; in
    managed organizations 115–116; origins
    of authority and 112–115
LEGO Ideas 171, 181
Le Guin, Ursula 79
Le Lay, Patrick 75
Levinas, Emmanuel 78
libertarian 173, 180
LiftShare 157
Linhart, Robert 108
Linux 4
Lombardi, Dominick 205
Lorde, Audre 51
Lumsden, Rick 205
Lyft 157, 159, 166

McGregor, Douglas 34–35
McQuinn, Jason **27**, 28, 31
Mahkno, Nestor 102
Malatesta, Errico 14, 16, 19, 147
management 1–3, 13; description of
    31–32; digital age and crowdsourcing
    in 170–172; diversity 42–44; freedom

and control 57; hierarchy of 26; inclusion 46–48; organizational sense of 3; organization and 6–7; prehistory of 21–23; self- 57–58; term 26; value in theory of 127–129; word 2
Manalo, Michael Vincent 205
marketing: brief history of 200–203; case of Charles Saatchi 204–206; case of Occupy Wall Street 206–208; concept of 199
markets, problem with 147–149
Marshall, Peter 19
Martínez, Saturnino 14, 15, 16, 19, 20–21, 24
Marti, José 18
Marx, Karl 20, 30, 87, 126, 129–130, 141, 142, 202, 216–217
Marxist thinking 173
May, Timothy C. 187, 188, 189
May, Todd **27**, 28, 30, 63
Mechanical Turk 157, 162, 165, 171, 181
Michel, Louise 9, 18–19, 53
Microsoft 149
Misfit Economy, The (Clay & Phillips) 221
Mission Tactics (MT) 33
Modotti, Tina 15
morality 69
moral responsibility 72
Moral Sentiments (Smith) 74
Mumford, Lewis 173
Musk, Elon 232
mutual 201; aid 136, 218; community 229–230
Mutual Aid (Kropotkin) **27**, 28, 227
mutualism 88, 158, 179–180
mutualist 20
mutual support 29, 105

Nakamoto, Satoshi 187, 190
National Health Service 214
National Highway Traffic Safety Administration (NHTSA) 131, 132
National School of Agriculture 15
neo-normative control 60
Netscape browser 192
Newman, Saul **27**, 28, 30–31, 63, 66
non-human life, value and 132–133

Occupy Wall Street 95, 199, 204, 206–208
Office for National Statistics 231
Omega boiler manufacturer 117–118, 120
Omnia Sunt Communia (everything for everyone) 134
open source software 4, 215; movement 233
organization(s): concept 3; labour markets 44–46; leadership in managed 115–116; management of 2–3; power and control in 86–89

organizational anarchism: US Marine Corps Forces Europe and Africa (MFE/A) 32–34; Zappos 34–36
organizational culture 98–99, 109; anarchism and 99–101; co-creating 105–109; fighting your own culture 103–104; struggling with difference 104–105; at work 102–105
Organization Man, The (Whyte) 31
othering 54; diversity management 42–44, 48–51; idea of 41; refusing group identity labels 51–52; social identities 49–50
Otherwise than Being (Levinas) 78
outsourcing 171

P2P lending 157
Pacioli, Luca 143
Paris Commune 18–19
Parsons, Lucy 44, 64, 129
participatory planning 151
Patio Volantin, self-management in Chile 118–119, 120
People or Personnel (Goodman) **27**, 28
Plato 200
politics 5–6
postanarchism 28, 30, 50, 62–63, 90
poststructuralism 30, 63
power 85–86; anarchist principles and 89; function of 87–88; in organizations 86–89; views on 87
practical anarchism 29
practical business ethics 70, 75–76
prefiguration 16–17, 50, 65, 78, 90, 98, 162
primitive accumulation 202
privacy, communication 185–186
productive labour 45
Proudhon, Pierre-Joseph 20, 43, 134, 138, 142, 172, 219
Pussy Riot 205

Rand, Ayn 213
Ravachol 142
Reclus, Élusée 28, 230
Reichardt, Carrie 205
reproductive labour 44, 45
return on capital employed (ROCE) 129, 138
Rhodes, Carl 74, 77–78
Ricardo, David 126
Ricoeur, Paul 112, 113
Rise of the Creative Class 161
Rivera, Diego 15
Roberts, John 74
Robertson, Brian 36
Rocker, Rudolf 228

Roíg San Martín, Enrique 14, 15, 16, 18, 19, 21, 22, 24
Rose, Nikolas 60

Saatchi, Charles 199, 204–206
Said, Edward 42
Scaruffi, Piero 189
Schumpeter, Joseph 216–217
Scott, James 135, 138
Second World War 144
Seeds for Change 93
self-exploitation 32
self-help 229
self-management 57–58, 66, 106; anarchic selves-growth 65–66; anarchist 61–64; capitalist 59–61; community centre in Chile 118–119; horizontality 116; Suma Foods 8
Shakur, Assata 51
sharing economy 160–161
Shirky, Clay 170
Smith, Adam 73–74, 125, 126, 127, 129
social entrepreneurs 32
social groups: concept of 42; diversity management 42–44
social marketing 201, 207
solidarity 17, 106
Spencer, Herbert 28
spontaneity 179
Springer, Simon 227
Stallman, Richard 4
Stirner, Max 30, 219–220
Sturdy, Andrew 60
Suma 100
Suma Foods 7–8
Swedish National Encyclopaedia 141
syndicalism 21, 106; anarcho- 65, 90, 106
Szabo, Nick 190, 192

Tag Del 172, 175, 176, 177, 178, 180
Tarde, Gabriel 79
TaskRabbit 157, 162
Taylor, Frederick 21, 143
Taylor, Henry 72
Taylorism 143
technology, in anarchism 172–175
techno-optimism 157, 170–171, 193
techno-pessimism 170
textbooks 238; accounting 141; management 1–3, 23, 85, 127, 235; topics 128, 224

Thomas, Roosevelt 47
Toffler, Alvin 88
Trade Union Congress 231
trust: from bitcoin to blockchain 190–192; from cryptoanarchy to bitcoin 189–190; digital profiling 186–187; private communication 185–186; third party transactions 184–185
Turkopticon 165
Twitter 173, 207
Two Cheers for Anarchism (Scott) 135

Uber 157, 159, 163, 166, 222
United Nations 5
United Nations Global Compact (UNGC) 77
Upwork 157
US Marine Corps Forces Europe and Africa (MFE/A) 32–34, 36, 37
US military headquarters 27

value 125; in accounting theory 129–130; anarchist theory of 133–138; of human life 130–132; in management theory 127–129; non-human life and 132–133; use and exchange 126–127
Vasai, Pietro 14, 15, 16, 18
Vieta, Marcello 116
Virgin 242

Walmart 144, 242
Ward, Colin **27**, 28, 29, 133, 226
Warfighting (US Marine Corps) 33
Wealth of Nations, The (Smith) 73, 126
Weber, Max 87, 114
Wikileaks website 187
Wikipedia 4
Wilson, Matthew 241
Woodcock, George 27
Woolgar, Steve 174
work: collaborative 158–160; precarious 163–165
Workbench, The (Linhart) 108
World Wide Web 174, 232

Zappos 27, 34–36, 37
Zerzan, John 171
Zipcar 159
Zooniverse 171, 180

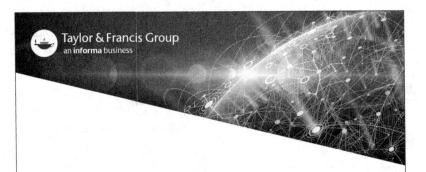

Printed in the United States
by Baker & Taylor Publisher Services